Epistemic Blame

Epistemic Blame

The Nature and Norms of Epistemic Relationships

CAMERON BOULT

Great Clarendon Street, Oxford, OX2 6DP,
United Kingdom

Oxford University Press is a department of the University of Oxford.
It furthers the University's objective of excellence in research, scholarship,
and education by publishing worldwide. Oxford is a registered trade mark of
Oxford University Press in the UK and in certain other countries

© Cameron Boult 2024

The moral rights of the author have been asserted

All rights reserved. No part of this publication may be reproduced, stored in
a retrieval system, or transmitted, in any form or by any means, without the
prior permission in writing of Oxford University Press, or as expressly permitted
by law, by licence or under terms agreed with the appropriate reprographics
rights organization. Enquiries concerning reproduction outside the scope of the
above should be sent to the Rights Department, Oxford University Press, at the
address above

You must not circulate this work in any other form
and you must impose this same condition on any acquirer

Published in the United States of America by Oxford University Press
198 Madison Avenue, New York, NY 10016, United States of America

British Library Cataloguing in Publication Data
Data available

Library of Congress Control Number: 2023945527

ISBN 978–0–19–289058–0

DOI: 10.1093/oso/9780192890580.001.0001

Printed and bound in the UK by
Clays Ltd, Elcograf S.p.A.

Links to third party websites are provided by Oxford in good faith and
for information only. Oxford disclaims any responsibility for the materials
contained in any third party website referenced in this work.

For Rosemary Scurfield

Contents

Preface xi
Acknowledgments xiii

Introduction 1

1. The Puzzle of Epistemic Blame 10
   1.1 Preliminaries 10
   1.2 Normative Parallels 13
   1.3 Blame in Epistemology 16
   1.4 The Authority of Epistemic Normativity 19
   1.5 The Puzzle 23
   1.6 Significance and Fittingness 26
       1.6.1 Significance and Normative Expectations 27
       1.6.2 Fittingness and Being "Independent of Practical Considerations" 29
   1.7 Conclusion 34

2. Negative Emotions and Frustrated Desires 35
   2.1 A (Very) Brief History of Blame 36
   2.2 Precedent in the Literature 39
   2.3 Varieties of the Emotion-Based Account 40
       2.3.1 The Bold Approach 40
       2.3.2 The Moderate Approach 43
       2.3.3 The Sui Generis Approach 47
   2.4 Moving On 49
   2.5 Moral Blame as a Set of Dispositions Organized Around a
       Belief-Desire Pair 51
   2.6 Brown on Epistemic Blame 54
       2.6.1 A Central Challenge for the Desire-Based Approach 56
       2.6.2 Other Worries 61
   2.7 Conclusion 63

3. A Relationship-Based Account of Epistemic Blame 64
   3.1 Blame and Relationships 64
   3.2 Refinements to the Relationship-Based Framework 67
   3.3 Epistemic Blame and Epistemic Relationships 74
   3.4 Conclusion 81

viii CONTENTS

4. The Significance and Fittingness of Epistemic Blame 82
4.1 Significance Revisited 82
4.2 Fittingness Revisited 93
4.3 Defending the Relationship-Based Account 98
4.3.1 Further Advantages of the Account 98
4.3.2 Objections and Replies 102
4.4 Conclusion 107

5. Blameworthy Belief, Assertion, and Other Epistemic Harms 108
5.1 Bad Thinking 108
5.1.1 Doxastic Control 110
5.1.2 Acts of Inquiry and Epistemic Bloat 113
5.2 Assertion 116
5.3 Testimonial Injustice 120
5.3.1 Testimonial Injustice and Deficient Normative Expectations 123
5.3.2 Contaminated Evidence Cases 129
5.4 Epistemic Relationships and Other Forms of Epistemic Harm 132
5.4.1 Testimonial Injustice through Credibility Excess 133
5.4.2 Epistemic Exploitation 136
5.4.3 Gaslighting 138
5.5 Conclusion 139

6. Standing 140
6.1 Standing to Blame: The Business Condition 140
6.2 The Business Condition and Epistemology 143
6.3 More Motivation for the Relationship-Based Account 145
6.4 Entitlements to Expect: The General Epistemic Relationship 147
6.5 Epistemic Expectations in Other Relationships 155
6.5.1 Professional Relationships 157
6.5.2 The Expert-Layperson Relationship 163
6.5.3 Institutional and Personal Relationships 166
6.6 Other Conditions on Standing to Epistemically Blame 168
6.7 Conclusion 171

7. The Value of Epistemic Blame 172
7.1 Preliminaries 172
7.2 Two Kinds of Political Epistemic Responsibilities 174
7.3 Interpersonal Political Epistemic Responsibilities 175
7.4 Comparing Accounts of the Epistemic Blame Claim 178
7.4.1 Responsibility to Resent 179
7.4.2 Responsibility to Desire 181
7.4.3 Responsibility to Adjust Epistemic Trust 182

CONTENTS   ix

7.5 The Value of Negatively Valanced Epistemic
    Relationship-Modification   184
7.6 More Arguments Against Epistemic Relationship Warming   190
    7.6.1 Inefficacy   190
    7.6.2 Social Justice   192
7.7 Conclusion   195

Conclusion   196

Bibliography   201
Index   211

Preface

I started working on epistemic blame about four years ago, with a draft paper called "Against Epistemic Blame." In that paper, I argued for the opposite of what this book concludes. At the time, it seemed to me that talk of "blame" in epistemology was at best misleading, and at worst deeply mistaken. But I soon found in conferences, workshops, and comments on the paper, that many were opposed to my ideas. "*Viva* epistemic blame!" I gradually became convinced that being *against* epistemic blame is not a straightforward matter.

The next draft of the paper was titled "Epistemic Blame?" I took a more tempered stance, outlining worries about epistemic blame, but also developing a more positive approach to the idea. This too was met with all kinds of objections. And they now came from the other direction. "Epistemic *blame*? Makes no sense!" Naturally, I was sympathetic, but because I'd also been convinced that things are not straightforward, it occurred to me that perhaps the most fruitful way of thinking about epistemic blame is in terms of a *puzzle*. There are competing sources of pressure in our intuitions about this concept, ones that are not easy to reconcile. To put it one way, the more *blame*-like a given response is, the less at home in the epistemic domain it seems—but the more at home in the *epistemic* domain a given response is, the less blame-like it seems. There is a kind of Catch 22 here. The puzzle is finding a way out.

What is exciting about this puzzle is that its solution has implications for fundamental issues in normative theorizing, including the nature of epistemic normativity, and the relationship between epistemology and ethics. By the end of this book, I will be saying that epistemic blame is like a *mirror* of epistemic normativity. Its properties reflect properties of the norms and values that structure our intellectual lives. By investigating these properties, we can put illuminating structure on the *parallels* and complex points of *interaction* between the epistemic and practical domains. Given the well-established and growing interest in the relationship between these domains, epistemic blame promises to be a valuable topic of study for many working in epistemology and beyond.

In my view, the most interesting and fruitful way to confront the puzzle of epistemic blame is to think about epistemic blame as a distinctive kind of *relationship modification*. Roughly, members of an epistemic community stand in a kind of "epistemic relationship," and epistemic blame is a distinctive way of modifying this relationship. This idea is inspired by the work of T.M. Scanlon, who famously argues that moral blame is a kind of relationship modification. When I read Scanlon's ideas in *Moral Dimensions*, they immediately struck me as a fascinating way of thinking about moral blame. But plans for extending these ideas to the epistemic domain were slow in the making. For a start, just as my initial work on the topic of epistemic blame was "against" epistemic blame, so too was my initial approach to Scanlon's framework against the idea that it could be extended to the epistemic domain. I even wrote a short paper about how this would mean embracing the idea of an "epistemic relationship," and arguing that we clearly have no such things... Coming at the epistemic domain from an individualistic perspective, thinking about things like proportioning one's beliefs to the evidence, the nature of perceptual justification, and whether knowledge of an external world is possible, it can of course be difficult to make sense of what this would even mean. But then I started thinking more about the *interpersonal* side of the epistemic domain—about how we rely on one another in pervasive ways for the most basic of information, and how we seem to have a corresponding set of *expectations* of one other, as potential sources of information. It occurred to me that there are plenty of materials in the epistemic domain for developing an account of epistemic relationships. It turns out that developing an account of epistemic relationships is a lot more interesting and fruitful than arguing they don't exist. It also leads to a way of solving the puzzle of epistemic blame.

By thinking of epistemic blame as a distinctive kind of relationship modification, we locate a response that is blame-like enough to warrant the term "blame," but also very much at home in the epistemic domain. Epistemic relationships can reconcile the competing sources of pressure generating the puzzle of epistemic blame. They can also do a lot more. In the second part of this book, I will be arguing that epistemic relationships help us make sense of a unique set of issues in the "ethics of epistemic blame," ones that broadly mirror a corresponding set of issues in the ethics of moral blame. I will examine the scope of appropriate epistemic blame, the idea of "standing to epistemically blame," and the role and value of epistemic blame in our social and political lives. These issues are unique in the sense that they take on their own character in the epistemic domain, and cannot be resolved simply by applying existing work in moral philosophy.

Our moral blaming practices give essential colour and shape to our experience as responsible agents. A vast literature is dedicated to analyzing, theorizing, and otherwise philosophizing about moral responsibility. Correspondingly very little has been done to analyze, theorize, or even *make sense* of the epistemic dimension of our blaming practices. And yet, epistemic blame plays a central role in our social and political lives. To my knowledge, this is the first book-length study of the nature and ethics of epistemic blame.[1] I hope that I have made a good start on these issues. But there is a lot of work to do.

---

[1] There are of course rich discussions of closely related and connecting topics in epistemology, including doxastic and epistemic responsibility. I explain how these discussions relate to this book in Chapter 1, section 1.3.

Acknowledgments

I have received helpful feedback and support from many people since starting this project. Most importantly, my wife Fiona has been there through all of my worries, ideas, and ruminations while battling "the beast"—our code-name for this project.

Robin McKenna and Sebastian Köhler also deserve special thanks. In some ways, my philosophy career feels like one big long extension of my time commiserating with these two in grad school reading groups: we've gone our separate ways, but we keep in touch and trade notes on all the major milestones. I owe a huge debt of gratitude to both of them for this project in particular. Robin was the first to read an entire early draft. He gave characteristically useful feedback, and has since been a source of advice on many practicalities. Sebastian has given lots of helpful feedback on the central ideas in this book, in various stages of development. He is also just always there with a quick reply to my text messages, which usually seek practical wisdom, or substantive reflection on some half-baked argument.

In the Fall of 2021, while on sabbatical, I benefitted from the amazing support of Chris Kelp and Mona Simion, and the entire COGITO group in Glasgow. We did a mini-workshop on the first draft of the book. The comments I received helped me write a much-improved second draft (and third and fourth ...). Chris and Mona are a central guiding inspiration and source of endless amounts of advice and good philosophy.

Another person who read an entire early draft is Eugene Chislenko. His incisive feedback and positive encouragement—particularly as someone with expertise in the moral blame literature—was a godsend. Eugene's comments made a significant difference to a big chunk of this book. At the other end of the writing process, Lani Watson very generously read the entire penultimate draft. I can't thank her enough for the careful attention to detail and constructive suggestions on a number of subtle but crucial issues. I also owe Sebastian Schmidt big thanks for his enthusiastic engagement with this project. His thoughtful comments have improved many pages, especially in Chapters 5 and 7. Others have read some chapters, given comments on related papers, or been helpful in conversation/ emails. I will forget important names here, but some that especially come to mind include: Craig Agule, Bob Beddor, Fernando Broncano-Berrocal, Jessica Brown, Daniel Buckley, Adam Carter, Matthew Chrisman, Marc-Kevin Daoust, Rachel Elliott, Davide Fassio, Miranda Fricker, Eric Bayruns García, Mikkel Gerken, Sara Ghaffari, Harmen Ghijsen, Sandy Goldberg, Thomas Grundman, Allan Hazlett,

xiv ACKNOWLEDGMENTS

Nick Hughes, Antti Kauppinen, Sophie Keeling, Carline Klijnman, Tim Kwiatek, Jennifer Lackey, Max Lewis, Arturs Logins, Veli Mitova, Adam Murray, Jordan Myers, Jesus Navarro, Francesco Praolini, Duncan Pritchard, Shane Ryan, Paul Silva Jr., Cory Spiegel, Susan Wolf, Elise Woodard, and Sarah Wright. My good friend Jessica Evans also deserves special thanks for help with the cover design. Finally, I would like to thank two anonymous referees for OUP for extremely helpful comments.

Material from this book was presented at the following workshops and conferences, and I would like to thank all audience members at those events for helpful feedback: Epistemic Wrongs and Epistemic Reparations Workshop, African Centre for Epistemology and Philosophy of Science, University of Johannesburg; Responsibility for Beliefs Workshop, University of Helsinki; The Social and Political Dimensions of Epistemic Risk, University of Seville; Epistemic Blame: Theory and Practice Workshop, University of Johannesburg; MANCEPT Workshops in Political Philosophy—Epistemic Responsibilities of Democratic Citizens, University of Manchester (online), Brown Bag Meetings, CONCEPT Cologne Center for Contemporary Epistemology and the Kantian Tradition, University of Cologne (online); 2021 Eastern APA Meeting, Symposium Session—commentators: Tim Kwiatek (Columbia University) and Sara Ghaffari (Bowling Green State University), New York, NY (online); Social (Distance) Epistemology: Weekly Virtual Events, Social Epistemology Network Online; COGITO Work in Progress Seminar, University of Glasgow (online); Philosophy Visiting Speaker Colloquium, University of Manitoba; GOGITO New Directions in Social Epistemology Speaker Series, University of Glasgow; 55th Annual Meeting of the Western Canadian Philosophical Association, University of Calgary.

On a more personal note, I want to thank Mikias, Angelika, Ulla, and the "Dream Team" from Dreamville Apartments, in Addis Ababa, Ethiopia. I wrote a lot of this book while there on sabbatical in Fall 2021. You guys were amazing companions and I will never forget those times. This book is dedicated to the memory of my mother, Rosemary Scurfield. I have such a vivid memory of early Spring in 2019, we were walking Logan in Assiniboine Park, and I was telling her about my idea for this book. She would not believe me if I told her what the world has been through since 2019. But one thing that stayed pretty much the same is my idea for the book.

My aim has been to create a book that stands by itself, something that unifies, develops, and takes in new directions a number of ideas I've had since I started thinking about epistemic blame. Much of the book is new, including the Introduction, most of Chapters 1, 2, 4, 5, and 6, large chunks of Chapter 3, and all of Chapter 7 and the Conclusion. The book includes passages that have been published elsewhere. In many cases these passages have been gradually re-written or slightly changed—hopefully improved. I am grateful to Wiley and Springer for permission to adapt and include the following material: Chapter 1, section 1.5,

Chapter 3, sections 3.1 and 3.3, and Chapter 5, section 5.1.1 contain adapted material from "There is a Distinctively Epistemic Kind of Blame," *Philosophy and Phenomenological Research* 103(2021): 518–34; Chapter 1, sections 1.2 and 1.3 adapt some material from "Epistemic Blame," *Philosophy Compass* 16–18(2021); Chapter 2, sections 2.6 and 2.7, and Chapter 4, section 4.3 includes and expands upon material from "The Significance of Epistemic Blame," *Erkenntnis* 88 (2023): 807–28; Chapter 6, sections 6.1, 6.3, and 6.4 include and expand upon material from "Standing to Epistemically Blame," *Synthese* 199(2021): 11355–75.

Introduction

This book is about the interpersonal side of thinking. It is about how our beliefs, biases, and methods of inquiry, matter to other people.

We often regard the epistemic dimension of our lives as a comparatively private affair. Belief and inquiry are of course bound up with action in innumerable ways, and so equally bound up with other people in at least that sense. But it also seems true that when I form a belief, for example, that it's going to rain tonight, this belief is somehow more my *own*, something that largely concerns *me*, in a way that my act of betraying your confidence is not. And yet, we clearly do keep an eye on one another's intellectual conduct. People are often exercised and engaged—in both negatively and positively valanced ways—by their perceptions of the intellectual conduct of others. We can be deeply impressed by someone's wit or cleverness, or the ingenuity with which they solve a problem. Words of intellectual praise, such as "clever" or "brilliant," are sometimes used to express this. Conversely, when we're not so impressed, we sometimes call one another "short-sighted," "irrational," "silly," or even "stupid." We sometimes rebuke, feel frustrated by, and demand better from people for beliefs they hold, assertions they make, or methods of inquiry they pursue.

And this seems fair. Some of us get justifiably upset when certain politicians appear to *believe* that humans have no impact on climate change. Some of us get justifiably frustrated by colleagues, or friends, who form their beliefs about contemporary issues solely on the basis of their social media news feed. How people conduct their intellectual lives is important—regardless of whether they are colleagues, friends, loved ones, or leaders of large countries. So, naturally we have an interest in doing so skillfully, and with success. It is also natural that we have ways of responding to one another when things don't go so well. This book is about that response: I call it *epistemic blame*.[1]

To bring my topic into sharper focus, consider a scenario:

THE OFFICE: One day while sitting at their desks, Dwight reveals to Jim that he believes there is a conspiracy amongst their coworkers. The aim of this supposed

---

[1] Why not examine "epistemic praise" and other related positively valanced responses? First, doing so would probably require a book in its own right. Second, epistemic blame will give us plenty to grapple with in what follows. I will discuss positively valanced responses in Chapter 7, sections 7.5 and 7.6. For recent overviews of work on praise, see Stout (2020) and Telech (2022).

Epistemic Blame: The Nature and Norms of Epistemic Relationships. Cameron Boult, Oxford University Press.
© Cameron Boult 2024. DOI: 10.1093/oso/9780192890580.003.0001

2 EPISTEMIC BLAME

conspiracy is to ensure that Dwight will be laid off in the company's upcoming plans to downsize. Dwight is so convinced, he secretively entreats Jim to form an "alliance" to counteract the efforts of the conspiracy. It doesn't take long for Jim to realize Dwight's conspiracy beliefs are unfounded; he has no evidence in support of them. When Jim realizes this, he criticizes Dwight, quite severely (mainly privately, but also through certain overt actions, such as requests for reasons—"how could you think this, Dwight?"—or sighs of exasperation). He criticizes Dwight in a way that goes beyond merely assigning him a bad epistemic grade for his epistemic failing.

Readers familiar with US TV series *The Office*[2] will know the dynamics of this situation. For those unfamiliar, a salient feature of the case is Dwight's tendency to get too wrapped up in his own thoughts. He's a smart enough guy. But he also tends to lose perspective. In our case, Jim realizes that this is one of those moments—a particularly bad instance. So, he reacts in a negatively valanced way. Jim criticizes Dwight for believing something so silly, without any supporting evidence. Importantly, however, he does not think Dwight has done anything *morally* wrong. In essence, what Jim is exercised and engaged by is the fact that Dwight has gone down another rabbit hole. He is being unreflective, careless, and irrational. Jim's response is an example of what I am calling "epistemic blame."

Epistemic blame is not simply a negative form of epistemic evaluation. It is not the same as merely judging that someone is being irrational, or has an unjustified belief. I might judge that you are being irrational, but take a certain pleasure in this fact because of a friendly rivalry between us. Epistemic blame, as I have already implied, is a more exercised or engaged kind of response than a negative epistemic judgment. It involves something more than merely noticing or believing that someone has fallen short of an epistemic standard. It turns out that this "something more" is quite difficult to articulate. One reason it is difficult to articulate is because, whatever it is, the "something more" of epistemic blame seems to have a complex and at times deeply intertwined relationship with the kind of engagement that characterizes *other* forms of blame, such as moral blame.

This book concerns a puzzle about the very idea of epistemic blame. The puzzle arises when reaching for two closely related, but distinct theoretical goals. These goals are: (i) to explain what makes epistemic blame more *significant* than mere negative epistemic evaluation—to explain what the engagement characteristic of epistemic blame consists in; and (ii) to do so without invoking attitudes, behaviors, or practices that seem out of place in the epistemic domain. A related challenge exists in the moral domain—the challenge of explaining what makes moral blame more significant than judging that someone has done something

---

[2] Based on the BBC series of the same name.

wrong, without invoking attitudes, behaviors, or practices that invite clear coun-terexamples. Interestingly, many of the most prominent responses to that chal-lenge do not seem like helpful models upon which to build an account of epistemic blame. Many of our best ways of understanding the significance of moral blame seem ill-suited to helping us understand the significance of epistemic blame. Or so I will argue.

In what sense is this a *puzzle*, as opposed to a set of theoretical desiderata? Making sense of epistemic blame generates a puzzle because goals (i) and (ii) are in tension. A helpful way of understanding this tension is in terms of opposing sources of pressure. On the one hand, epistemic blame seems like a kind of *blame*, in ways that somehow parallel the moral domain. Accounting for this intuition is one source of pressure. As Adam Piovarchy puts it: "if our conception of epistemic blame is too distinct from our conception of moral blame, there is a risk that there won't be any shared features that warrant considering both to be a species of blame" (Piovarchy 2021a, 2). On the other hand, typical ways of understanding what blame is—for example, in terms of negative emotions, or as a kind of protest to wrongdoing—can easily seem out of place in the epistemic domain. It is far from clear how to capture the *engagement* characteristic of blame with attitudes, behaviors, or practices that also seem at home in the epistemic domain. The project of keeping things epistemic, so to speak, is a competing source of pressure.[3]

One way of responding to this puzzle is to simply reject the idea that there is an epistemic kind of blame. Perhaps our sense that Jim blames Dwight for his epistemic failing can be explained in some other way. Another approach is to double down and insist that blame—*whatever* it is—is as equally at home in the epistemic domain as anywhere else. In my experience, people tend to be sympa-thetic to one or the other of these stances in equal measure. Some find it obvious that blame just is a moral notion. Others find talk of epistemic blame perfectly natural. People seem pulled in opposing directions. Why is this? In my view, it is because it is easy to inadequately appreciate *both* of these competing sources of pressure. We really *do* seem to react to one another for culpable epistemic failings in a way that goes beyond negative epistemic evaluation—and appropriately so. But it also seems true that people aren't fitting targets of ordinary forms of moral blame just for epistemically failing. My aim is to solve this puzzle, not by rejecting one or the other of these plausible ideas, but rather by explaining how they can both be true.

Solving the puzzle of epistemic blame requires developing an account of epistemic blame that can achieve goals (i) and (ii), while satisfying a number of other desiderata, ones that will be articulated throughout this investigation. I will

---

[3] Thanks to Elise Woodard and Mona Simion for helpful discussion about ways of framing the puzzle.

4   EPISTEMIC BLAME

argue that the key to solving this puzzle lies in focusing on the distinctive way our epistemic lives are *interpersonal*. Many paradigmatic epistemic failings do not amount to direct personal harms or wrongs, but they are not devoid of an interpersonal dimension altogether. I will argue that people have certain *expectations* of one another as epistemic agents. When someone falls short of an epistemic standard, often they also fall short of a normative expectation that others may legitimately hold them to. This is a kind of interpersonal failing. Making sense of it as such is key to locating a kind of response that has the requisite significance, while fitting neatly within the epistemic domain, to deserve the label "epistemic blame." Developing these ideas is a central aim of this book. The result is what I call the *relationship-based* account of epistemic blame.

According to the relationship-based account, epistemic blame is a distinctive kind of *relationship-modification*. The account draws on some influential, but admittedly controversial ideas in the literature on moral blame. It draws on approaches to moral blame that understand blame as essentially involving a kind of relationship modification.[4] At the heart of the account is the idea of an "epistemic relationship," a kind of relationship that people have insofar as they are epistemic agents in an epistemic community. This book will develop a unique understanding of what it is to *modify* one's epistemic relationship with another person (and oneself), and it will argue that certain ways of modifying one's epistemic relationship with another (or oneself) can, under the right conditions, amount to a kind of blame response. One interesting feature of my development of these central ideas is that, as an account of epistemic blame, the relationship-based approach avoids some of the most important controversies it faces in the moral domain. Some of its perceived weaknesses as a theory of moral blame are precisely what make it promising as a solution to the puzzle of epistemic blame.

Along the way, we will encounter a number of alternative accounts of epistemic blame, alternatives that fall short in instructive ways. Our primary focus will be accounts that model epistemic blame as a kind of *negative emotion*, and accounts that model epistemic blame as the manifestation of a kind of *frustrated desire*. Investigating these options, including my preferred one, is key to resolving the puzzle of epistemic blame. But it also has broader implications. Most importantly, engaging with the puzzle of epistemic blame reveals a great deal about the relationship between the epistemic and practical domains. More precisely, finding an adequate account of epistemic blame deepens our understanding of how the epistemic and practical domains *parallel* and *interact* with one another. This point is worth pausing to elaborate.

It seems clear that when we appropriately blame people for epistemic failings, practical factors often play a role in what *makes* blame appropriate. Consider an

---

[4] Most notably the framework of T.M. Scanlon (2008).

employee who earns an unfair salary because of their boss's culpably prejudiced and irrational beliefs about the employee's competences. Other things being equal, it is natural to suggest that the practical *harm* or *wrong* done to the employee is what makes blaming the boss for their prejudiced beliefs seem called for. But is that the whole story? Must there *always* be something moral or practical at stake when blame for epistemic failings is appropriate? Studying epistemic blame forces us to get clear on the role that non-epistemic factors play in our responses to epistemic failings. I will be arguing that "epistemic relationship modification" can play a role in our blaming practices *independently* of moral and practical considerations, and, in this sense, constitutes a genuine kind of blame in its own right—one that *parallels* the moral domain. That said, I will defend this idea while accounting for the platitude, just noted, that most of the time the character, or force, of our responses to one another for epistemic failings is clearly influenced by non-epistemic factors. In fact, this is yet another way in which epistemic relationships are useful tools. Understanding epistemic blame in terms of relationships positions us, not just to make sense of an epistemic kind of blame, but also to put a new kind of *structure* on our understanding of its interaction with moral blame. One of my aims is to model abstract questions about epistemic blame's connection with the moral and practical domains in very familiar and concrete terms—ones having to do with relationship dynamics. This in turn is interesting because it gives structure to the broader notion that the epistemic domain itself is deeply intertwined with other normative domains. This is of course a familiar idea. Early forms of pragmatism, the literature on practical reasons for belief, and more recently the literature on pragmatic and moral encroachment, all tell us a great deal about (potential) points of interaction between the epistemic and practical domains. I will argue that epistemic blame provides a novel angle, one that is interesting not least because it illuminates an important aspect of this interaction independently of commitments about things like pragmatic or moral encroachment, or whether there are practical reasons for belief.

Perhaps most interesting of all, with an adequate understanding of the possibility of epistemic blame in hand, a wide range of new questions come clearly into view—many of which broadly mirror the sorts of questions that moral theorists have been engaging with in increasing detail over the last twenty years or more. The most pressing of these questions concern the *ethics* and *value* of epistemic blame. What are the appropriate targets of epistemic blame? What, if anything, does it take to have the proper *standing* to epistemically blame? What is the purpose and value of our practice of epistemically blaming others? Is it possible that we would be better off abandoning this practice for some other form of responding to one another for epistemic failings? The relationship-based account of epistemic blame can shed useful light on these questions. More specifically, I will be arguing that epistemic relationships can help us achieve the following surprisingly disparate set of goals: set principled limits on appropriate targets of

6 EPISTEMIC BLAME

epistemic blame; explain why some people but not others have the standing to epistemically blame; and explain why our epistemic blaming practice has distinctive value. We will also see that there is much to be done in this new area of social epistemology—including examining the connections between epistemic blame and social power, and using epistemic relationships to illuminate a wide range of epistemic harms, such as testimonial injustice, epistemic exploitation, and gaslighting.

Here is the plan of the book. Chapter 1 introduces the very idea of epistemic blame. It motivates the thought that there is a distinct form of epistemic blame. It does so in two ways: first, by arguing that we should *expect* there to be an epistemic kind of blame, in light of considerations about the parallels between ethics and epistemology; second, it does so by explaining the role that the concept of epistemic blame already plays (often implicitly) in a number of central debates in epistemology, including debates about epistemic norms and epistemic justification, doxastic control, and the "authority" of epistemic normativity. Motivating the idea that there is an epistemic kind of blame is intimately connected with the project of accounting for the *nature* of epistemic blame. Successfully accounting for the nature of epistemic blame is first and foremost a matter of solving the puzzle of epistemic blame. The rest of Chapter 1 lays out that puzzle.

Laying out the puzzle requires articulating a clear way of understanding just what it means to talk about the "significance" and "fittingness" of a blame response. I propose that the significance of blame has something crucial to do with the *interpersonal* nature of blame, which I in turn cash out in terms of normative expectations. In blaming others, we hold them to normative expectations in a distinctive way, underlining the significance of blame. Regarding fittingness, I propose that a response counts as fitting to a failure in the epistemic domain just in case an epistemic failing can be sufficient to render the response legitimate. That is to say, there must be circumstances under which it can be legitimate to direct the response toward someone for an epistemic failing, as opposed to downstream practical consequences of the epistemic failing. As we'll see, developing this condition requires a fairly in-depth examination of just what it means for an evaluation to be made "independently of practical considerations," and this is something that will come up in various places throughout the book.

Chapter 2 examines two ways we might try solving the puzzle of epistemic blame. These are: understanding epistemic blame in terms of a kind of negative emotional response, and understanding it as a characteristic range of dispositions, unified insofar as they are manifestations of a desire that people not "believe badly." I argue that both of these approaches fail, but instructively so. What's common and instructive about their respective failures is that both approaches lean quite heavily in the direction of understanding epistemic blame as having something essential to do with our *relationships* with one another. The problem with these accounts is that they either do not go far enough with this idea, or they do so in the wrong sort of way. In a word, emotion-based accounts cannot do justice to the requirement of *fittingness*, while desire-based accounts have a hard time with epistemic blame's *significance*.

Chapter 3 takes a cue from this observation and develops an account of epistemic blame that appeals directly to relationship modification. The key to successfully doing this is to develop an account of "epistemic relationships." The bulk of the chapter is dedicated to doing so. The chapter develops an account of what modifications to our epistemic relationships consist in, and how this can be understood as a form of blame. The chapter also addresses a number of initial concerns we might have about the relationship-based approach to epistemic blame, setting the stage for an argument that the account successfully resolves the puzzle of epistemic blame.

It is worth noting again that the relationship-based framework is controversial as an account of (moral) blame. In the process of developing my epistemic extension of the account, I take it upon myself to defend the framework against a number of challenges it has been presented with in moral philosophy. One of the more significant proposals I make in this regard involves some substantive adjustments to a few key ideas in the Scanlonian account, largely in response to recent worries from Angela Smith (2013) and Eugene Chislenko (2020). To the extent that the basic approach I take to the framework diverges from Scanlon, it should be emphasized that I am not engaged in a project of Scanlon exegesis. Some may find that what I call an "epistemic extension" of the relationship-based framework bares resemblance to Scanlon's original work in fairly superficial respects only. I leave it to the reader to decide for themselves what to make of my interpretation of Scanlon, in addition to whether they consider my revisions to the account a welcome development—though I will of course be doing my best to make the case that they are.

Chapter 4 argues that the relationship-based account resolves the puzzle of epistemic blame. The relationship-based account can explain the significance of epistemic blame without invoking practices, behaviors, or attitudes that seem out of place in the epistemic domain. The key to the former claim is arguing that— contrary to proponents of emotion-based approaches to blame—we can account for what it is to hold one another to *normative expectations* without giving a central role to negative emotions. The key to the latter claim is arguing that epistemic relationship modification is something that we can appropriately do "independently of practical considerations." This goes a long way toward demonstrating the relationship-based account's promise in resolving the puzzle of epistemic blame. But it is also important to ensure confidence that the account is well-motivated on independent grounds, and that it is not itself vulnerable to obvious fatal objections. So, the chapter also advertises some further advantages of the account over the alternatives, and responds to the most pressing remaining objections.

8 EPISTEMIC BLAME

With the puzzle of epistemic blame resolved, Chapters 5 to 7 turn to new avenues of exploration. The primary foci are a number of issues in the ethics of epistemic blame. The first of these concerns the *scope* of appropriate epistemic blame. People are typically regarded as appropriate targets of epistemic blame for things like dogmatism, wishful thinking, and other forms of biased cognition. Is this really the case, and what other sorts of things might be appropriate targets of epistemic blame? In Chapter 5, I address this question by taking a step back and considering whether dogmatism, wishful thinking, and other forms of biased cognition really can be failings for which people are appropriate targets of epistemic blame. I examine whether doxastic states, acts of inquiry, and assertions can be appropriate targets of epistemic blame, ultimately arriving at the conclusion that they can. Expanding the discussion, I then examine how epistemic blame connects with the growing literature on *testimonial injustice,* and other related epistemic harms. I consider the possibility that another central and important kind of failing for which people can be appropriate targets of epistemic blame is the harm of testimonial injustice. This opens the door to a unified framework for making sense of a wide range of epistemic harms, including testimonial injustice through credibility excess, epistemic exploitation, and gaslighting.

In addition to examining who the appropriate *targets* of epistemic blame are, we can also examine who the appropriate epistemic *blamers* are. In Chapter 6, the second issue in the ethics of epistemic blame I explore concerns the "standing" to epistemically blame. My main focus is resolving a seeming tension between the so-called "business condition" on standing to blame, and the fact that it is not immediately obvious in what way a person's typical epistemic failing is the business of anybody else. As will be clear by the time we reach this point in the book, the relationship-based approach is well-suited to make good sense of this apparent tension. But spelling this out carefully requires connecting the relationship-based account to recent work from Sandy Goldberg (2017, 2018) on "practice-based entitlements to expect." The chapter puts structure on a wide range of ways our epistemic blame responses can be differentiated, partly with the help of Goldberg's work on entitlements to expect. Exploring this connection between epistemic relationships and the epistemic expectations involved in other kinds of relationships ends up being a central way the relationship-based account gives concrete shape to epistemic blame's interaction with the moral and practical domains. More specifically, I will argue that the extent to which our epistemic relationships are impacted by intentions and expectations constitutive of other kinds of relationships, is the extent to which epistemic blame interacts with normative domains beyond the epistemic. A key advantage of my approach, we will see, is that it frames this issue in terms of some familiar ideas about how the dynamics of our relationships can change.

Finally, Chapter 7 asks the question: should we epistemically blame one another? Might there be other, better ways of responding to one another for epistemically blameworthy conduct? The discussion has two main parts. First, I develop a positive defense of the value of epistemic blame, understood as a negatively valanced form of epistemic relationship modification. I focus on *democratic participation* as a case study to highlight one important role for epistemic blame in our social lives. The connection between responsibilities of citizens in a democracy and epistemic blame also generates further support for the relationship-based account of epistemic blame. In the second part of the chapter, I turn my attention to the question of whether negatively valanced relationship modification is the best way to respond to people for epistemic failings. I examine an alternative proposal, namely that *positively* valanced epistemic relationship modification is a better way to respond to epistemic failings. I challenge this proposal on the grounds that, in many circumstances, positively valanced epistemic relationship modification would be paternalistic, inefficacious, and demanding it of epistemic agents will track social and material inequalities in unjust ways.

1

The Puzzle of Epistemic Blame

This chapter motivates the idea that there is an epistemic kind of blame. One reason to take this idea seriously comes from reflections on parallels between epistemology and ethics. Another comes from considerations about the role that blame and blameworthiness play in contemporary epistemology. I examine the role that epistemic blame plays in debates about epistemic norms and epistemic justification, doxastic control, and the "authority" of epistemic normativity. I then introduce a puzzle. The puzzle arises when aiming to achieve two distinct, but closely related and equally important theoretical goals: (i) explaining what makes epistemic blame more significant than mere negative epistemic evaluation, and (ii) doing so without invoking attitudes, behaviors, or practices that seem out of place in the epistemic domain. These goals push in opposing directions, generating a puzzle about epistemic blame. A core aim of this chapter is to carefully articulate these competing sources of pressure, developing criteria that an account of epistemic blame must meet in order to resolve the puzzle.

1.1 Preliminaries

What are we talking about when we talk about *blame*? According to Justin Coates and Neal Tognazzini, "(b)lame is a reaction to something of negative normative significance about someone or their behavior" (Coates and Tognazzini 2014). Beyond this bare statement, not much can be said without controversy. Indeed, the project of analyzing *moral* blame has not led to a great deal of consensus (Fricker 2016; Sliwa 2019). There are live debates about such central questions as whether moral blame necessarily requires emotion, or judgment, or some conative component. Disagreement persists on the relationship between moral blame and control, and what exactly serves as an appropriate target for blame (an action, attitude, character trait, person, etc.).

Views in the literature do display some common features. These features allow us to divide the terrain into prominent groupings. *Cognitive* approaches understand blame in terms of a kind of judgment. Jonathan Glover holds that blame is a judgment that someone has "stained their moral record" (Glover 1970, 64). Michael Zimmerman holds that blame is a judgment that an agent has done something to reduce their normative "score" (Zimmerman 1988, 38). *Emotion-based* approaches understand blame in terms of the manifestation of negative

---

Epistemic Blame: The Nature and Norms of Epistemic Relationships. Cameron Boult, Oxford University Press.
© Cameron Boult 2024. DOI: 10.1093/oso/9780192890580.003.0002

emotional responses. P.F. Strawson is widely taken to have inspired the view that blame essentially involves the manifestation of reactive attitudes, such as indignation, resentment, and guilt (in the case of self-blame) (Strawson 1962).[1] *Conative* approaches understand blame in terms of its connection to motivational states, such as desires, or intentions. George Sher has argued that blame is a set of dispositions to feel and behave organized around a certain belief-desire pair (Sher 2006). T.M. Scanlon defends an account in terms of relationship modification which will ultimately serve as my preferred model for developing an account of epistemic blame (Scanlon 2008, 2013). We will spend a considerable amount of time in Chapters 2 and 3 looking further into these ideas in an epistemic context.

Still others approach the nature of blame by theorizing first and foremost about its *function*. For instance, consequentialists have tended to think of blame in terms of its utility, and have argued that it plays the particular societal role it does by being the expression of disapproval and contempt (Arneson 2003; Smart 1970). More recently, authors such as Miranda Fricker, Paulina Sliwa, David Shoemaker, and Manuel Vargas have developed theories of the function of blame, arriving at very different views about the nature of blame as a result (Fricker 2016; Shoemaker and Vargas 2021; Sliwa 2019). This is by no means an exhaustive list of the ways theorists approach the nature of moral blame, and I will not be engaging with all of these frameworks in this book.[2] The taxonomy is nevertheless helpful to have on hand when investigating the nature of epistemic blame.

An important note of clarification: all parties to the dispute about the nature of blame agree that blame and its expression come in many varieties. Sometimes we blame with a light rebuke, other times we announce the end of a friendship. Being able to explain what these varieties have in common is a central part of the project of developing an account of blame. While all agree there are varieties of blame, the accounts just categorized differ on what they think makes various attitudes and behaviors instances of *blame*. In this book, I will sometimes use the expression "vehicles of blame" to refer to the varieties of ways we can manifest or express blame.

---

[1] It is far from clear whether Strawson himself endorses this view. He and many others who have been inspired by his work seem to regard blame as a sui generis attitude *alongside* attitudes like resentment and indignation. Nevertheless, many writers on the topic of blame have adopted the practice of labeling approaches that give negative emotions a central role "Strawsonian." I will follow suit.

[2] I will not engage much with questions about blame's function. One reason is because function-talk strikes me as hostage to empirical issues in challenging ways. Of course, this depends on what notion of function is at play in function-talk. Claims about *etiological function* come with significant empirical commitments. Other notions of function less so. To my knowledge, the precise notion of function that is at play in much discussion of the function of blame tends not to be specified in much detail. In any case, pretty much everything I say in this book should be consistent with a variety of views about the function of blame. I simply won't be taking epistemic blame's function as my starting point. I do, however, engage with issues surrounding the *benefits* of epistemic blame in Chapter 7. See Queloz (2021) for helpful critical discussion of function-based approaches to blame.

12 EPISTEMIC BLAME

We have already intuitively fixed the target of my discussion. But what does it really mean to speak of "epistemic blame"? What exactly makes this notion *epistemic* as opposed to something else, such as moral? In the present context— one characterized by an interest in finding the correct account of the nature of epistemic blame—some ways of understanding the very idea of "epistemic blame" will be more useful than others.

For example, some theorists appear to understand "epistemic blame" as a kind of blame that attaches to *belief* (or other doxastic states, such as disbelief, or suspension of belief). This can easily lead to confusion, since there are cases of blame for doxastic states that seem *moral* in nature, perhaps in addition to being epistemic.[3] Tara believes there is no point in respecting other people's feelings, simply because she has had enough with the world and doesn't care anymore. She has not yet acted on this belief. But in conversation, her sister Toni learns about this unsettling turn in Tara's moral outlook, and blames her for even thinking this way. It is natural to think of this as a kind of moral blame, as opposed to, or perhaps in addition to something deserving the title "epistemic blame." There may also be cases of epistemic blame that do not target a person's doxastic states, at least not directly, or primarily. Epistemic blame may target an *assertion*, some- one's actions of *inquiry*, or a particular *inference* someone makes.

On a wider usage, epistemic blame is not merely blame for belief, though beliefs and other doxastic states may be paradigm targets; rather, epistemic blame is a kind of blame directed at someone for an epistemic failing. Consider again the example of THE OFFICE. In this case, an epistemic norm has been violated, the target of Jim's response has epistemically failed in some way. On the wider approach, the idea is that an epistemic blame response is a response to *that* failing. Still, there are at least two ways of understanding this wider view. First, we might take it to entail simply that people can be morally blamed for epistemic failings.[4] Perhaps blame for epistemic failings is the same sort of thing as moral blame, even though what is at issue is a distinctive kind of failing. One challenge for this approach is that it seems we can blame people for epistemic conduct that is not immoral. As Quassim Cassam argues, it seems overly moralistic to maintain that all epistemically blameworthy conduct is also worthy of moral blame (2019, 18).[5] The example of Dwight is a potential case in point.

An alternative approach holds that epistemic blame is a distinctive form of blame for epistemic failings. One way to articulate this idea is in terms of the kinds

---

[3] See Begby (2018), Basu (2018, 2019, 2021), Basu and Schroeder (2019), and Marusic and White (2018) for helpful discussions of morally blameworthy belief, and the closely connected idea of "doxastic wronging." See Saint-Croix (2022) for the morality of *attention*. See Enoch and Spectre (forthcoming) for skepticism about the idea that beliefs can morally wrong.

[4] Or blamed in some other practical way, such as professionally.

[5] See also Brown (2020a, 2020b) for a prominent example of somebody who argues that we can be blameworthy for not complying with what we epistemically ought to do, where this is true independ- ently of any moral or practical considerations.

of goods that epistemic blamers, as such, are in some sense concerned with. We might say that epistemic blame is a kind of blame for epistemic failings oriented distinctively around the promotion of epistemic goods such as believing truly and avoiding believing falsely (Boult 2023, 2021a, 2021c; Brown 2020a, 2020b; Piovarchy 2021a; Schmidt 2021).[6] On this approach, many targets of epistemic blame may also be targets of moral blame, or other kinds of blame. But they need not be.[7] This way of articulating epistemic blame may raise some worries of its own, particularly the question of whether it leads to a kind of "epistemic bloat."[8] But I will not be in a position to address these worries until my preferred account of epistemic blame is on the table. I return to them in Chapter 5. For now, I think the basic idea is intuitive enough. From this point onward, unless I note otherwise, I will have this notion of epistemic blame in mind when I use the term "epistemic blame."

1.2 Normative Parallels

To a large extent this book takes the idea of epistemic blame at face value, and attempts to make sense of it by developing an account of its nature. What are we doing when we epistemically blame one another? As I explain below, the project of arguing for the existence of epistemic blame, and arguing for a particular account of what it is, are deeply intertwined. However, it is worth motivating these intertwined projects a bit more before getting under way. It is worth motivating them in a way that goes beyond soliciting intuitions. The first source of motivation comes from reflections on parallels between epistemology and ethics.

It has become commonplace in philosophy to treat ethics and epistemology as importantly related to one other. They are often both regarded as normative domains, in the sense that ethics is about what we ought to do, and epistemology is about what we ought to believe. This is a large oversimplification. But it is a

---

[6] I leave the connection between epistemic blame and the promotion of epistemic goods purposely imprecise. It is difficult to say anything more precise without taking on theoretical commitments about the function of epistemic blame. However, note that I do not mean to imply here that a person must *consciously endorse* epistemic norms in order to count as epistemically blaming someone. A more plausible way of understanding the connection might go via a causal-historical story about the *practice* of epistemic blame, connecting this practice to the needs that an epistemic community has for the acquisition and maintenance of epistemic goods (see Chapter 4, section 4.2). Also note that there may be other epistemic goods that are not reducible to true belief—perhaps knowledge is one (Kelp 2018), or some epistemically irreducible form of understanding (Kvanvig 2003).

[7] This point will become increasingly important as we explore the ethics of epistemic blame in Chapters 5 and 6.

[8] In a nutshell, the worry is that many things which seem evaluable from the perspective of promoting epistemic goods do not intuitively seem like appropriate targets of epistemic blame. Dealing with the problem of epistemic bloat requires setting a principled limit on what sorts of things can be appropriate targets of epistemic blame. I do this in Chapter 5.

14 EPISTEMIC BLAME

useful starting point for further illuminating some ways ethics and epistemology seem to parallel one another. To begin, consider the widely held view that there are at least two fundamentally different kinds of normative *reasons*—practical and epistemic. To a rough approximation, a practical reason is a fact, proposition, or some other kind of feature or consideration that favors *acting* in a certain way. To an equally rough approximation, an epistemic reason is a fact, proposition, or some other kind of feature or consideration that favors *believing* in a certain way.[9] Epistemic reasons are said to have a bearing on *truth*, whereas practical reasons have a bearing on what to *do*. There is a live debate about whether there can be practical reasons for belief. From at least as far back as Pascal, philosophers have debated the precise relationship between belief, truth, and practical considerations. But this debate presupposes a distinction between practical and epistemic reasons.

The same questions asked about practical reasons arise for epistemic reasons: What is the normative force of an epistemic reason? Where does that force come from? How can we weigh our epistemic reasons? Are epistemic reasons perspective-dependent? This appears to highlight a significant parallel between ethics and epistemology: both are domains containing something that is widely regarded as a fundamental normative unit, namely that of a reason. They are domains that raise parallel questions arising from the concept of a reason.[10]

"Justification" has a distinctively epistemic use. As with reasons, the difference between epistemic and moral justification centers on considerations about truth as opposed to moral goods. Epistemic justification is paradigmatically taken to be a status enjoyed by beliefs and other doxastic states. While it also seems true that beliefs can be morally justified (or unjustified, as the example of Tara suggests), it is one thing for an action or attitude to be justified from the point of view of morality, and quite another for it to be justified from the epistemic point of view. The same kinds of questions asked about moral justification are asked about epistemic justification: When is a belief or attitude epistemically justified? What is it in virtue of which this justification consists? What is the difference between being epistemically justified in a belief or attitude and merely excused? This appears to highlight another significant parallel between ethics and epistemology: both are domains in which actions or attitudes can be regarded as justified or unjustified. They are domains that raise parallel questions arising from the concept of justification.

---

[9] Or forming or maintaining some other doxastic state, such as disbelief, or suspension of belief.

[10] Of course, there are theorists who maintain that there are fundamental differences between epistemic and practical reasons. Recently, Maguire and Woods have argued that only practical reasons can be "authoritatively normative" (2020). Relatedly, Susanne Mantel (2019) argues that epistemic reasons are not "substantively normative." Interestingly, other theorists have begun deploying the very idea of epistemic blame to defend just the opposite claim. I return to discussion of this point in section 1.4.

THE PUZZLE OF EPISTEMIC BLAME   15

Similar points hold for rationality,[11] and deontological terms such as "obligation," "permission," and "ought."[12] There is also a large literature on the epistemic (or intellectual) virtues (Baehr 2011; Roberts and Wood 2007; Zagzebski 1996). Such virtues are said to resemble moral virtues in their structure (character traits with a certain motivational component, etc.), but are nevertheless taken to be epistemic in nature. It is common to find theorists drawing or at least presupposing parallels between ethics and epistemology in other, perhaps less central ways. For example, there is a growing literature on epistemic *injustice*—a kind of injustice that shares basic central features with distributive and other forms of injustice, but which is distinctively epistemic (I return to an in-depth discussion of this topic in Chapter 5). Other recent work engages with "epistemic dilemmas" (Hughes 2019, 2021, forthcoming; McCain et al. 2021), "epistemic rights" (Watson 2021), "epistemic enhancement" (Carter et al. forthcoming), and "epistemic expressivism" (Beddor 2019; Chrisman 2012; cf. Boult and Kohler 2020; Boult 2017c). In each case, a basic assumption is at play: there is a normative parallel between ethics and epistemology, one that makes sense of the idea that we can pick out a concept that shares basic features with a concept in the moral domain, but which is also importantly different—somehow *epistemic*.[13]

What relevance do any of these parallels have for epistemic blame? I want to make two key claims about this. The first involves an admittedly weak inductive argument whose flaws are instructive. It goes like this: *blame* is a central concept of ethics; there are many parallels between ethics and epistemology; if these parallels run deep, we should expect there to be a kind of blame in epistemology—perhaps an *epistemic* kind of blame; the fact that there are so many parallels between ethics and epistemology suggests that they do run deep; so, since these parallels run deep, we should expect there to be a kind of blame in epistemology.

This line of reasoning is perhaps dubious. After all, there might be some important difference between blame and other normative phenomena which makes all these parallels an unrepresentative basis upon which to reason inductively like this. However, and this is my second point, rather than simply being a random collection of similarities, most of these parallels are *systematically interconnected*. For instance, the concept of a reason is connected to the concept of rationality; the concepts of permission and obligation are connected to the

---

[11] Just as actions can be rational, so too can doxastic states.

[12] Just as actions can be permitted, so too can doxastic states; just as certain actions can be the ones we *ought to* do, so too can certain doxastic states be the ones we *ought* to have.

[13] Some theorists see the relationship between ethics and epistemology as more intimate than one of parallel. For example, Linda Zagzebski has argued that "epistemology is a *branch* of ethics" (Zagzebski 1996, xiv, 6). Others say things that seem to imply the two domains are not really distinct at all—perhaps one is simply a sub-domain of the other, or perhaps all evaluative claims in one are grounded in or in some way reducible to claims in the other. Such theorists will likely be skeptical of the idea of a distinctive form of epistemic blame. Notice, for now, that these ideas simply seem to reinforce the claim being made in this section: namely, that drawing *parallels* between ethics and epistemology is a way of motivating epistemic blame.

16 EPISTEMIC BLAME

concept of justification; and so on. We should expect these parallels to run deep because they are part of an interrelated web of concepts.

This leads to a key insight: in the moral domain, *blame* and *blameworthiness* are part of a family of interrelated concepts. For example, "ought"-judgments, reasons, and many other normative concepts in the moral domain stand in an intimate relationship with blame. A minimal condition on being the appropriate target of blame is that you've done something you *ought* not to have done, or that you weren't *permitted* to do. One cannot be blameworthy for doing something that one had no *reason* not to do. Thus, if the parallels run deep, perhaps we should expect there to be an epistemic kind of blame. Perhaps we should expect parallel concepts of (epistemic) "ought," (epistemic) permission, and (epistemic) reasons to bear a family connection to epistemic blame and blameworthiness.

1.3 Blame in Epistemology

Besides the argument from parallels—which concludes that we should *expect* there to be such a thing as epistemic blame—there are other considerations that motivate taking epistemic blame seriously. Precisely in line with the expectations we concluded we ought to have last section, epistemologists increasingly deploy the notion of epistemic blame in debates about other epistemological issues. Jessica Brown is one of the leading theorists to point out the fundamental role that appeals to epistemic blame, blameworthiness, and blamelessness play in epistemological theorizing. She notes:

> [T]he notion of blame has become of increasing interest to epistemology. In part, this is because of the increasing interest in the idea of epistemic norms, the idea that certain epistemic conditions, say knowledge, are the norm for belief, assertion or practical reasoning. Just as in the ethical case, we might expect cases in which such epistemic norms may be blamelessly violated.   (Brown 2017, 1)

This highlights the importance of blame-talk for the epistemic norms debates. But it appears that blame-talk is equally important for debates about epistemic justification. Regardless of whether one is a radical externalist,[14] a standard reliabilist, or an internalist evidentialist about epistemic justification, it seems one must draw a distinction between justified and merely blameless belief in order to account for a fundamentally diverse range of cases (Brown 2020a; Boult 2019, 2017a, 2017b; see also Williamson forthcoming; Littlejohn forthcoming). Let's examine this in more detail.

---

[14] A radical externalist endorses a *factive* conception of epistemic justification (Littlejohn 2012; Sutton 2007; Williamson forthcoming).

THE PUZZLE OF EPISTEMIC BLAME   17

Starting with radical externalists, Brown has pointed out that, because these externalists maintain that epistemic norms are factive, there can be pairs of cases in which both agents fail to count as justified with respect to a norm, but where there is nevertheless an intuitive normative difference between the cases. Perhaps one person formed a false belief by wishful thinking, and the other was carefully deceived. Because both agents have unjustified beliefs by radical externalist lights, we might worry whether radical externalists have a correct understanding of the nature of justified belief. In order to respond to this sort of worry, the radical externalist typically appeals to the idea that the difference here comes down to differences in blamelessness/blameworthiness. The first person is unjustified and *blameworthy*, while the second is unjustified but blameless.

A similar point can be made about simple forms of reliabilism, such as process reliabilism. Roughly speaking, simple reliabilists count a belief justified just in case it was formed by a reliable process, such as perception. This is so regardless of whether the agent forming the belief is subject to defeaters. Intuitively, however, an agent who believes that p despite being subject to defeaters against the truth of p is in some sense worthy of negative evaluation. Thus, there are cases of agents counting as justified by simple reliabilist lights whom it is nevertheless fitting to evaluate negatively. In order to respond to this worry, the process reliabilist must regard such agents as blameworthy as opposed to having an unjustified belief (since the belief is, by stipulation here, nevertheless "justified").

Finally, even internalists rely on the notion of blameless/blameworthy belief. Take an internalist who defends certain non-factive epistemic norms, such as the norm that one ought to proportion one's beliefs to the evidence. Subjects can fail to meet this norm in different ways. For example, one agent may falsely believe that p as a result of seemingly good but fallacious reasoning—perhaps she lacks the ability to see this for herself because she's never been taught to beware this form of fallacious reasoning. Another agent may falsely believe that p as a result of the same fallacious reasoning, despite all the training they've received on how to avoid it. Although both agents form unjustified beliefs with respect to the relevant norm, the former subject seems blameless, while the latter does not. It seems we need the notion of blamelessness/blameworthiness to account for the difference between the cases (Brown 2020a).[15]

In addition to playing this role in debates about epistemic norms and epistemic justification, the concept of epistemic blame—or something closely related—has also been a central focus of the very large debate about the kind of *control* we have

---

[15] Someone might object that uses of "blameworthy" and "blameless" in the justification debates do not imply the sort of distinction I am most interested in this book, namely that between negative evaluation and something more engaged. If not, I would be interested to hear more about what exactly differentiates an unjustified belief from a blameworthy one. One alternative usage of "blame" is what some theorists call the *causal sense* ("I'm sorry we're late, but I blame the flat tire"). This clearly isn't what epistemologists have in mind. I return to this issue in the book's Conclusion.

18 EPISTEMIC BLAME

over our doxastic states. The main driver of that debate is more or less the question of how, given the seeming lack of *voluntary control* we have over our doxastic states, people can ever be appropriate targets of blame, or other deonto-logical forms of evaluation, concerning their doxastic states. A related literature directly explores the concept of "blameworthy belief": theorists have developed highly complex accounts of the *conditions* under which someone can be blame-worthy for their doxastic states. There is a firm connection with the doxastic voluntarism literature here, insofar as theorists have typically sought to find conditions on blameworthy belief that do justice to the kind of control (or lack thereof) people seem to have over their doxastic states (Alston 1988; Chrisman 2008, 2012; Chuard and Southwood 2009; Montmarquet 1992; Nottelmann 2007; Owens 2000; Peels 2016; Ryan 2003; Steup 2008; and many others).[16]

The amount of work that has been done in this area might make it seem as though the topic of epistemic blame is quite well-worn. But this would be a mistaken assumption. There are of course many different philosophical issues surrounding blame and blameworthiness. Two importantly different questions about blame are: what *is* blame? And when is blame *appropriate*, or *justified*? Answering the first question requires articulating the nature of blame, explaining what attitudes, actions, feelings, or dispositions it consists in. Answering the second question requires developing an account of the *norms* of blaming. It requires developing an "ethics of blame." This sort of question obviously gives rise to a wide range of further issues, many of which comprise distinct areas of study, including issues surrounding the standing to blame, the nature of excuses and forgiveness, and whether we ought to blame at all. A third sort of issue might be classified as making sense of the *metaphysical possibility* of blameworthiness. This is essentially the problem of moral responsibility and free will. If it turned out our actions and attitudes are ultimately not really "down to us," could we really be blameworthy for them? Much of the literature on "blameworthy belief" has focused on the metaphysical possibility of epistemic blameworthiness, which is essentially a narrower version of this larger problem—one focused on the distinc-tive kind of control (or lack-thereof) we seem to have over our doxastic states. While important in its own right—I will make my own contributions to it in Chapter 5—this issue is subtly different from the basic question of what it *is* to epistemically blame someone, as well as various questions about whether and when we *ought* to do it. It is striking that most of that literature simply assumes (implicitly or explicitly) an understanding of the nature of epistemic blame, or doesn't say much about what they have in mind. This is striking because the adequacy of answers to questions in the ethics and metaphysics of blame would

---

[16] Contributors to these debates about doxastic control and blameworthy belief do not always seem to be interested in the conception of epistemic blame I narrowed discussion down to in section 1.2. In many cases, I find it somewhat unclear what conception of blame is at issue in these debates.

THE PUZZLE OF EPISTEMIC BLAME   19

seem to depend on our understanding of what blame is. Even more striking is that the standardly assumed view is probably mistaken (as we shall see in Chapter 2).

We've done a fair bit to motivate the idea that there is an epistemic kind of blame. The argument from parallels suggests we should expect as much. In line with that expectation, considerations about the role of blame and blameworthiness in epistemology suggest that there is a wide practice of endorsing the idea of epistemic blame among experts.

1.4 The Authority of Epistemic Normativity

A final consideration motivating the importance of epistemic blame—one that might even explain *why* the concept of blame plays a central role in epistemology—is the connection between blame and what is sometimes called "authoritative normativity." Recently Antti Kauppinen (2018; forthcoming) and Sebastian Schmidt (2021; ms) have independently pointed out the relevance of this connection for the debate about the authority of *epistemic* normativity.

What does it mean to call normativity "authoritative"? Notice that not all "ought"s are created equal. You ought to play only optimal moves in chess. But, other things being equal, you also ought to avoid getting punched in the face. If you are playing chess and someone tells you they'll punch you in the face if you play the optimal move, is it still true that you ought to play the optimal move? Probably not (Maguire and Woods 2020, 217). So, it seems there is something you *really* ought (not) to do here, even though it is true that you ought to play only optimal moves in chess. If you like, we can allow that there is some kind of normativity governing chess play—Kauppinen calls it "formal normativity," a kind of normativity generated "by way of conventions or the internal standards of success that many activities have" (forthcoming, 3). Formal normativity isn't *authoritative* normativity. Only the latter tells us what we *really* ought to do. Or so the idea goes.[17]

Recently, a central and live debate in meta-normative theory concerns the question of whether epistemic normativity is authoritative.[18] You ought to proportion your beliefs to the evidence. But you also ought to do what you can to be

---

[17] I am not attempting to provide an informative definition of "authoritative normativity," something it is notoriously difficult to do. The idea that it has something essential to do with what we "really" ought to do is standard in the literature. The connection I am about to discuss, between *blameworthiness* and authoritative norm violation, is deployed by Kauppinen and Schmidt explicitly as a "mark" of authority. The idea that there is a meaningful distinction between formal and authoritative normativity is of course controversial. See Howard and Laskowsky (forthcoming) for an insightful critique. In my view, this distinction—or something like it—is prominent enough to warrant highlighting its relevance for epistemic blame.

[18] See Boult (2017c), Côté-Bouchard (2017), Cowie (2019), Cuneo (2007), Hazlett (2013), Kiesewetter (2022), Maguire and Woods (2020), Mantel (2019), Reisner (2018), and many others.

20 EPISTEMIC BLAME

happy. If forming some belief in proportion to the evidence (say, about how bad at chess you are) will make you less happy, is it still true that you ought to form the belief? This is a somewhat artificial example, but the basic idea is simple. It seems we can ask what we ought to do from the epistemic perspective; but we can also ask what we ought to do from other perspectives (moral, prudential, etc.). Does the epistemic "ought" carry any authoritative weight in this nexus of "ought"s? Does it have a bearing on what you *really* ought to do? Or is it more like an "ought" of chess?

There are a number of views we might take on this question. Three sorts of stance include:

(i) Epistemic "ought"s are not authoritative; they depend entirely on other normative considerations for their weight.

(ii) Epistemic "ought"s are authoritative, and their authority is a sui generis kind. There is a question about what you *really ought* to do from the epistemic perspective; and there is a question about what you *really* ought to do from the practical perspective. These authoritative domains are incommensurable.

(iii) Epistemic "ought"s are authoritative, but they can also be weighed against other authoritative "ought"s, such as prudential or moral ones. In addition to a variety of authoritative "ought"s, there is an all-things-considered "ought."

My aim is not to settle which of these stances is correct. Rather my aim is to point out the connection between this debate and epistemic blame. The connection is comprised of two claims. The first claim is that there is a link between authoritative norms and blameworthiness or criticizability. Kauppinen and Schmidt argue (independently) that the link is roughly this:

- If it can be fitting to blame a person for failing to comply with norm N, N is authoritative.

The second claim is that people can be blameworthy (or criticizable)[19] for violating epistemic norms. As Schmidt puts it:

Violations of epistemic norms in non-culpable and trivial cases can well deserve [epistemic blame].[20] The presented analysis of these cases thus calls into doubt

---

[19] I return below to an important qualification about Kauppinen's precise formulation of the link.
[20] The original text says: "suspensions of epistemic trust if they are manifestations of epistemic vice". On Schmidt's view this is what epistemic blame amounts to. He draws in part on my own account of epistemic blame as developed in Chapter 3 (which develops on work originally published in Boult 2021a). In order to keep things less complicated for the time being, and since we will not have the

[the skeptic of the authority of epistemic normativity][21] by revealing a *purely epistemic* kind of blame that might be appropriate in these cases—a blame that reflects the normative significance we attach to *purely epistemic norms.*

(2021, 21 my italics)

If the linking claim is correct, and *if* we can be blameworthy for violating epistemic norms, then it seems epistemic norms are authoritative. This in turn would be interesting because it has a direct bearing on our understanding of the relationship between practical and epistemic norms, as well as our understanding of normativity in general.

There are of course ways we can put pressure on all this. Is something as full-blooded as "authoritative" normativity really necessary for opening us up to blame? Perhaps we should be more liberal with blameworthiness. For example, some hold that people can be appropriately blamed for bad chess moves. Perhaps the same goes for other games, like sudoku. Bad chess and sudoku moves are paradigm examples of *non*-authoritative norm violations (violations of formal norms). So, perhaps norm authority is not necessary for opening people up to blame. If that's so, perhaps the question of epistemic blame has no bearing on the authority of epistemic normativity.

In response, I do not find it plausible that people can be genuinely blameworthy for bad chess moves or bad sudoku play—not when these things are considered independently of additional practical, moral, or perhaps even epistemic factors. In my view, something of additional prudential, moral, or perhaps epistemic significance would have to hang in the balance for a bad chess move to seem blameworthy. For example, if a bad chess move is the proximate cause of doing something else that is objectionable, such as patronizing one's opponent, then perhaps it is blameworthy. Of course, people can be *negatively evaluated* for bad game play, and harshly so. Anyone who has played a spirited game of just about anything knows this. But that does not yet establish that people can be blameworthy for violating the norms of games. More is needed to challenge the link between blameworthiness and authoritative normativity.[22]

---

resources to make sense of my preferred account until much later, I have simply replaced the original phrasing with "epistemic blame." The point is to highlight Schmidt's claim that the appropriateness of a "purely epistemic kind of blame" is evidence of the authority of epistemic normativity.

[21] The original text here is "anti-normativism about evidence," which means the same thing as skepticism about the authority of epistemic normativity. I have opted for the latter since it's the terminology I've already introduced.

[22] The following occurred to me after having a conversation with Chris Kelp about the concept of authoritative normativity. Perhaps those who feel inclined to blame others (and/or themselves) for bad chess moves should consider whether the response they have in mind is actually an *epistemic* blame response ("what a horrible move—I'm so *stupid!*"). To flip the worry above on its head, then, perhaps "chess blame" just is a form of epistemic blame. Perhaps chess is useful for getting a grip on the authority of *epistemic* normativity. I return to this example in the context of epistemic self-blame in Chapter 4.

22   EPISTEMIC BLAME

Might there be other non-authoritative norms that more plausibly open us up to blame than norms of games? I will leave that to the opponent of the linking principle. My aim for present purposes is simply to highlight how a prominent defense of the authority of epistemic normativity depends for its success on existential claims about the very phenomenon that is the subject of this book. It depends on epistemic blame. Thus, an additional motivation for taking epistemic blame seriously is its implications for the debate about the "authority" of epistemic normativity.

Before moving on, a brief word about Kauppinen's approach to this debate. Strictly speaking, Kauppinen does not claim that there is a connection between authoritative "ought"s and *blame*, but rather *criticizability*. His view is that people can be criticizable in a distinctively epistemic way. One burden Kauppinen takes on with this approach is that, in order to avoid proliferating authoritatively normative domains without end, he must argue for a serious restriction on the sorts of things for which people can be criticizable. For example, he must argue that—despite how things may seem—people are *not* criticizable for making suboptimal moves in chess (especially not if they had overriding reasons to do so). To assuage conflicting intuitions about this, Kauppinen draws a distinction between criticizability of the *agent* and criticizability of the *action* (or attitude). In the chess case, our feeling that some criticism may be warranted when someone makes a bad move (call it "chess criticism") is to be explained in terms of the idea that the *move* is criticizable. According to Kauppinen, no *agent* is ever criticizable for making a bad chess move. And this is because chess isn't authoritatively normative.[23]

In my view, this is a fairly implausible and counterintuitive position. I think it's quite clear that people (agents) can be criticizable for making bad chess moves. They are criticizable from the point of view of good chess. In my view, the connection Kauppinen is really interested in is that between authoritative normativity and *criticism that amounts to blame*—not just any criticism. We might even think that this is what "criticism of the agent" basically amounts to. Perhaps, roughly speaking, it's blame. In my preferred vocabulary, blame is a form of criticism that is somehow more *engaged* or *exercised* than mere negative evaluation. It's a way of holding someone to an expectation. So, while Kauppinen may disagree that there is an epistemic kind of blame, a case can be made that there is an important connection between his (and others') work on the authority of epistemic normativity and epistemic blame.

---

[23] Kauppinen might allow that a person can be criticizable for making a bad chess move as the proximate cause of doing something else that's criticizable (e.g., as in the example above, in order to patronize their opponent).

1.5 The Puzzle

Whatever blame is, we have seen it's a response that goes beyond mere negative evaluation. According to many, a central aim in developing an account of blame is explaining *what it is* about blame that goes beyond mere negative evaluation. Were blame no different from negative evaluation (such as a judgment of wrongdoing), it is far from clear why we would need distinct concepts in our conceptual repertoire. Certain proponents of purely cognitive accounts of blame might disagree, but it is widely held that whatever the difference is, blame is somehow more significant, or weightier than mere negative evaluation.

R.J. Wallace (2011, 367) has proposed we model the distinction between negative evaluation (including judgments of blameworthiness) and blaming on the familiar distinction between judging that something is *valuable*, and actually *valuing* it. The difference between judging X valuable and actually valuing X comes down to a difference in one's engagement with X. When one values X, one is engaged and exercised by X. One gets excited by opportunities to X, disappointed by missing opportunities to X. Meanwhile, in judging X valuable, one merely recognizes that there are reasons for someone to be so exercised, without necessarily being that way oneself. According to Wallace, something similar is true of blame. When one blames someone for X, one is engaged and exercised by what they have done. It matters to one that this person has done something bad, or flouted some norm, and by blaming them for it one manifests this concern in an engaged way. Meanwhile, in judging someone blameworthy, one merely judges that there are reasons for one (or someone else) to be so engaged, without necessarily being that way oneself. As Pamela Hieronymi puts it, blame has a characteristic "sting, force, and depth" that merely assigning someone a bad grade does not (Hieronymi 2004, 116–17).

This idea goes hand in hand with some familiar features of blame. For instance, blame seems governed by norms of *standing*. Not just anyone can justifiably blame anyone else, even if the target of blame is blameworthy. It is widely held that one needs to meet certain conditions on standing that make blame an appropriate thing for one to do. For example, according to some, there is something flawed about blame that is in some way "hypocritical" (Fritz and Miller 2018, 2019; Lippert-Rasmussen 2020; Piovarchy 2020, forthcoming; Rossi 2018, 2020; Tierney 2021). Perhaps relatedly, there may be something flawed about blaming someone for a wrongdoing in which you are somehow "complicit" (Coates and Tognazzini 2014; Cohen 2006; Cornell and Sepinwall 2020; Engen 2020). In Chapter 6, I return to the so-called "non-hypocrisy" and "non-complicity" conditions, and also focus in detail on yet another standing condition, known as the "business condition." For now, the important point is that meeting such conditions seems less important, if important at all, when merely negatively evaluating others.

The appropriateness of blaming someone also seems tied to questions about what is under their *control*, and what they are in a position to *know*, in a way that merely negatively evaluating someone does not. The literature on doxastic voluntarism reflects the first point. There is also an enormous literature on the general idea that "ought implies can,"[24] as well as the idea that (non-culpable) ignorance can excuse.[25] The latter does not examine the question of whether ignorance excuses one from being the target of merely negative evaluation. It examines whether ignorance excuses one from being the appropriate target of *blame*, or other more engaged kinds of evaluation and sanction. Arguably something similar goes for discussions of the ought implies can principle. These differences—the ones surrounding standing, control, and ignorance—highlight a characteristic significance that blame has. Any theory of blame should be able to explain what this significance consists in, what makes blame the sort of thing that has these properties. For short, sometimes I will simply refer to this explanatory goal as SIGNIFICANCE.

The puzzle of epistemic blame is the puzzle of how to explain the significance of epistemic blame without invoking practices, attitudes, or behaviors that seem out of place in the epistemic domain. How to account for the engagement characteristic of blame in a way that fits with familiar features of the epistemic domain? To get an intuitive sense that there is indeed a puzzle here, briefly consider some options. Note right away that it seems cognitive approaches are especially ill-suited to solving the puzzle, since they seem tantamount to rejecting SIGNIFICANCE in the first place. I have already stated my position on going that route. In contrast, emotion-based accounts look like a natural starting place. As we have seen, according to a large number of moral philosophers who take a broadly "Strawsonian" approach to blame (Menges 2017; Strawson 1962; Wolf 2011), moral blame essentially involves negative reactive attitudes such as indignation, resentment, and guilt (in the case of self-blame). We might take a cue from this approach and argue that the "sting, force, and depth" of epistemic blame is to be explained in terms of the idea that blame is essentially a kind of *negative emotional response*.

The trouble with going this route is that negative emotional responses such as indignation and resentment can easily seem somewhat out of place in the epistemic domain. It will take me a large part of Chapter 2 to fully argue for this claim, but here is an opening observation. Consider judging that Bob is epistemically unjustified in believing that there are 799 motes of dust on his desk, or that Tim ought to know how many states there are in the USA. It seems one can make such judgments, and a wide range of similar others, without feeling any sort of emotion or concern for the matter. Of course, not all epistemic judgments concern trivial

---

[24] See Alex King (2019) for a recent book-length discussion.
[25] See Robichaud and Weiland (2017), Rosen (2003), and Zimmerman (1988, 2008).

matters, and some may indeed be quite heated in nature. But the coolness of epistemic judgment seems to be a characteristic feature of many forms of epistemic judgment. Now, we have just said that an essential property of blame is that it goes *beyond* mere negative evaluation. So, even if negative evaluation in the epistemic domain is characteristically cool in nature, this need not imply anything about the nature of epistemic blame. However, the characteristic coolness of epistemic evaluation strikes me as defeasible evidence that whatever kind of response epistemic blame is, it will most plausibly be characterized by behaviors and attitudes that are in some sense less heated than the behaviors and attitudes that tend to characterize moral blame. Indignation and resentment are suspicious resources for filling out an account of epistemic blame in this regard.[26]

Of course, there are other approaches to the nature of blame, and not all of them put negative emotional responses at the center of the account. According to Angela Smith, for example, what makes blame distinctive is that it is a response that necessarily involves the disposition to register *protest* in light of one's judgment that one has been *wronged* by another (2013, 36). Pamela Hieronymi argues that blame necessarily involves the judgment that the target of blame has shown the blamer (or someone else) *ill will*, and reacting accordingly (2004, 116). And as we have seen, George Sher argues, roughly, that blame is the manifestation of a frustrated desire that the target of blame not have acted badly (2006, 101–8).

Each of these approaches comes with its own explanation of what it is about blame that goes beyond mere negative evaluation. What is important for present purposes is that, while none of them gives as central a role to negative emotional responses as emotion-based accounts, it is not clear that the features they appeal to in explaining the significance of blame would be any more at home in the epistemic domain than negative emotional responses. Registering protest in light of a judgment that one has been *wronged* by another does not seem like a fitting response toward that person for fallaciously reasoning about their scratch 'n' win lotto ticket. The same point seems true with respect to judgments that the target of blame has shown one *ill will*. It seems odd to think of many of the most typical kinds of epistemic failings frequently presented as epistemically blameworthy failings (fallacious reasoning, wishful thinking, intellectual laziness) as involving one person *wronging* another, or showing another person *ill will*.[27]

---

[26] A second, related, argument against a negative emotional account of epistemic blame is based on a more direct appeal to paradigm cases. Consider how you might respond to a colleague upon learning that they'd formed a belief about Prince Harry's love life, merely on the basis of the tabloids they read; or think of how you might respond to a friend for believing that they've got a winning scratch 'n' win lotto ticket, just because they have not won in quite some time. While the details of the cases require filling out, it's hard to imagine what would make indignation and resentment fitting responses *to these epistemic failings*. Insofar as we keep the distinctively epistemic dimension of someone's failure in mind, negative emotional responses such as indignation and resentment do not really seem like typically fitting responses.

[27] In Chapter 5, I discuss perpetrators of epistemic injustice as possible targets of epistemic blame. Perhaps such cases are ones in which a judgment that someone has shown you ill will, or at least

26 EPISTEMIC BLAME

Perhaps Sher's account is more applicable in this regard. We will consider his account, and the possibility of extending it to the epistemic domain, in detail in the second half of Chapter 2. For now, if indignation and resentment are out of place in the epistemic domain, it seems on first blush that so are judgments of ill will and protestations to wrongdoings. For short, sometimes I will simply refer to the explanatory goal of finding practices, behaviors, or attitudes that seem at home in the epistemic domain as FITTINGNESS.

An important note to avoid potential confusion. It may seem obvious that almost *any* theory of moral blame deploys resources that are out of place in the epistemic domain, simply in virtue of imposing conditions like the judgment that someone has done something *morally* wrong. This even applies to my preferred approach, which draws on ideas from T.M. Scanlon. But the point at issue here is not simply the trivial observation that theories of *moral* blame cannot serve as theories of *epistemic* blame. Rather, the point is that, in virtue of their particular ways of explaining the significance of moral blame, it is far from clear whether any of the above accounts can serve as a *basis* or *model* upon which to build an account of epistemic blame.

The puzzle of epistemic blame is not merely a puzzle for emotion-based approaches to the nature of blame. There appears to be a more general tension between the observation that blame is a kind of response that goes beyond mere negative evaluation—that it has a certain "sting, force, and depth"—and the observation that epistemic judgment is in some sense a typically cool (or cooler) sort of normative judgment than moral judgment. The more engaged a given response is, the less distinctively *epistemic* it will tend to seem. Meanwhile, the more at home in the epistemic domain a given response is, the less it may seem to resemble an actual form of *blame*. What sort of response, if any, can accommodate both sources of pressure here? It will take the better part of this book to answer this question, and thereby fully resolve the tension. But in order to put ourselves in a position to do that, we must first develop a more precise way of thinking about what this tension amounts to, thus bringing into view a clearer understanding of what it will take to resolve the puzzle of epistemic blame.

1.6 Significance and Fittingness

Developing a more precise way of understanding the tension I have identified requires precisifying the two sources of pressure generating the puzzle: What does it really mean to say that blame responses are more "significant" than mere negative evaluation? And what does it really mean to say that some responses

---

wronged you, would be fitting. As we will see—especially in section 5.6—the connection between epistemic blame and various forms of epistemic harm is complex, and well worth examining in its own right.

are "out of place" in the epistemic domain? In this section, I flesh this out in more detail. My aim is to develop criteria that an account of epistemic blame must meet in order to resolve the puzzle of epistemic blame.[28]

1.6.1 Significance and Normative Expectations

I have been somewhat loosely connecting the "significance" of blame to things like being *engaged* and *exercised* in a certain way, as well as Hieronymi's idea that blame has a certain *sting, force, and depth.* Is there a single unifying concept that can help us get a grip on what this suggestive cluster of ideas amounts to?

Wallace is again helpful here. He argues that to blame someone, minimally one must judge or in some way take it that they have fallen short of certain relationship-constituting *expectations* (1994, 18–51). According to Wallace, the key thing that takes blame beyond negative evaluation is that blame involves holding someone to an expectation in a way that mere negative evaluation need not imply. The idea of an "expectation" that Wallace has in mind is admittedly tricky to pin down further. But I think the basic concept is intuitive, and thus useful for cashing out the significance of blame. In reflecting on moments of blame, we are all familiar with the sense that an expectation has not been met, that someone has in some way or another let us down, or fallen short of what is demanded of them by virtue of certain facts about your relations with them, or their relations with others. According to Wallace, what it is to "hold someone to an expectation" in the relevant sense, just is to be susceptible to the *reactive attitudes* as he narrowly understands them (resentment, indignation, and guilt) when one judges someone to have fallen short of those expectations. Here is Wallace:

> Reactive attitudes as a class are distinguished by their connection with expectations, so that any particular state of reactive emotion must be explained by the belief that some expectation has been breached. It is the explanatory role of such beliefs about the violation of an expectation that is the defining characteristic of the states of reactive emotion as a class.   (Wallace 1994, 33)

In defense of this claim, Wallace points out the difference between expectations in the *predictive* sense ("I expect it to rain later"), and expectations in what we might call a *demand-making* sense. According to Wallace, the *only* way to adequately

---

[28] The way I understand "significance" and "fittingness" in what follows is only as precise and representative as it needs to be in order to facilitate this aim. That said, I do aim to fill out these notions in a way that is neutral on the question of what the correct account of epistemic blame is. In Chapter 4, I will revisit whether my approach in this section should be refined, or altogether replaced, when I assess my account of epistemic blame's ability to resolve the tension.

delineate the sense of expectation that is relevant to the domain of holding responsible, is in terms of susceptibility to the reactive attitudes narrowly construed (2011, 369). (From now on, when I use the phrase "reactive attitudes narrowly construed," I mean paradigm negative emotional responses such as indignation and resentment.)

I think Wallace is onto something with his focus on relationships and expectations. But, as will become clear in later chapters, I disagree that the *only* way to make sense of holding someone to an expectation is through the reactive attitudes narrowly construed. It is a substantive dispute at the heart of this book exactly what holding someone to an expectation requires. Doing this, in my view, is a core part of the project of defending an account of the nature of blame. For now, I am simply in the business of articulating what blame's *significance* amounts to. My proposal is to borrow Wallace's idea that the significance of blame should be understood in terms of holding someone to an expectation in the demand-making sense. Henceforward, I will call this a *normative* expectation. To understand what it means to epistemically blame someone, we need to get a grip on what sorts of behaviors, practices, or attitudes can constitute holding someone to a normative expectation in the epistemic domain. Whatever epistemic blame is, it must be a way of holding others (or oneself) to a normative expectation.

Here is a potential worry about this way of articulating the significance of (epistemic) blame. Perhaps normative expectations are just as much a part of mere negative epistemic evaluation as they are epistemic blame. Sinan Dogramaci (2012) appears to defend something along these lines in discussing the interpersonal impacts of sincere assertions that someone is (being) "irrational." According to Dogramaci,

> when we make our evaluations of others' beliefs, we are *intending for them to follow the correct rules*. Actually, I'll claim something slightly stronger; I claim this: our evaluations have an overall tendency to *influence our audience to follow the endorsed rules*. (Dogramaci 2012, 520, emphasis added)

In this quote, Dogramaci seems to connect mere negative epistemic evaluation with something like a normative expectation, or at any rate a fairly serious kind of engagement—namely, the *intention* that people follow correct rules, and exerting an *influence* on the audience to follow those rules. If Dogramaci is right, perhaps the significance I have attributed to epistemic blame is something that is in fact shared by many other sorts of responses, including sincere assertions involving terms of epistemic appraisal, such as "irrational." If so, it would seem that I have failed to pick out anything particularly interesting and important about epistemic blame.[29]

---

[29] After this book began proof production, I noticed that Smartt (2023) raises a similar concern.

I don't think I have failed to pick out something important here. In my view, merely (sincerely) asserting (or judging, for that matter) that someone is being irrational does not amount to holding them to a normative expectation, or in other words does not have the sort of interpersonal importance that Dogramaci appears to claim it does. To see why, notice that we can sincerely assert that someone is being irrational in a light-hearted way, or in a way that amounts to taking a kind of pleasure in someone's irrationality. Consider asserting that one of your friendly rivals, or a political opponent, is being irrational. Evaluations such as "S is being irrational" may express an *understanding* of, and perhaps even *endorsement* of, certain normative expectations. But there is an important distinction between endorsing those expectations and *holding* someone (or oneself) to them. My claim is that the significance of blame is best captured in terms of the idea that, in blaming someone, we hold them to normative expectations, as opposed merely to manifesting an understanding or even endorsement of them. A sincere assertion that someone is being irrational does not amount to holding them to normative expectations, unless perhaps it is done in a certain mode, or accompanied by other attitudes or behaviors. In my view, one way of characterizing the mode I have in mind is precisely when a sincere assertion that someone is being irrational (partially) comprises an epistemic blame response.

Notice that we have not yet pinned down a list of attitudes, actions, or practices that can serve as vehicles for epistemic blame. Ultimately, I will take a *variable* approach to this list, according to which many different sorts of responses can be vehicles for epistemic blame. I am not alone here. My most sophisticated opponent, Jessica Brown, also takes a variable approach. I think many would agree that we sometimes (perhaps often) epistemically blame people *by* sincerely asserting that they are being irrational—as long as certain other conditions are met. Thus, views such as Dogramaci's about sincere assertions that people are being irrational need not conflict with my account of what makes epistemic blame more significant than mere negative epistemic evaluation. A sincere assertion that someone is being irrational, when it has the sort of interpersonal weight identified by Dogramaci, just is a form of what I have in mind when I talk about epistemic blame. I suggest the same is true of negative evaluations and/or assertions involving other negative terms of epistemic appraisal, such as "unjustified," "ignorant," and "unreasonable."

1.6.2 Fittingness and Being "Independent of Practical Considerations"

What does it take for a response to be "out of place" in the epistemic domain? In my view, a response is out of place in the epistemic domain just in case it is not a fitting sort of response to an epistemic failing. My proposal is that something counts as a fitting response to an epistemic failing just in case it is a type of response that can be rendered legitimate by an epistemic failing, *independently of*

30 EPISTEMIC BLAME

practical concerns. What does it take to be legitimate "independently of practical concerns"? This is a complex question, and we'll return to it in a number of places throughout the book. But the basic idea is this. A response is rendered legitimate by an epistemic failing independently of practical concerns just in case the epistemic failing, as opposed to downstream practical consequences of the epistemic failing, legitimizes the response in question.

Note right away that, understood as such, pursuing the goal of FITTINGNESS does not require us to presuppose a "purist" or "intellectualist" view of the nature of epistemic evaluation. In particular, while it may appear to, it does not assume the falsity of the increasingly prominent thesis of pragmatic encroachment.[30] According to pragmatic encroachers, whether someone knows that p or has a justified belief that p is in part a function of what is at stake for that person in getting things right. The well-known bank cases frequently employed in defense of subject sensitive invariantism (SSI) about knowledge-ascriptions are a good illustration of the idea of stakes.[31] The primary motivation for the idea that stakes can affect knowledge or justified belief is the shiftiness of our intuitions about who can appropriately be ascribed knowledge or justified belief across cases in which all truth-relevant factors remain fixed but there is a change in the practical stakes. Additional motivation comes in the form of principles connecting knowledge and justified belief to reasons for action (Fantl and McGrath 2009; Hawthorne 2003; Hawthorne and Stanley 2008; Ross and Schroeder 2012). It can easily seem that whether you have sufficient reason to φ can in part be affected by how much is at stake in φ-ing. If reasons for action are as tightly connected to knowledge as many pragmatic encroachers have argued, then perhaps it is a short further step to the conclusion that knowledge itself is partly determined by practical factors.

The debate about pragmatic encroachment is one of the central live debates of contemporary epistemology. As such, I have no intention of predicating my discussion of the puzzle of epistemic blame on either the rejection or endorsement of pragmatic encroachment. Happily, we can stay neutral on this issue. To see this, notice that the thesis of pragmatic encroachment as prominently understood involves a story about the mechanisms by which practical factors affect the *epistemic threshold* an agent needs to meet in order to count as knowing that p, or be justified in believing that p (a threshold determining the strength of their evidence). Taking this on board, it is clear that my proposal does not assume the rejection of pragmatic encroachment. To see this, perhaps an example will be useful.

---

[30] I discuss moral encroachment shortly below.

[31] See Fantl and McGrath (2009). Contrast SSI with views that claim the *assessor's* practical context affects whether the subject being assessed knows that p. These include contextualism and various kinds of relativism (DeRose 2009, 2005; McKenna 2015; McKenna and Hannon 2020).

Sticking with the bank cases, assume that Jack's practical circumstances are such that the threshold he needs to meet in order to count as justified in believing that the bank is open on Saturday is a bit higher than it is for Jill. Jack does something intellectually remiss when reasoning about the bank—say, he lets wishful thinking move him to believe that the bank will be open, rather than proportioning his belief to the evidence (thus meeting the relevant threshold). Jill does precisely the same thing. We can equally ask of both Jack and Jill whether their failure to proportion their beliefs to the evidence is itself sufficient to render a given response legitimate. It's just that—if some version of pragmatic encroachment is correct—what it *takes* for each of them to count as having adequately proportioned their beliefs to the evidence is different, because of what is at stake for each of them. Jack's intellectual failing may seem worse because the stakes are higher for him, and as a result, his wishful thinking leaves him with a doxastic state that is further from the appropriate evidential threshold than Jill's. His failing is *epistemically* worse, partially as a function of the stakes.

But this is neither here nor there for present purposes. An epistemic blame response, as I understand it in this book, is a response directed at Jack *for his epistemic failing*, as opposed, for example, to any downstream practical consequences of this failing (such as losing his house). My proposal simply requires that an *epistemic* failing—however the nature of that failing itself may or may not be impacted by practical factors—be sufficient to render a given response legitimate. Of course, as in many cases of epistemic blame, and as I have remarked, responses to one failing can overlap in important ways with responses to others. Someone can be the target of epistemic and other kinds of blame simultaneously. And again, I explore dimensions of this complexity in detail throughout this book—it's part of why the topic of epistemic blame is interesting. But for now, the key point is simply that considering whether a response targets an epistemic failing itself, as opposed to any downstream practical consequences of it, and asking whether that epistemic failing is sufficient to render the response legitimate, does not presuppose the falsity of pragmatic encroachment.

There are surely further issues to explore at the intersection of epistemic blame, pragmatic encroachment, and related concepts. The thesis of *moral* encroachment is a case in point. At the broadest level, this is the idea that moral factors can impact the epistemic status of a doxastic state. As Renée Jorgensen (Bollinger 2020a) explains, we face a number of choice points in theorizing about moral encroachment, leading to a range of moral encroachment views. One choice point concerns the *mechanism* by which moral factors influence the normative status of a belief. Following Jorgensen, roughly, three main options are: (i) moral considerations influence the *threshold* of evidential support required for justified belief, or some other epistemic status (Basu and Schroeder 2019; Fritz 2017; Guerrero 2007; Pace 2011); (ii) moral considerations influence the *sphere of error possibilities* that must be ruled out for justified belief, or some other epistemic status

(Bollinger 2020b; Buchak 2014; Gardiner 2020; Moss 2018); (iii) moral considerations can themselves constitute reasons for belief, directly influencing what one ought to believe (Basu 2019). On this last (most controversial) view, a belief can be unjustified, in part, because of an insufficient sensitivity to moral reasons.

I won't take a stand on whether any of these views is correct. What is important here is that my approach to FITTINGNESS is consistent with all of them. I think this is for the same reason it is consistent with the prominent approach to pragmatic encroachment just discussed. We can put the point as follows: a response complies with FITTINGNESS just in case an *epistemic* failing—however the nature of that failing itself may or may not have been impacted by moral factors—is sufficient to render the response legitimate.[32]

In Chapters 2 and 4, I will examine two other ways that we might understand the idea of being "independent of practical considerations." In considering a defense of the emotion-based view in Chapter 2, I will point out that there is a general *explanatory* sense in which our assessment of an epistemic failing can be "dependent on practical considerations." The basic idea is that, because good epistemic conduct tends to be conducive to practical goods, this *explains* why good epistemic conduct matters, and thus, an assessment of any epistemic failing is dependent on practical considerations in light of this explanatory connection. In defending my own relationship-based account in Chapter 3, I will point out that there is also a *genealogical* sense in which our assessment of an epistemic failing can be "dependent on practical considerations." The basic idea is that, because the epistemic concepts we deploy in making epistemic evaluations took the shape they have in light of practical pressures, an assessment of any epistemic failing is dependent on practical considerations in a genealogical sense. As we will see, it is best to hold off discussion of the details of these ideas until they arise naturally in their respective contexts. But the key point to flag here is that neither of them is equivalent to the central sense of being "independent of practical considerations" I have in mind in FITTINGNESS. Call this the *target-based* sense. Again, FITTINGNESS simply states that a response counts as rendered legitimate by an epistemic failing independently of practical considerations just in case:

> the epistemic failing, as opposed to downstream practical consequences of the epistemic failing, legitimizes the response in question.

How can we tell whether a given response is rendered legitimate by a given failing? Often, I will be relying on direct intuitive judgments about cases. But I will also do

---

[32] My point jibes with how most moral encroachers conceive of their views. As Jorgensen puts it: "Quite importantly, moral encroachment does not commit a theorist to thinking that moral norms conflict with, and sometimes overrule, epistemic norms. In fact many explicitly reject this suggestion (including Basu [2020]; Bollinger 2020b; Johnson-King and Babic [2020]; Schroeder 2018). Instead, the picture is just that moral norms explain why the range of epistemically permissible attitudes is narrower in some cases of interest" (2020a, 16).

what I can, when appropriate, to provide more substantive ways of adjudicating this. For example, a helpful way to approach this question is to think about what is *disvaluable* about a given failing, and determine whether that sort of disvalue is, under the right circumstances, *sufficient* to render a given response legitimate.

When my good friend fails to keep an important secret of mine, one thing that is disvaluable about this is that it's a kind of betrayal. Arguably, the harm of betrayal amounts to a kind of *personal* disrespect, one rooted in relationship-specific norms of friendship, or partnership (Seim 2019). When I *resent* my best friend for not keeping the secret, my resentment has features that may be rendered legitimate by the disvalue at issue here, in the sense that the harm of betrayal is, under the right circumstances, sufficient to make resentment a legitimate response to direct toward my friend.

What kinds of disvalue do epistemic failings have? This is obviously a large question, and I don't want my view about epistemic blame to be hostage to substantive commitments in epistemic axiology. However, it is useful to have a broad sense of some options here. I find it easier to start with claims about what epistemic disvalue is *not*. For instance, it seems fairly clear that the disvalue of many paradigmatic epistemic failings does not consist in *directly personal* harm in the way that failing to keep a secret can be a directly personal harm. It can seem difficult to get a grip on what this would even mean, given that many paradigmatic epistemic failings—like failing to proportion one's beliefs to the evidence—quite simply do not in any straightforward sense involve actions or attitudes directed toward features of a specific individual's personality, preferences, or allegiances, *as such*. My discussion of testimonial injustice and other epistemic harms in Chapter 5 may complicate this point. Indeed, I will remain open to the possibility that some epistemic failings, as such, can amount to direct personal harms. But my primary point here is that many epistemic failings seem to abstract away from these kinds of particulars. To think of the point one way, the distinctive disvalue of failing to proportion one's beliefs to the evidence has something to do with the disvalue of not doing one's part to get at the *truth* and to avoid falsity. Those are not direct personal harms, as such.

A natural thought is that epistemic disvalue just amounts to the disvalue (perhaps intrinsic, perhaps instrumental) of obstructing epistemic goods like the acquisition of true belief, and the avoidance of false belief. However, I doubt this can be the whole story. For one thing, such obstructions can come about in ways that have nothing to do with, let alone reflect the competence of, an individual person or group of people. A computer might crash and thereby obstruct me from forming all kinds of true beliefs. Sometimes we fail to get at the truth through no fault of our own. In my view, epistemic failings can also have disvalue insofar as they reveal certain facts about epistemic *agents* and their regard for the epistemic community. I find it natural to think that epistemic failings, as such, can have disvalue by being ways in which a person fails to live up to certain normative expectations that we have of them. As I will explore throughout this book, this reveals a sense in which epistemic failings, even when not *directly* personal, nonetheless have an important *interpersonal* dimension. Thus, even if epistemic failings do not amount to direct personal harms, they amount to more than merely the obstruction of epistemic goods like truth and knowledge. When determining whether a given response can be rendered legitimate by an epistemic failing, we must take into account the distinctive interpersonal dimension of epistemic failings, too.

Foundational issues remain about the relationship between the value of truth, the value of epistemic agency, and intellectually responsible conduct. Perhaps all epistemic value reduces to just one type of epistemic value. Perhaps there are a plurality of epistemic values, and corresponding *dis*values (Haddock et al. 2009). I leave it open whether any item in the picture just sketched ultimately reduces to any other. For now, my elaboration of SIGNIFICANCE and FITTINGNESS amounts to a way of articulating the available *space* for a concept of epistemic blame. The first part of this book is devoted to finding a kind of response that can fill that space.

1.7 Conclusion

This chapter articulated and motivated the idea of epistemic blame. Primary considerations in favor of the idea focus on parallels between epistemology and ethics, the role that epistemic blame already plays in central debates in epistemology, including recent work on epistemic norms and epistemic justification, doxastic control, and the "authority" of (epistemic) normativity. I then put a puzzle on the table when it comes to taking the idea of epistemic blame seriously. We now have the materials needed to move forward and consider some different approaches to solving that puzzle.

2

Negative Emotions and Frustrated Desires

I suggested last chapter that an emotion-based approach to blame seems ill-suited as a basis for building an account of epistemic blame. On the face of it, such an approach does not seem well-suited to accounting for SIGNIFICANCE without invoking attitudes or practices that seem out of place in the epistemic domain. But as I've indicated already, emotion-based approaches to blame are perhaps the most prominent in the literature. Moreover, not everyone will agree that negative emotions—in all their possible varieties—are out of place in the epistemic domain. I begin this chapter by giving the option of an emotion-based approach to epistemic blame a more thorough hearing. I consider three ways of pursuing such an approach—a *bold*, *moderate*, and *sui generis* version. I argue that all three approaches are inadequate. Importantly, however, a diagnosis of what goes wrong provides an initial source of evidence that there is an important role for relationships in epistemic blame.

The chapter then turns to the most developed, competing account of epistemic blame in the literature, due to Jessica Brown (2020a). Brown draws on influential work by George Sher (2006), who identifies moral blame with a characteristic set of dispositions to feel and behave, unified by a particular belief-desire pair. The nutshell idea is that blame is the manifestation of a kind of unsatisfied desire. Extending this idea to the epistemic domain, Brown argues that epistemic blame is the manifestation of an unsatisfied desire with distinctively epistemic content. This account makes headway over emotion-based accounts. It makes headway by accounting for SIGNIFICANCE with a *conative* component—something that seems more at home in the epistemic domain than negative emotions. Nevertheless, I will argue that it falls short of being an adequate account of epistemic blame. Brown's approach to the conative component of epistemic blame doesn't go far *enough* in accounting for SIGNIFICANCE. But this again is instructive. As we'll see, the way Brown's account falls short provides another clue that there is an important role for relationships in epistemic blame.

Epistemic Blame: The Nature and Norms of Epistemic Relationships. Cameron Boult, Oxford University Press.
© Cameron Boult 2024. DOI: 10.1093/oso/9780192890580.003.0003

36 EPISTEMIC BLAME

2.1 A (Very) Brief History of Blame

Before diving in, it will be helpful to motivate thinking of blame in terms of negative emotional responses in a bit more depth.[1] To do so, this section briefly traces the history of a number of earlier approaches to the nature of blame. The inadequacy of these approaches partially explains the prominence of emotion-based accounts of blame.[2]

Blame has not until relatively recently been explored in detail as a self-standing topic. Questions about blame have typically surfaced in discussions of the nature of responsibility, the problem of free will, and normative ethics more generally. Philosophers historically speaking have been less interested in the nature of blame itself than in the relevance blame has for these wider issues. One idea, endorsed by J.J.C. Smart (1970), and other consequentialist moral philosophers, is that moral blame is the outward *expression* of disapproval. Such an idea has historically found favor with consequentialists in part because it conceptualizes blame in terms of the function or consequences of our blaming practices, a function that in turn fits neatly with a consequentialist view of moral rightness. For example, speaking of the related notions of praise and "dispraise," Smart says:

> Praising a person is...an important act in itself—it has significant effects. A utilitarian must therefore learn to control his acts of praise and dispraise, thus perhaps concealing his approval of an action when he thinks that the expression of such approval might have bad effects, and perhaps even praising actions of which he does not really approve.   (Smart 1970, 49–50)

Presumably, the idea is that, qua form of disapproval, blame (or "dispraise") acts as a kind of social deterrent. After all, people tend to have a strong aversion to being disapproved of. While questions about the function of blame are of course important to be able to answer, it seems fairly clear that moral blame cannot be understood as the outward expression of disapproval. This is for the simple reason that there are clear cases of *private* or otherwise unexpressed moral blame. For example, it seems entirely possible for me to blame you for failing to take the garbage out while concealing my blame, perhaps as part of some broader strategy for getting something else I want. In general, it is important not to mistake *symptoms* or *expressions* of blame for blame itself.

---

[1] The notion of "negative emotion" needs disambiguation, in a way that cuts across the three-pronged distinction I draw in this chapter. Kristján Kristjannson argues that there are no fewer than six senses of "negative emotion" one can find in moral psychology, philosophy, ordinary life, and other areas. I will be using this term in this book to refer to what Kristjannson calls "negatively evaluating emotions" (2003, 357). These are emotions that evaluate their object or their object's situation as negative (357).

[2] Parts of this section are indebted to Sher (2006, 71–92).

For these and other reasons, moral philosophers have developed accounts of moral blame that do not require appeal to outward expression. Some approaches conceive of moral blame as a kind of belief or judgment—we saw last chapter that these are known as *cognitive* accounts of blame. On the most plausible versions of such accounts, blame is not merely a belief that the target of blame has done something wrong or blameworthy—i.e. a negative judgment about the person or their actions and attitudes. If it were, such accounts would be straightforwardly unable to meet the moral analogue of our puzzle for epistemic blame. On the most plausible versions of cognitive accounts, the significance of blame is to be understood in terms not only of a belief that the target of blame has done something wrong or blameworthy, but also an *additional* belief, namely that the person has, in some sense, "stained their moral record" through their wrongdoing. To put it another way, the idea is that to blame someone is to believe that they have incurred a negative balance in their "moral ledger," or "moral scorecard" by doing something wrong (Glover 1970; cf. Zimmerman 1988).

The basic issue for even these more plausible versions of cognitive accounts is that, when it comes to the business of explaining the significance of blame—what blame is beyond a negative judgment—it is not clear how such accounts can contribute to this project simply by appealing to an additional "ledger belief." As critics have pointed out, it is something of a mystery how adding a belief that a person's moral record has been tarnished can contribute anything to such an explanation, over and above any contribution already made by the belief that the person is blameworthy (Scanlon 2008, 127; Sher 2006, 77). The fact that a blamer believes the blamee has done something wrong or blameworthy already seems to go *further* toward explaining the significance of blame than any fact about the blamer's beliefs about the blamee's moral record. This approach can easily make the practice of blaming seem like trivial tally-keeping. Blame seems more important than that.

The apparent inability of mere judgment—even of a seemingly special kind—to explain the significance of blame leads us to negative emotional response accounts. We are all familiar with the feeling of anger that can accompany the judgment that someone has wronged us. Rather than try to explain this further emotional element of blame *via* some cognitive component, we might *identify* blame with that emotional element itself. This is the Strawsonian picture. On this picture, blame is a negative emotional response, paradigmatically manifested in reactive attitudes, such as indignation (third-person blame), resentment (second-person blame), and guilt (self-blame). As George Sher points out, going this route has the advantage of preserving the attractive features of the previous two approaches, while avoiding their pitfalls (Sher 2006). It can help explain why being blamed is so undesirable and acts as a social deterrent: people typically have a strong aversion to being on the receiving end of resentment and indignation. But it allows for private blame: one can keep one's indignation and resentment to oneself.

38   EPISTEMIC BLAME

A number of prominent contemporary moral theorists have embraced this approach, in one way or another (Cogley 2013; Graham 2014; Menges 2017; Pereboom 2014, chapter 6; Pickard 2013; Tognazzini 2013; Wallace 2011; Watson 1996; Wertheimer 1998; Wolf 2011). Wallace is perhaps the most prominent defender of the view. As we have seen, he has defended it by arguing that there is a conceptual connection between the significance of blame and the reactive attitudes narrowly construed. According to Wallace, negative emotions just are an integral—even essential—part of what it is for human beings to be engaged and exercised—to hold each other to normative expectations—in the way characteristic of blame. According to Wallace, someone who claims to blame another (or oneself) for a wrongdoing without feeling any emotion whatsoever would raise suspicion: according to Wallace, it would be natural to judge that they are not actually engaged by the norms they claim to be engaged by, and so do not actually *blame* the person, though they may nevertheless judge them blameworthy.

Prominent as it is, the emotion-based account of moral blame has also been attacked with counterexamples. Some find it obvious that there are instances of "affectless blame," cases in which we blame someone but do not feel any negative emotional reaction. Sher offers examples of blaming dead people in the distant past, blaming one's child for a relatively innocuous lie, or blaming a criminal for committing a burglary we read about casually in the Saturday morning paper. Here's another kind of case from Miranda Fricker:

> If I am listening to the news with a friend, and we hear that certain pay negotiations in France have failed so that the French lorry drivers are likely to go out on strike, my friend might say he blames French union leaders for driving too hard a bargain, while I may blame the management for being too inflexible. But neither of us need have any emotional investment whatever in these matters, so that the blame has no emotional charge even while each of us is certainly finding fault and, as we say, "pointing the finger."   (2016, 170)

This is a useful example because it highlights a fairly ready reply on behalf of proponents of the emotion-based account. Fricker's case is quite plausibly a case of one person merely judging another person blame*worthy*, as opposed to actually blaming them. One reason to think so might be because, presumably, neither of these characters stands in much of a relationship with the lorry drivers, nor the union leaders. As such, the actions and attitudes of the union leaders perhaps lack the right kind of import or meaning, for the characters in Fricker's story, in order for blame to be appropriate.

In response to cases of apparently affectless blame, Wallace himself points out that: "[o]n the reactive account, blame requires that you actually are subject to a reactive emotion, but an emotional response of this sort is not necessarily required

NEGATIVE EMOTIONS AND FRUSTRATED DESIRES   39

for you to hold your colleague morally blameworthy" (see Sher 2006, 90). One can judge that someone *would* be warranted in feeling such emotions toward another person, without happening to feel that way oneself. The strategy, then, is to argue that in all cases of apparently affectless blame, the supposed blame responses are not genuine blame responses; they are mere judgments of blameworthiness (judgments that the relevant emotional responses would be *appropriate*).

There are of course challenges for this strategy. For now, I believe the negative emotion account has enough independent plausibility to make looking into its prospects worthwhile. Perhaps it can help us make sense of epistemic blame.

2.2 Precedent in the Literature

The plausibility of emotion-based approaches may explain why they seem to be in the background of many discussions in the ethics of belief and epistemology more generally. In this section I look briefly at the prominence of emotion-based approaches to blame in epistemology. This provides yet further (albeit of course defeasible) motivation to take such an approach seriously.

A good example is Lindsay Rettler, who says, after presenting three paradigm cases of epistemic blame, "[the] blame specifically targets the faulty belief of another agent. The blaming agents hold others responsible for their beliefs by feeling resentment, indignation, and guilt, respectively" (Rettler 2018, 4). Conor McHugh says, "We blame and even *resent* people, when, for example, they form foolish or hasty beliefs on matters of importance, and when they fail to believe what they should" (McHugh 2012, 66; emphasis mine). Nikolaj Nottelmann is also implicitly committed to a negative emotional response view, even though at times he seems to explicitly reject it (Nottelmann 2007, 42). Here is Nottelmann:

> It seems highly plausible that an agent's epistemic blameworthiness may suffi-ciently justify attitudes such as resentment or indignation taken towards her, at least mild degrees of such attitudes. In short then, if we are in fact prone to feel resentment or even indignation towards one another for holding certain beliefs, an accurate grasp of the notion of epistemic blameworthiness could spell out conditions under which such attitudes are justified.   (2007, 3)

Finally, Rik Peels, one of the most prominent authors in contemporary ethics of belief, laying out the basics of his approach to epistemic responsibility, says:

> To be responsible, I will argue, is to be the proper object of one or more normative attitudes, such as praise, blame, and neutral appraisal. But what kind of attitudes are they? Normative attitudes, perhaps with the exception of neutral appraisal, are *affective* attitudes that we adopt primarily toward people on

40 EPISTEMIC BLAME

the basis of their actions, desires, beliefs, virtues and vices, and character. We adopt them toward other people, but also toward ourselves. Thus, we can be *angry* at someone's decision to remain silent and I can feel *remorse* about what I said to my friend last night. Normative attitudes are as varied as blame, praise, *resentment, outrage,* gratitude, forgiveness, *indignation,* respect, compunction, and *remorse.*   (2016, 17–18; emphasis mine)

This is about as close as Peels gets to saying what he means when he talks about blame. As is evident, it's not particularly close, for at least two reasons. First, Peels is here explaining what he takes to be a minimal condition on "being responsible," as opposed to saying anything directly about the nature of blame. Second, he classifies blame as itself belonging to a category of *normative attitudes,* some of which are themselves negative emotional responses. So, while Peels may not define blame *in terms of* negative emotional responses, he does seem to want to group it alongside them in a significant way. This, in combination with the fact that Peels explicitly claims to endorse a Strawsonian approach to responsibility (2016, 22), is evidence enough that he endorses a negative emotional response theory of epistemic blame.[3]

Not only does the emotion-based approach have independent plausibility in the moral domain, it also seems to be at play in a lot of prominent epistemology. Is an epistemic extension of the account viable? Let's examine the options for developing an emotion-based account of epistemic blame.

2.3 Varieties of the Emotion-Based Account

2.3.1 The Bold Approach

One way to go is to simply deny the claims made in Chapter 1 about the prima facie oddness of indignation and resentment in the epistemic domain (as Nottelmann appears to do in the quote above). According to the bold version of the approach, epistemic blame is a manifestation of negative emotional responses such as indignation and resentment, directed toward an agent, in response to a judgment of epistemic failing. This is of course a rough statement of the view, and details would need working out. But I'm interested in whether the basic idea has any plausibility whatsoever.

---

[3] McHugh (2012), too, may take blame to be a kind of sui generis attitude, *alongside* resentment, as opposed to something that can be understood *in terms of* resentment. I set aside whether this entails that he should not properly speaking be considered an advocate of the emotion-based account of epistemic blame.

One way to motivate the bold approach is to emphasize the importance of our roles in the information gathering and distributing economy. We continually rely on one another for information about things such as when the next bus arrives, where the nearest gas station is, and so on. Not infrequently, it's a matter of great importance whether someone provides you with the correct information. It's $-30°$C, and you are running on a quarter tank. You need to know whether you should fill up here, or can afford to wait until the next station. When someone tells you how far the next station is, the accuracy of their statement is of great importance. Similarly, the beliefs of people in positions of power can have significant consequences: consider an ignorant leader who believes that humans have no influence on climate change, or that gay couples do not have the same rights to marriage as heterosexual ones. Obviously, the beliefs of this leader have the potential for enormous impact on the lives of citizens. On a more structural level, certain forms of biased cognition are deeply linked to systematic sources of injustice in society—they can lead to things like gender-based employment inequity, over-representative incarceration rates amongst marginalized groups, and so on. Finally, note that we sometimes form beliefs about matters that are *themselves* of grave importance for both ourselves and others. Consider, for example, someone who believes, against all the available evidence, that the holocaust didn't happen. It is not hard to imagine this belief itself being immensely hurtful to another individual, for example, someone who was directly affected by the holocaust, or who had family who was so affected (or is simply a member of a group who was affected).

All of these examples reveal ways in which the intellectual conduct of others can be a serious matter. So why shouldn't certain failures of intellectual conduct license negative emotional responses? The thought is that such responses are entirely proportionate to the significance of our intellectual conduct. When things go badly in this regard, people can be deserving of heated negative emotional responses. Of course, given the way I've spelled out FITTINGNESS, this proposal might seem like a non-starter. It appears to directly flout a condition of FITTINGNESS, namely, that an epistemic blame response must be capable of being rendered legitimate by an epistemic failing, independently of practical considerations. A response counts as rendered legitimate by an epistemic failing independently of practical considerations just in case the epistemic failing, as opposed to downstream practical consequences of the epistemic failing, legitimizes the response in question. The present proposal appears to build practical considerations right into its account of what makes the manifestation of reactive attitudes in response to an epistemic failing legitimate.

However, as we have already seen with our brief discussion of pragmatic encroachment in Chapter 1, the idea of being "independent of practical considerations" is fairly nebulous, and open to interpretation. Perhaps the proponent of the bold view has a way of arguing that the proposal does not give practical

42   EPISTEMIC BLAME

considerations a problematic role vis-à-vis the condition of FITTINGNESS. For example, perhaps they can argue that the *general* moral and practical importance of getting things right is just a way of explaining why token epistemic failings matter, independently, at a given time t, of whatever downstream consequences they may happen to have. The thought might be, the general practical import of conducting our intellectual lives carefully and reliably imbues epistemic failings with a kind of import that it can be entirely fitting to be indignant and resentful about, independently of any particular consequences that may or may not occur downstream of a token epistemic failing. This is the *explanatory* sense of being "dependent on practical considerations" I mentioned in Chapter 1.

This idea sounds promising. But I think it leaves a serious worry intact. Even if this proposal gets around the worry that the bold approach directly flouts FITTINGNESS, this may not be enough to make it plausible. After all, even if getting things right has general moral and practical importance, it is nevertheless implausible that many token epistemic failings, considered independently of their downstream practical consequences, are typically sufficient to render attitudes like resentment or indignation legitimate. As we have seen (Chapter 1, section 1.5.2), such attitudes are fitting responses to direct personal harms, whether those harms have been done to oneself (by another)—as in the case of resentment—or to others (by others)—as in the case of indignation. Many paradigmatic epistemic failings, as such, do not seem to be direct personal harms.

In all of the examples just offered, it seems that it's precisely the *moral* dimension of the case—perhaps in addition to an epistemic one—that plays a central role in our understanding of how it might be appropriate for someone to feel indignation or resentment. For example, it is true that, from a purely epistemic point of view, the political leader (since they are a political leader, with access to all kinds of evidence) should know better about climate change. But it's also true that, as someone in such an important position of power, they should—from a moral point of view—be properly informed and clear-headed about the issue. Perhaps we are entitled to be indignant toward the leader because of this dereliction of political duty to the people the leader represents. This dereliction of political duty is an affront *to his people*. So, someone *is* directly harmed or wronged in this case. But not directly in an epistemic way. Likewise, when someone hastily and mistakenly tells you that the nearest gas station is fairly close by, they commit the epistemic blunders of not thinking carefully about how far away it is, and asserting something inaccurate. But, at least when it's $-30°C$ outside, they also commit a moral blunder: they are putting you at significant risk of harm. Thus, the person is directly harming or wronging you.[4] But this harm or wrong is not an epistemic one.

---

[4] See Maheshwari (2021), Placani (2017), and Rowe (2022) for discussion of whether putting someone at risk of harm is itself a harm.

I find it plausible that moral failings—as opposed to epistemic ones—are what generate intuitions about the appropriateness of negative emotional responses in these cases. As such, it seems plausible that the sort of responses argued fitting in these scenarios should count as moral (or professional, or political) blame responses, not something appropriately understood as an epistemic kind of blame response. At the very least, this is a ready reply available to anyone wanting to reject the bold approach. The bold approach seems unsatisfyingly vulnerable and prone to leave matters unsettled in this respect.

Worse, any account of epistemic blame should be able to explain what all cases of epistemic blame have in common (or at least, the closer it can get to such an ideal, the better). Even if the sorts of cases just sketched can be accommodated by the bold approach, it's far from clear what the bold approach has to say about intuitive cases of epistemic blame that are not about climate change, systemic prejudice, or the holocaust. What can the bold approach say about THE OFFICE from the Introduction, for example? Of course, they might reject cases like THE OFFICE as genuine cases of epistemic blame. I do not intend to rule such a move as out of line. However, many seem to find cases like THE OFFICE—along with other cases in which an assessor does not seem to manifest negative emotional responses toward someone for an epistemic failing—intuitive as examples of a kind of blame. As our reflections last chapter suggest, the epistemic domain seems to be *characteristically* cooler in nature than the moral domain. The point here is that the bold view simply seems out of step with that observation. So, going this route puts the theorist of epistemic blame in a rather limited dialectical position. My strategy is to avoid it if possible.[5]

2.3.2 The Moderate Approach

Perhaps negative emotional responses are a more variegated and nuanced bunch than we've so far been presupposing. As Roger Wertheimer points out, even some of the more robust forms of negative emotional response, such as *condemnation*, need not amount to massive surges of rage: "[c]ondemnation isn't defined by liters of blood lusted for. A condemner may hanker for the slightest of suffering: a quick squirm under a mild scold may suffice" (1998, 493).[6] We might think, then, that among the wide range of responses that may count as negative emotional

---

[5] For those worried that my objection to the bold view trades on problematic assumptions about the relationship between the moral and epistemic domains—namely, that they somehow stand in pristine isolation from one another (i.e. that something like pragmatic or moral encroachment can't be true)—please see Chapter 1, section 1.6.2 where I address this issue in detail. Note also, as indicated in the Introduction, I will be developing my preferred account of epistemic blame with a clear eye on the fact that epistemic blame interacts with the moral and practical domains.

[6] As discussed in Sher (2006, 89–90).

44   EPISTEMIC BLAME

responses, some of them can be fitting in the epistemic domain. Here are some potential candidates:

- flickers of irritation
- vague annoyance
- frustration
- disappointment

The moderate approach argues that epistemically blaming always involves negative emotional responses. However, because it emphasizes the variegated nature of these responses, it adds that sometimes they are easy to miss, or mischaracterize as such. Some of these responses may be easier to overlook, or misidentify, than full-fledged indignation and resentment. So perhaps we are simply mistaken in thinking that negative emotional responses are out of place in the epistemic domain—perhaps there are milder forms we simply fail to recognize as such when testing our intuitions.

In response to the moderate approach, I readily admit that frustration, vague annoyance, and disappointment are common responses to epistemic failings, ones that may comply with FITTINGNESS. However, it is far from clear that something like vague annoyance has the significance needed to constitute a genuine blame response. It is not clear that vague annoyance can explain what takes epistemic blame beyond negative epistemic evaluation. But what about the other examples above? Perhaps most saliently, what about disappointment? When a parent says to a misbehaving child, "I'm very disappointed in you," is this not as significant as any blame response? Perhaps there are forms of disappointment that are significant enough to count as kinds of blame and are also at home in the epistemic domain. Disappointment will come up in a few places later on, so it is worth pausing to consider this in detail.

First, consider *propositional* disappointment, as in when we say, "Sam is disappointed that the game is cancelled." According to Daniel Telech and Leora Dahan Katz, propositional disappointment is distinctive in that it is rationalized by "*predictive* hopes":

> When some hoped-for state of affairs fails to obtain, the hoping agent will intelligibly be disappointed. For her hope was constituted in part by the belief that the hoped-for state of affairs was possible (but not guaranteed) and by the desire that that state of affairs obtain.   (Telech and Katz 2022, 14)

People can be propositionally disappointed about cancelled games, spoiled sunsets, and other states of affairs that need not be anyone's fault. Propositional disappointment is simply what results when we thought something was possible, and wanted it to happen, but it didn't happen. Propositional disappointment can of course also concern *agents* and states of affairs involving *moral* goods, as in "I am disappointed that Sheila couldn't bring herself to tell the truth." But according to Telech and Katz, so long as it is an attitude rationalized by predictive hope, it is not yet a kind of *blame*. We do not blame states of affairs or agents when they fail to do or be X, just because we thought it was possible they might do or be X, and wanted them to do or be X. I will refer to this sort of attitude as "mere disappointment." Some theorists explicitly rely on mere disappointment as an *alternative* to blame, for example in the context of recommending revisions to our blaming practices in light of worries about free will (Pereboom 2001).

Contrast this with what Telech and Katz call *reactive* disappointment. The distinctive feature of reactive disappointment, in contrast with propositional disappointment, is that it is rationalized by what they call "*normative* hopes": "Normative hope is hope invested in an agent; it is essentially agent-directed, as it is for some agent to meet, or aspire toward, the attainment of some normative standard or ideal" (14). According to Telech and Katz, reactive disappointment is a genuine vehicle of blame, and this is precisely in virtue of its role in our interpersonal relations, specifically the "normative hopes" we have of one another, which clearly resemble the idea of a normative expectation (even if they are in some sense "weaker" than full-blown expectations).[7] In my view, pressing on disappointment in a moderate approach to the emotion-based account of epistemic blame will not work. This is because either we end up relying on *mere* disappointment, and thus failing to meet SIGNIFICANCE, or we end up relying on *reactive* disappointment, leading us back to the problem faced by the bold view. As a response rationalized by the sorts of direct personal harms or wrongs that make sense of the reactive attitudes narrowly construed, reactive disappointment is as suspect in the epistemic domain as the reactive attitudes narrowly construed.

It also seems to me that vague annoyance and disappointment, along with each of the other examples above, are more appropriately classified as *conative* responses, rather than emotional ones. It seems that a more central feature of frustration, annoyance, and disappointment is that one *desires* something to be the case (which, presumably, one takes *not* to be the case). It does not seem essential that one *feels* something that might appropriately be understood as a negative emotion. Consider: I can be disappointed or vaguely annoyed with you for φ-ing without feeling anything as such, perhaps because I'm currently distracted or overwhelmed by feelings I have about something else (it is interesting to compare the phenomenology of mere disappointment versus reactive disappointment in this regard—Telech and Katz appear to classify reactive disappointment as essentially a negative emotion, in which case the present point may not apply; but again, then the previous point about running into the bold view's issues seems

---

[7] See also Menges (2020) and Blustein (2014) for helpful discussion of the relationship between disappointment and blame. See Telech and Katz (2022), fn11, for a critique of these accounts.

46   EPISTEMIC BLAME

all the more pressing). Meanwhile, it seems odd or even inconsistent to say that I am annoyed with you for φ-ing but have no desire whatsoever that you not do whatever it is that you are doing, or have done.

This is important because, as we'll see shortly, these points imply that going the moderate route effectively amounts to taking a significant step in the direction of endorsing an entirely different approach to blame—one that has been championed most prominently by Sher. In other words, the defender of the moderate approach appears to face the following dilemma: either the negative emotional responses they appeal to remain out of place in the epistemic domain, or the "negative emotional responses" they appeal to aren't really negative emotional responses.

At this point, the defender of the moderate approach may find a distinction drawn in recent work by Leonhard Menges useful. Menges (2017) argues that emotional responses are essential to blame, but maintains that there is an important distinction to draw between different kinds of emotional responses. Menges argues that we should distinguish between an emotion *episode* and emotion *stance*. To have an emotion episode is to be in the grip of an emotion for a comparatively short period of time, perhaps a few minutes or maybe a few hours. To have an emotion stance is to have a long-term set of dispositions, during which time one does not necessarily feel anything typically associated with emotions. Consider someone whose good friend died three years ago. They still think about the friend on many occasions, and indeed have been sad about their friend's death since it happened. But they have not experienced a *feeling* of sadness for the entire duration of that time. It is worth pausing to explore this distinction in a bit more detail.

According to Menges, emotion episodes are typically characterized by three properties. First, they have phenomenological character: having an emotion episode of anger, for example, typically involves a feeling of hotness and tension, which supervenes on certain bodily activity such as increased heart rate (Menges 2017, 3). Second, emotion episodes have a systematic and reliable motivational profile. We associate anger in the emotion episode sense with aggressive and sanctioning behavior (Menges 2017, 3). We associate fear in the emotion episode sense with running away. Third, emotion episodes have representational content. Emotion episodes are *about* something specific—being scared of a lion in an episodic way involves representing that lion as dangerous. This condition is necessary, many agree, for distinguishing between emotion episodes and *moods*, which do not necessarily have distinct representational content, but which share some of the other features of emotion episodes.

Emotion stances do not require the agent to undergo any of these things at a particular time. But they do require the agent to be *disposed* to undergo emotion episodes under certain circumstances. "[If] Barbara does not have the tendency to be in the grip of anger when she thinks about Alice, then it would be false to say that she is angry at her" (Menges 2017, 5). Emotion stances may also involve the tendency to see the target of one's emotion in a certain light. "Barbara's emotional stance will also involve the tendency to see Alice in a certain light and to take certain things to be particularly striking about her. For example, Barbara might take the fact that Alice's desk is a mess as supporting her evaluation that she is unreliable" (Menges 2017, 5). These disparate facts, among others, combine to comprise a stance that Barbara takes toward Alice, which in turn gives the disparate range of feelings, beliefs, desires, and behavior Barbara tends to manifest toward Alice a specific "meaning and importance" (Menges 2017, 5). We can say that Barbara is angry with Alice, in the emotion stance sense of angry.

With this distinction in mind, perhaps the idea that epistemic blame (and moral blame, for that matter) is essentially tied to negative emotions becomes more plausible. After all, it is one thing to maintain that blaming someone requires having an occurrent feeling with the phenomenological and motivational profile of resentment. It is quite another to maintain that blaming someone merely requires being disposed to enter into such states under certain circumstances.[8] Perhaps in some cases of epistemic blame, that disposition never manifests, though it would under particular circumstances.

The basic issue with this approach is that it is not clear that it really solves the problem faced by the bold view. It simply moves that problem further down the line. Even if we understand emotion stances in terms of dispositions, thus avoiding the need to say that anyone occupying one must *occurrently* have a certain phenomenological profile, in order to count as a kind of stance that's relevant to the negative emotion-response approach to blame, presumably those dispositions must, in principle, be able to appropriately manifest at some point. Even if they never manifest, it needs to be the case that their manifestation *would* be appropriate, under certain circumstances. And at that point we can simply press the worries we did for the bold emotion-response approach in section 2.3.1.

2.3.3 The Sui Generis Approach

A third way of embracing an emotion-based approach to epistemic blame is to abandon negative emotional responses that may also be at home in the moral domain, and argue that the epistemic domain is home to its own distinct kind of negative emotional response, or perhaps some sort of functional analogue.[9]

---

[8] As we'll see in section 2.5, this idea may foreshadow the role that Sher gives to dispositions in his own approach to blame.

[9] Perhaps this is what Nottelmann had in mind with his "mild forms" of indignation and resentment. I think the objection I level against the sui generis approach below equally applies to talk of "mild forms" of indignation and resentment.

48 EPISTEMIC BLAME

Here is one suggestion: epistemic blame consists in the manifestation of *epistemic* indignation and *epistemic* resentment (and *epistemic* guilt, in the case of epistemic self-blame). Just as there can be epistemic forms of injustice, rationality, and angst,[10] perhaps there can be epistemic forms of indignation and resentment. Of course, given that—as far as I am aware—I have just now invented these terms, their meaning is purely technical. What reason do we have to adopt such terminology? One cannot simply appeal to their usefulness as a way out of the puzzle of epistemic blame. That would seem to be a straightforwardly ad hoc solution to the problem. At the very least, we'd need to demonstrate some independent theoretical fruitfulness to adopting these terms. For example, we'd need to know more about whether other issues might become more tractable by adopting such terms, as understood on some stipulative definition. The trouble is, it's not entirely clear what these terms *could* mean, such that they are useful even in the present context.

Consider: what exactly is it about epistemic indignation that differentiates it from moral indignation? A proponent of this approach might say that the difference comes down to a difference in the content of the indignation. Epistemic indignation takes epistemic failings, of a certain kind, as its object, while moral indignation takes moral failings, of a certain kind. This might seem promising as far as it goes. However, if what these responses have in common is that they both involve a distinctive negative emotional component—the *indignation* part—then this proposal of course takes us no further than any of the other attempts at defending a negative emotional response approach to epistemic blame. Simply stipulating that a response is, by its nature, putatively directed toward an epistemic object, so to speak, does not make it any more at home in the epistemic domain—not if that response has features that seem out of place in the epistemic domain. Indeed, going this route seems to amount to postulating a kind of response that, while different in some ways, nevertheless has the very features we've been worried about all along, rather than providing some kind of helpful alternative. And the real problem here is that it is difficult to see any other way of differentiating epistemic and moral indignation such that they both count as species of a broader genus.

Another way of pursuing the sui generis approach might be to think of something that parallels the *significance* of resentment and indignation, as opposed to positing epistemic analogues of resentment and indignation themselves. For example, as we saw Wallace point out, what seems to underpin the significance of indignation and resentment is that they are fitting responses to perceived *relationship* impairment—to violations of relationship-constituting expectations. Perhaps we can more directly focus on that idea and find a response

---

[10] For a book-length discussion of "epistemic angst," see Pritchard 2015.

that is fitting to a kind of relationship impairment that is somehow more episte-mic in nature.

Recent work by Antti Kauppinen might be understood as falling somewhere in this category. Kauppinen argues that, under the appropriate circumstances, the fitting response to someone for their epistemic failing is simply to *reduce your epistemic trust* in that person, and possibly let them know it (Kauppinen 2018, 6). Might reductions of epistemic trust be a sui generis kind of "negative emotional response," or some functional analogue for the epistemic domain?[11] This doesn't strike me as obvious. I'm not sure how one would argue for such a claim. The most plausible idea that comes to mind is that "reductions in epistemic trust" function as an epistemic analogue of negative moral emotion through a shared connection with the idea of relationship impairment. But in my view, rather than ground the claim that reductions in epistemic trust should be understood as an epistemic analogue of negative emotional response, this proposal suggests that there is a deeper core to blame than negative emotional responses—perhaps in *both* the epistemic and moral cases. As I have said, I agree that blame has something essential to do with our relationships with one another. Rather than taking this as the basis for an emotion-based approach to epistemic blame, however, I will argue in Chapter 3 that, by developing the notion of an epistemic relationship, we ought to more directly and broadly appeal to relationship impairment in filling out an account of epistemic blame.

The sui generis approach faces a similar dilemma to that of the moderate approach. Either it turns on an unmotivated terminological innovation that doesn't seem to track anything in reality; or, it collapses into a view that is no longer recognizable as a negative emotional response account. As will become clear, I would argue it collapses into something that paves the way for my preferred account. For these reasons, I consider the sui generis approach to warrant tabling as a last resort.

2.4 Moving On

We have raised a number of objections to the emotion-based account of epistemic blame. The central issue for the bold approach comes down to some insights from Wallace, and the other two approaches face the worry of collapsing into something else, or returning us to the central issue for the bold approach. We have seen that Wallace argues that indignation and resentment are the uniquely fitting responses to violations of moral norms, because of the "relational character" of

---

[11] Kauppinen himself argues that this sort of response is better understood merely as a kind of "holding accountable," than as a kind of blame response. He denies that there is an epistemic kind of blame (Kauppinen 2018, 2; cf. Kauppinen forthcoming, 24).

50   EPISTEMIC BLAME

moral norms. I have suggested that epistemic failings, *as such*, are often not plausibly "relational" in the sense that Wallace has in mind.

Still, even when not "relational" in that way, it is highly implausible that epistemic failings are completely devoid of interpersonal significance. For a start, recall from Chapter 1 that epistemic disvalue goes beyond the disvalue of obstructions to the acquisition of true belief and the avoidance of false belief. Sometimes—perhaps often, or even always—it has to do with the disvalue of violations of our normative expectations of one another. This seems like one way of getting at the idea that epistemic failings are *interpersonal* in some sense. In Chapters 3 and 4—as part of a defense of my relationship-based account—I will develop a detailed account of how epistemic blame reflects the interpersonal nature of epistemic failings. The slogan idea is this: while people tend not to stand in direct personal relationships *as* epistemic agents, members of an epistemic community stand in *epistemic relationships*—and this, while perhaps not sufficient to ground emotional responses such as indignation and resentment, can nevertheless ground a wide range of responses that are helpfully understood as epistemic blame responses.

I have so far been concerned with explaining why negative emotional reactions such as indignation and resentment ought to drop out of our theoretical picture. It is worth pointing out that the central issue for the emotion-based approach seems to apply equally to two other prominent approaches to moral blame I briefly mentioned in Chapter 1—Smith's protest view and Hieronymi's ill-will view. Recall, according to Smith, moral blame necessarily involves registering protest in light of a judgment that one has been *wronged* by another. This account seems applicable only to cases involving wrongdoings that are interpersonal in exactly the way I have argued epistemic failings are not. The same point seems true with respect to judgments that the target of blame has shown one *ill will*. For this reason, I will not delve further into discussion of how we might use these accounts of moral blame as bases for building an account of epistemic blame. I do acknowledge that such a project may be worth pursuing elsewhere.[12]

Before getting to my preferred account, it is well worth examining another very different sort of approach to epistemic blame—one that seems promising at least insofar as it appears to have resources to account for SIGNIFICANCE without relying on attitudes, practices, or behaviors that seem out of place in the

---

[12] The same point goes for any number of other accounts of moral blame. One reason I restrict the number of accounts of moral blame I consider as candidates for accounts of epistemic blame is that many of them have features shared by the accounts I do consider in this book, which render them problematic for the same sorts of reasons. Another is that I am not interested in arguing that there is *no other possible way* of developing an account of epistemic blame than my preferred approach. I am interested in arguing that the relationship-based account is an especially promising and fruitful way to go.

NEGATIVE EMOTIONS AND FRUSTRATED DESIRES 51

epistemic domain. This is Jessica Brown's prominent Sher-based approach to epistemic blame.

2.5 Moral Blame as a Set of Dispositions Organized Around a Belief-Desire Pair

A central feature of Sher's approach to moral blame is his *broadening* of the range of responses that count as manifestations of blame beyond what we find in a negative emotional response approach. He puts these into four basic categories, comprised of *anger, hostile behavior, reproach,* and *apology*:

- **Anger:** Under this broad heading we can include emotional responses such as resentment, irritation, bitterness, hostility, fury, rage, outrage, disappointment, contempt, disdain, or disgust.
- **Hostile Behavior:** Unlike the relatively circumscribed set of emotional responses that can accompany blame, the range of hostile behavior that can accompany blame is indefinite. As Sher puts it, it is "determined partly by the particulars of our situation, partly by the conventions that determine what count as hostile gestures in situations of that sort, and partly by our own particular mixture of cleverness and caution" (Sher 2006, 94). For example, hostile gestures range from certain facial expressions, to crossing someone's name off a guest list, to throwing a pancake across the room, and so on. Importantly, to count as an expression of blame, this behavior must be rooted in, or in other words caused by, the belief that the relevant person has acted badly or is being a bad person.
- **Reproach:** Under this heading we can include reproaching, reprimanding, remonstrating, and the like. What distinguishes these responses is that they have an intentional object. For example, one always reproaches another person *for* some reason. The content of one's reproach, so to speak, is precisely the content of whatever it is that one believes the target of reproach has done that counts as acting badly, or being a bad person. Reproach, and its cousins, seems to have a *communicative* function that hostile behavior may lack. In reproaching someone, we allude to whatever it is that we reproach them for, and thereby aim to make it understood that we reproach them for that thing.
- **Apology:** This is a manifestation of *self*-blame. It is a lot like reproach, in the sense that an apology is always *for* something. Similarly, an apology is always *to* someone, and so appears also to have a communicative function.

According to Sher, blame cannot be identified with any one of these responses on its own. He argues that it is possible to blame someone without manifesting any of these responses. But perhaps the following is true. Perhaps we can articulate the sting, force, and depth of blame in terms of the belief that someone has acted badly plus the *disposition* to manifest a range of these responses (under certain conditions).[13]

This is promising because we can then explain how non-expressed and affect-less blame are possible. We can do so by maintaining that the various responses typical of blame are not necessarily what it is to *blame*, but they are what one is necessarily disposed toward when blaming. Promising as this idea may be, it can't be the whole story. The above list amounts to a highly disparate range of responses. What do they have in common? Being able to explain what they have in common would seem to be crucial for our understanding of why we have a single notion of blame, and why we care about it. The present proposal seems unable to do that.

We also need to be able to explain the *relation* that holds between one's negative evaluation of someone—one's belief that they have acted badly, or are being a bad person—and the above set of dispositions. By simply identifying blame with these dispositions to respond, we have not yet done that. That said, it seems clear that the relation is a causal one. These are dispositions one has *because* of one's negative evaluation of the target of blame. Could such dispositions be caused merely by the belief that the target of blame has acted badly? It seems not. This is for the simple reason that one can negatively evaluate someone—can believe they have acted badly, or have a bad character—without blaming them. This is something we established in Chapter 1. Therefore, such negative evaluation alone cannot explain why these dispositions are present in certain circumstances, but not others. It seems we need some additional state in combination with negative evaluation to explain what gives rise to these dispositions.

Sher's idea is to appeal to a past-oriented standing *desire* that the target of blame not have acted badly, or manifested some bad character trait. The thought is to model our understanding of blame on a familiar idea: namely, our ability to explain a person's otherwise disparate set of behaviors by attributing a particular goal to that person. If I see you hanging around Jen's office, joining Jen's gym, and browsing often on Jen's Facebook page, I might be able to explain why you are doing all these things by positing that you've got a (potentially worrisome) goal to be around Jen. In a similar way, replacing goal-talk with desire-talk, I might be able to explain a variety of responses typical of blame that you are disposed to manifest by attributing to you a standing desire that the target of your blame-responses not have acted badly, or manifested bad character traits. How might the

---

[13] Hence the apparent connection to Menges's proposal regarding emotion-stances versus emotion episodes I mentioned in section 2.3.2.

explanatory connection between this desire and these responses be more fully articulated?

For the first two kinds of response (anger and hostile behavior), a fairly straightforward and explanatorily satisfying connection can be identified. Note that in general we tend to *feel* negative things and behave in retributive ways when our desires are not satisfied. This is something most of us are surely familiar with starting from a very early age. But, according to Sher, that's just what these blame-responses *are*: feelings and behaviors typical of an unsatisfied desire—in this case, the past-oriented desire that the target of the response not have acted badly.

What about the other dispositions characteristic of blame, namely reproach and apology (when one blames oneself)? Note that neither reproach nor apology need be identical with, nor necessarily accompanied by, negative feelings or retributive behavior. So, we must take a different approach to understanding the connection between blame's belief-desire pair and these dispositions. As Sher puts it: "We cannot trace these reactions to the bad feelings that often accompany our failure to get what we want because reprimands and apologies are neither bad feelings themselves nor always accompanied by them" (2006, 108). Sher presents an alternative connection between blame's belief-desire pair and these dispositions. According to Sher, the connection here is the same as the one found more generally between having an unsatisfiable desire (such as desiring to win the race, which you will certainly not win) and the attempt to achieve the *next best thing* (such as coming in second place). We reproach people because we wish they hadn't acted badly. And even though the fact that they acted badly can't be changed, reproaching them might get them to appreciate the reasons they failed to see, or it might encourage them to not do the same thing again in future. Achieving these things may amount to satisfying the next best thing to the original unsatisfied desire.

According to Sher, when one blames oneself, one desires that one hadn't acted badly. The fact that one acted badly cannot be changed any more than the fact that someone else did. However, according to Sher, *apologizing* allows one to achieve the next best thing: by apologizing one communicates to others *that* one has the past-oriented desire not to have acted badly, that one appreciates the reasons they had failed to adequately respond to at the time of the transgression. Sher concludes: "Because these last two blame-constituting dispositions are thus also rendered intelligible by [the putative desire component of blame], we may conclude that [this desire component] is indeed an essential element of blame" (111).[14]

---

[14] I find Sher's explanation of the connection between desire frustration and dispositions toward anger fairly compelling. But I do not find his explanation of the connection between desire frustration and either *reproach* or *apology* particularly convincing. This may be significant in its own right, given that these dispositions seem quite central to our blaming practices. I explain my concern in section 2.8.

54 EPISTEMIC BLAME

2.6 Brown on Epistemic Blame

Brown imports the structure of Sher's framework straightforwardly into the epistemic domain. According to Brown, all that needs modifying are the characteristic dispositions to feel and behave, along with the contents of the belief-desire pair. According to Brown, dispositions to feel and behave typically associated with epistemic blame include anger and publicly expressed rebuke, as well as attempts to get the target of blame to appreciate the reasons they had previously failed to appreciate.[15] The content of the belief-desire pair unifying such dispositions is, of course, epistemic in nature. That is to say, the relevant belief involved in epistemic blame is that the target of blame has *"believed* badly"—which Brown uses as shorthand for the idea that the target has culpably flouted some epistemic norm (she remains neutral on what the correct epistemic norm(s) is/are).[16] The relevant desire is that the target not have believed badly, or otherwise culpably flouted the relevant epistemic norm. Instances of epistemic blame can be understood as one or another of the characteristic dispositions, brought about through the frustration of the desire that the relevant epistemic norm not be violated.

Brown draws connections between the unsatisfied desire and epistemic blame's characteristic dispositions in a way that parallels Sher (though she doesn't discuss epistemic self-blame in this regard). If someone experiences "negative feelings such as anger" toward someone for their epistemic failing, this can be explained as the manifestation of a typical disposition toward such feelings when one of our desires is frustrated. If someone reproaches another—for example, through verbal expression such as "How can you believe the president is in New York given that the TV is showing that he is in Washington?!" (Brown 2020a, 400)—this can be explained as the manifestation of a disposition to try to achieve the next best thing to an unachievable goal (in this case, that the person not have believed badly), namely, to get them to appreciate the epistemic reasons they have and perhaps conduct their intellectual lives more carefully in the future.

This looks like a promising way of explaining how epistemic blame goes beyond mere negative epistemic evaluation. The idea would be that epistemic blame's characteristic significance can be explained in terms of a certain connection to

---

[15] Some comment is warranted here on the fact that this view about what's characteristic of epistemic blame seems to be at odds with the conclusion of the first half of this chapter. This tension need not concern us, since Brown is simply advertising her account's ability to be *consistent* with a wide range of views about what we might think constitute manifestations of epistemic blame. This flexibility is a feature shared by my own preferred account, which I will explain in the next chapter. In any case, while the first half of this chapter ultimately argues that anger (at least in the form of negative emotional responses) is not a fitting response to epistemic failings per se, it also includes discussion of why the opposing claim is not completely without merit.

[16] The account does not require that ordinary speakers have the explicit concept of an "epistemic norm violation." Rather, the contents of blame's belief-desire pair can be more specific: they can concern failures to conform belief to the evidence, assertions of falsehoods, etc.

motivation that is lacking in cases of mere negative evaluation. One may judge that someone has fallen short of some epistemic standard without being moved to do *anything*. But when one person blames another for falling short, this goes beyond mere negative evaluation because they are thereby motivated in certain distinctive ways. To put this in terms of the conditions laid out by SIGNIFICANCE, we might say that by desiring that the person not have violated an epistemic norm in this way, a blamer holds that person to a normative expectation. Moreover, it seems the account can readily handle FITTINGNESS. After all, the account locates the *content* of the relevant belief-desire pair at the heart of epistemic blame explicitly in the epistemic domain. If we agree with Brown that it's possible to desire that an epistemic norm not have been culpably violated, it seems a short step further to agree that such a norm violation—such an epistemic failing—can be sufficient to render legitimate the sorts of attitudes and behaviors that Brown identifies as the sorts of things we manifest when such a desire is frustrated, in the way specified by FITTINGNESS. I am prepared to grant that the account readily handles FITTINGNESS.[17] As I have said, my main concern is the account's ability to meet SIGNIFICANCE. We will assess the account on this score shortly. A couple of clarificatory questions are in order first.

Must epistemic blame be accompanied by a desire that the target of blame not have believed badly? One might be suspicious of this idea for the reason that ordinary people seem to lack a general desire for truth and knowledge. Cases of trivial truths and trivial knowledge abound. Sometimes people seem to desire the *absence* of true belief and knowledge (consider reactions to movie spoilers (Kelly 2003, 20)). If that is so, why must it be the case that, when epistemically blaming someone, and thereby believing that they have believed badly, we must also desire that this is not the case? What if the target of epistemic blame believed badly and thereby failed to form a true belief about the number of "8"s on page 406 of the Yellow Pages? Perhaps the account does not fit with our actual epistemic practices after all.

Brown responds that it does not matter whether people have a general desire for truth and knowledge. All she maintains is that in each case of epistemic blame, the blamer has a desire that the target of blame not have believed badly. In all cases of epistemic blame, the blamer desires that *this* person in *this* case not have believed badly. One might be tempted to challenge this claim, too, and argue that there can be cases of epistemic blame that do not involve a desire that some epistemic norm has not been violated. Here is a possible case:

---

[17] Some may want to challenge the idea that the sorts of attitudes and behaviors (the disposition toward which) Brown says are typical manifestations of the frustration of the desire that people not "believe badly," can really be rendered legitimate by an epistemic failing, independently of practical considerations. Since I think there are deeper worries about the connection between Brown's belief-desire pair and the dispositions characteristic of epistemic blame, I won't pursue this challenge here.

56 EPISTEMIC BLAME

ROOMMATE RIVALS: Mikias and Tsehaye are old roommates; they compete over just about everything. One of Tsehaye's character flaws is that he is a sucker for tabloids. He tends to believe things about celebrities and current events simply on the basis of his favorite tabloid magazine. Mikias has just realized that Tsehaye has formed yet another tabloid-based belief. Mikias believes that an epistemic norm has been violated (e.g. the rational credibility norm of belief, or the knowledge norm, etc.). He also manifests many of the dispositions to feel and behave that Brown says are typically associated with epistemic blame—he publicly expresses rebuke, and attempts to get Tsehaye to appreciate the reasons he seems to fail to appreciate. But, out of a sense of rivalry, Mikias also takes a twisted pleasure in Tsehaye's tabloid problem. He takes pleasure in Tsehaye's formation of a shoddy tabloid-based belief.

It seems Mikias lacks a desire that the epistemic norm not be violated. After all, he takes *pleasure* in the fact that an epistemic norm has been violated. It also seems Mikias epistemically blames Tsehaye. After all, he believes Tsehaye has violated an epistemic norm, and manifests a range of dispositions Brown claims are typical of epistemic blame.

Brown has room to maneuver here. According to Brown, even if there seem to be cases of epistemic blame without the relevant desire, this may simply be due to the fact that the relevant desires in such cases are either very weak, or overridden by other desires (or both) (Brown 2020a, 398). Appealing to differences in strength of desire can also help explain the variable strength of epistemic blame. Stronger expressions of epistemic blame may correspond to stronger desires that the relevant epistemic norm has not been violated. According to Brown, the fact that epistemic blame seems less common and less strong than moral blame can be explained by noting that the desire that people not believe badly, in token situations, is usually less strong (thus more easily overridden) than in cases of morally wrong action.[18]

2.6.1 A Central Challenge for the Desire-Based Approach

I agree that some sort of motivational component is necessary for epistemic blame. However, I am not convinced that understanding the motivational component as a *desire that the target of epistemic blame not have believed badly* is the best way of pursuing this more general idea. To start, a worry that Angela Smith (2013, 35) has presented against Sher's original account also seems problematic for Brown.

---

[18] I am suspicious of the need to posit weak or overridden desires as a way dealing with cases in which the relevant desire does not seem present. However, I will remain neutral on that issue.

Suppose a mother judges that her son has done something morally wrong, and is blameworthy for doing so. She desires very much that her son not have committed this morally wrong deed; she knows that his implication in the wrongdoing will make his life more difficult. The mother has the belief-desire pair at the heart of Sher's account. She believes her son blameworthy, and desires that he not have culpably violated the relevant moral norms. However, suppose she falls short of manifesting any of the dispositions characteristically associated with blame. Perhaps she simply feels a great deal of remorse and sadness about the whole thing. These are not dispositions characteristically associated with blame. Crucially, it seems *entirely natural* to imagine the mother manifesting these attitudes toward her son as a result of having Sher's belief-desire pair. The case is not a far-flung possibility. For this reason, it seems there is work to do in order to show that the dispositions characteristic of moral blame are the sorts of things we should *expect* to manifest when the desire component of the belief-desire pair at the heart of Sher's framework is frustrated. Why is it the case that sometimes dispositions manifest which have seemingly not much to do with blame, and at other times, dispositions characteristic of blame do manifest? What makes the difference between these sorts of cases?

Sher addresses something close to the concern I am raising here in Sher (2006, 112–13). In particular, he argues that he is *not* claiming that for every person imaginable, the belief-desire pair at the heart of blame will give rise to the dispositions characteristic of blame in all situations. He argues that he does not need such a commitment in order for his account to work. Rather, according to Sher, it merely needs to be the case that for all cases of people with a "standard" (112) psychology, the belief-desire pair will tend to give rise to the dispositions characteristic of blame. But this is why I have emphasized that the mother-son case is *not* an unusual case. Doing so, I explicitly distinguish it from the sort of thing Sher considers in the neighborhood: namely, "imaginary" or "far off" cases in which a person has the belief-desire pair, but not the dispositions characteristic of blame. My aim here is to point out that the mother-son case seems like a normal sort of case.

A parallel point can be made in the epistemic domain. A mother believes that her son is epistemically blameworthy for dogmatically buying into everything his new circle of friends thinks about "sexism against men."[19] She also desires that her son not have violated the epistemic norms he has violated; she fears that these epistemic failings have a good chance of making his life more difficult. Despite having the belief-desire pair at the heart of Brown's account, the mother falls short of manifesting any of the dispositions characteristically associated with epistemic blame. She simply feels a certain degree of regret or sadness over the matter. Once

---

[19] She may of course believe her son has failed in other ways besides epistemically.

58 EPISTEMIC BLAME

again, it seems entirely natural to imagine that the mother manifests these attitudes toward her son as a result of having Brown's belief-desire pair. The case is not unusual. So, it seems there is work to do in order to show that the dispositions characteristic of epistemic blame are the sorts of things we should expect to manifest when the desire component of the belief-desire pair at the heart of Brown's framework is frustrated. Indeed, at this point, it is fair to wonder whether something more might be involved in cases in which the dispositions characteristic of epistemic blame are present, something over and above a belief that the target of blame has believed badly, and the desire that they not have believed badly. Perhaps some further component is required to explain the difference between the cases I have in mind.

Framing this issue in terms of the puzzle of epistemic blame as articulated in Chapter 1, what I take these considerations to suggest is that Brown's account has trouble meeting SIGNIFICANCE after all. That is to say, one way of diagnosing the problem—namely, the fact that it is not difficult to imagine ordinary agents having the belief-desire pair at the heart of Brown's account frustrated without manifesting the dispositions characteristic of epistemic blame—is to say that the materials with which Brown attempts to analyze epistemic blame do not themselves amount to ways of holding others to normative expectations. That the "frustration" of one's desire that S not violate an epistemic norm can lead to dispositions of disappointment and regret, as opposed to dispositions characteristic of blame, is an indication that having such a desire is not really a way of holding S to a normative expectation in the first place.[20] If the significance of epistemic blame comes down to the idea that epistemic blame involves holding others to normative expectations in a way that mere negative epistemic evaluation does not, then this is a problem for an account of epistemic blame that uses these materials.

Brown responds to Smith's mother-son case in Brown (2020a). However, I am not convinced that her response addresses the heart of the problem. Brown interprets the objection as a straightforward counterexample in which all of the conditions of the Sher-based account of blame are supposedly satisfied and yet intuitively there is no blame. Interpreted as such, I agree with Brown that the objection clearly misses the mark. After all, the dispositions characteristic of blame (a condition on blame, according to the account) are missing. However, in my view, this feature of the case is precisely the point. As I have presented it—and I will leave it open whether my objection here is ultimately the same as Smith's or simply a new objection—the case is not intended as one in which all of the

---

[20] Recall the discussion from section 2.3.2 where I distinguished between *mere* disappointment and *reactive* disappointment. This distinction is equally relevant here. To put the point one way, it is entirely natural to imagine cases in which the frustration of Brown's belief-desire pair manifests in *mere* disappointment—perhaps a kind of disaffected giving up. And that, in my view, is not a way of holding to someone to a normative expectation.

conditions of the Sher-based account of blame are satisfied and yet intuitively there is no blame. Rather, it is meant to be an illustration of how, under very normal circumstances, a person can have the belief-desire pair involved in the Sher-based account of blame without this giving rise to the sorts of dispositions that are characteristic of blame. Again, a central feature of the Sher-based account is that the dispositions characteristic of blame just are a special case of what people do when their desires are frustrated. This is supposed to be part of the explanatory power of the account. The belief-desire pair is supposed to explain why the reactions characteristic of blame are ones we would expect people to have under the relevant circumstances. My aim here is to bring out a central challenge that this explanatory claim of the account faces.

Here is another way of framing how Sher's belief-desire pair seems inadequate to the task at hand. Note first that, despite the fact that Sher appeals to a belief-desire *pair* to explain what unifies our blame responses, the desire component is arguably what's doing the heavy lifting. Recall that the belief in this belief-desire pair is the belief that the target of blame has "acted badly." Recall that, by this, Sher does not simply mean that the target of blame has violated some moral norm. Again, people can blamelessly do what is morally impermissible. They can also do morally permissible things in blameworthy ways. By "acting badly," Sher means acting in a *blame*worthy way. But then, as Sher has pointed out in the context of developing his own account, the account must appeal to the desire condition in order to have anything to say about what the belief condition amounts to—that is, in order to have anything to say about what it is that a blamer believes a person is *worthy* of when one blames them (Sher 2006, 75). This, in my view, is why the desire component is doing the heavy lifting in Sher's account (as well as Brown's). Appropriate targets of blame are judged worthy of being on the receiving end of the dispositions the blamer manifests as a result of the blamer's *desiring* that the blamee not have acted or believed badly.

Second, it seems to me that when people manifest the dispositions characteristic of blame, it is not simply because they *want* it to be the case that someone hadn't acted badly. Something else seems to be involved. Consider how people typically react when they hear about some natural disaster, such as a hurricane striking a populated center, or a wildfire destroying people's homes. When we respond to such events, we typically *want* it to be the case that these horrible things not have happened. And yet, it would be irrational to direct genuine blame responses toward avalanches or wildfires, no matter how much destruction they may have caused. Of course, the content of one's desire that a natural disaster not have occurred is different from the content of one's desire that a person not have acted badly. Perhaps people manifest the dispositions characteristic of blame only when, and precisely because, they have a desire with a very specific sort of content. But it is not clear that the content of the desire in the Sher-based framework can do the work needed here. This is what the mother-son case seems to illustrate.

60 EPISTEMIC BLAME

Again, there seem to be very natural sorts of cases where an agent can desire *that someone not have acted badly* and yet fail to manifest any of the dispositions characteristic of blame. Desiring that someone not have acted badly simply does not seem capable of underpinning the kind of normative expectation that constitutes the significance of blame.

Returning to Brown's account, a structurally similar point can be made in the epistemic case. Consider how we might respond when we discover that, despite appearances to the contrary, some significant portion of our beliefs are unjustified and false; there is much less knowledge in the epistemic community than we had previously thought. One would typically desire that such an unfortunate state of affairs not have occurred. But it seems clear that our dispositions to react, when this desire is frustrated, will not amount to epistemic blame responses. In any case, it would seem irrational to epistemically blame anyone in such a scenario. Of course, the content of one's desire that an "epistemic mishap" not have occurred is different from the content of one's desire that a person not have believed badly. But, as in the moral case, it remains unclear that this point alone can do the work needed. This is what the epistemic analogue of the mother-son case seems to effectively illustrate. Again, there seem to be very natural sorts of cases where an agent can desire *that someone not have believed badly* and yet fail to manifest dispositions characteristic of epistemic blame. Desiring that someone not have believed badly simply does not seem capable of underpinning the kind of normative expectation that constitutes the significance of epistemic blame.

It is not clear that Brown's desire condition can make sense of the idea that epistemic blame is something over and above mere negative evaluation. Following Smith, I take this to suggest that the motivational component of epistemic blame involves something other than, or in addition to, a desire that the target of blame not have believed badly. Still, Brown's appeal to a motivational component in her account of the nature of epistemic blame contains an insight. It enables her account to have a much easier time with FITTINGNESS than appealing to negative emotions. It is well worth thinking about whether the insight can be captured in other ways, which is precisely where I am headed in Chapter 3.

Of course, one of the most likely responses Brown will have to my central objection is that my preferred competing approach to epistemic blame will run into the very same issue I have raised for her. That is to say, Brown will likely contend that what I call "relationship modification" is itself something that comes apart from blame in important ways, thus equally implying that relationship modification is incapable of capturing the significance of blame (in both its moral and epistemic varieties). Since I won't be developing my preferred account until the next chapter, I won't address this issue here. I will simply assure the reader in advance that I will of course be taking this issue up later. In Chapter 4, I provide a detailed argument that the relationship-based approach can account for SIGNIFICANCE.

2.6.2 Other Worries

Before getting to my preferred account, I'd like to raise a few more issues with the Sher-based framework. I think this will help drive the point home that we should be looking elsewhere for a solution to the puzzle of epistemic blame.

I said earlier that I'm not convinced by some of the finer-grained details in the Sher-based framework concerning the alleged explanatory connection between frustrated desires and the characteristic dispositions of blame. Here I will elaborate on this worry, focusing first on Sher's original framework, but then showing how the worries carry over to Brown's extension.

According to Sher, the connection between blame's belief-desire pair and dispositions to *reproach* and *apologize* (two dispositions he claims are characteristic of blame) is an instance of a general kind: the connection between desire frustration and getting "the next best thing." We reproach people because we wish they hadn't acted badly, but of course the fact that they acted badly can't be changed. So, we reproach to get the next best thing, which is to get others to "appreciate the force of the reason they ignored or flouted" (2006, 111), or to see what is wrong with their current lack of reasons responsiveness (111). By apologizing for a moral transgression, according to Sher, we aim to get others to see that we have the relevant desire that we not have morally transgressed.

Starting with reproach, note that one can reproach another while nevertheless lacking any (predictive) expectation (or even desire) whatsoever that they will come to appreciate the force of the reason they ignored or flouted, or see what is wrong with their current lack of reasons responsiveness. Perhaps one simply writes the person off, or even wants the person to continue failing for some overriding consequential reason. Is this a problem for Sher's story about reproach and satisfying the "next best thing" to the desire that one not have acted badly? Not quite. Just because individuals can reproach one another in the absence of aims Sher attributes to reproach, does not impugn his story about our *practice* of reproach. Individuals might instantiate tokens of reproach for all kinds of reasons, where this has no bearing on the function of our general practice of reproach. Indeed, philosophers tend to defend views about the function of our blaming practice with genealogical or etiological arguments; none of these give a central role to the motivations or expectations of individual blamers on specific occasions.

However, note that reproach just *very often* seems to take place in the absence of any anticipation that one's reproach will get others to appreciate the force of the reason they ignored or flouted, or see what is wrong with their current lack of reasons responsiveness. To my mind, this is a typical feature of our blaming *practice*. Reproach often signals that we've had enough, flags personal limits, or simply makes it known that we've been wronged (end of story). These modes of reproach need not have any connection to desires that *other people* be a certain

62   EPISTEMIC BLAME

way, as such. They may simply be expressions of a desire concerning *one's own* state of being or situation. If so, reproach plays a more multifaceted role in our blaming practice than getting others to appreciate the force of the reason they ignored or flouted, or see what is wrong with their current lack of reasons responsiveness. This puts a burden on Sher to further defend the explanatory connection between reproach and the belief-desire pair supposedly at the heart of blame.

Sher's story about apology raises a different worry. Recall, according to Sher, apology is connected to frustrated desires in the following way: we apologize in order to show that we have the relevant desire—namely, the desire that one not have acted badly. This is supposedly the next best thing to avoiding the frustration of the relevant desire in the first place. But this strikes me as an odd explanation of why we apologize. More specifically, it seems like the wrong kind of reason to apologize to someone. It seems selfish and self-centered to apologize to someone *so that they see you have desire X about morality.* Good apologies are ones that are made, perhaps among other things, because you care about the person you're apologizing to—because you want *them* to be better off, which might of course be brought about through letting them know you care. But in my view the former, not the latter, is the primary motivation behind a good apology. On Sher's theory, it seems the latter is the content of your desire. So, by drawing the particular connections he does between frustrated desires and apologies, Sher may be licensing bad apologies.

Brown draws connections between epistemic blame's belief-desire pair and characteristic dispositions in a way that parallels Sher. According to Brown, if someone experiences "negative feelings such as anger" toward another for their epistemic failing, this can be explained as the manifestation of a typical disposition toward such feelings when one of our desires is frustrated. I won't spend much time on this claim except to suggest that the account's ability to explain cases of anger in the epistemic domain may be of limited utility in light of the considerations rallied against emotion-based views of epistemic blame in the first half of this chapter (but see fn15). According to Brown, if someone reproaches another—for example, through verbal expressions such as "How can you believe the president is in New York given that the TV is showing that he is in Washington?!" (Brown 2020a, 400)—this can be explained as the manifestation of a disposition to try to achieve the next best thing to an unachievable goal (in this case, that the person not have believed badly), namely, to get them to appreciate the epistemic reasons they have and perhaps conduct their intellectual lives more carefully in the future. Here, I think Brown's epistemic extension inherits a parallel worry to the one I have just raised for Sher: it seems we can epistemically blame others without any hope (or desire) that they will appreciate anything, or do anything differently in future (even if it is true that we do desire that they not have believed badly). Perhaps we've simply written them off.

Brown of course might reply with a structural analogue of the response I canvassed on behalf of Sher above. But here again the basic point is the following. Epistemic blame in the form of reproach *very often* takes place in the absence of any anticipation that one's reproach will bring about any desired change in the attitudes or behavior of one's reproach. This seems to be a characteristic feature of our *practice* of epistemic blame. Just consider epistemic blame in politics, if an example is needed. In my view, this puts a burden on Brown to defend the claim that the practice of reproach really has the function she appears to presuppose in her extension of Sher's account to the epistemic domain.

Again, I mention these issues simply with the aim of casting further doubt on the general idea that we can understand the significance of epistemic blame in terms of a connection to *desire*, even one with a special sort of content. There are serious worries about our ability to tell a compelling story about the connection between such a desire and the dispositions characteristic of epistemic blame.

2.7 Conclusion

Sher and Brown have taken us some way beyond the shortcomings of emotion-based accounts of (epistemic) blame. The desire component of Sher's framework looked well-positioned to help with SIGNIFICANCE without relying on attitudes, behaviors, or practices that seem out of place in the epistemic domain. However, on closer inspection, the desire component doesn't go *far enough* in accounting for SIGNIFICANCE. It cannot make adequate sense of the idea that blame requires holding to normative expectations. I have agreed with Brown that some kind of motivational component is needed in order to do this job. An alternative approach to this motivational component—one that is looking increasingly promising—is to examine the modifications we make to intentions and expectations constitutive of our *relationships* with one another. Perhaps if we can make sense of the notion of an *epistemic* relationship, we can thereby make sense of an epistemic kind of blame.

3

A Relationship-Based Account of Epistemic Blame

A number of considerations now point in the direction of a role for relationships in our solution to the puzzle of epistemic blame. It is time to give this idea a run for its money. According to the account I develop in this chapter, epistemic blame just is a kind of relationship-modification. At the heart of the account is the notion of an epistemic relationship, a kind of relationship that people have with one another insofar as they are epistemic agents in an epistemic community. The chapter develops an account of what it is to modify one's epistemic relationship with another person, and argues that certain ways of modifying one's epistemic relationship with another amount to a kind of blame response.[1] As we'll see, the account works by taking as its starting point the idea that normative expectations are importantly connected to blame. The account makes sense of epistemic blame in terms of modifications to relationships that are themselves partly comprised of normative expectations.

Of course, as I have said, the relationship-based framework is the subject of controversy in the moral domain. I will be developing some of the framework's central concepts in a bid to allay some of the challenges facing this framework in the moral domain. In this chapter, my main aim is to motivate the claim that the framework can fruitfully be extended to the epistemic domain. A full defense of the account's ability to resolve the puzzle of epistemic blame, and other advantages over the competition, is taken up in Chapter 4.

3.1 Blame and Relationships

As can be gathered from various points in our discussion of blame so far, a family of views connect blame and relationships in importantly different ways. The account that utilizes the concept of a relationship most directly and centrally is T.M. Scanlon's. Like many philosophers, Scanlon develops his account of blame within a broader context. In Scanlon's case, it is a discussion about the role that an agent's intentions can play in determining the permissibility of their actions and

---

[1] I take up the question of *self*-blame in the next chapter.

Epistemic Blame: The Nature and Norms of Epistemic Relationships. Cameron Boult, Oxford University Press.
© Cameron Boult 2024. DOI: 10.1093/oso/9780192890580.003.0004

attitudes, an issue centrally connected to his widely discussed approach to *contractualism* in normative ethics. According to Scanlon, an agent's intentions are never directly involved in determining the permissibility of their actions and attitudes. In the process of developing his argument, he draws a distinction between *permissibility* and *meaning*. While an agent's intentions are never directly relevant to determining the permissibility of their actions and attitudes, they are directly relevant to the meaning of their actions and attitudes. In a word, the meaning of an action or attitude is essentially the significance it has for oneself and the other people with whom one stands in various sorts of relationships.

According to Scanlon, *blameworthiness* is a species of meaning, and *blame* is a response to a judgment about the meaning of someone's action or attitude. I plan to avoid getting involved in a deeper analysis of the concept of "meaning," since it would only distract from my main purposes. We can delve into other details of Scanlon's work on blame largely in abstraction from this broader theoretical background—and, in fact, I think it is helpful to do so since the account of epistemic blame I ultimately wish to develop should not be understood as hostage to the bigger-picture commitments in the background of Scanlon's framework, such as his contractualist account of moral permissibility.

I follow Scanlon in using the term "relationship" in a somewhat technical sense. As I shall be understanding the term, relationships are constituted by certain intentions, expectations, and attitudes people have concerning how to act and feel toward one another—intentions, expectations, and attitudes that are justified by a wide range of facts about parties to the relationship, depending on those involved and the kind of relationship it is. Strictly speaking, relationships also consist in dispositions people have toward each other (in addition to their *intentions*, for example), as well as the reasons why they have those intentions and dispositions. I will bracket these additional two points for the sake of presenting the basic idea of the account.

We can distinguish between relationships as normative ideals—idealized sets of intentions, expectations, and attitudes that would be constitutive of a *good* relationship, whether friendships, romantic relationships, or something else—and actual token relationships. The latter are instances of actual relationships which will approximate to a better or worse degree the relevant normative ideal. To illustrate, consider the example of friendship. What is the normative ideal of friendship? According to Scanlon, paradigm intentions and expectations include, "intending to give help and support when needed, beyond what one would be obligated to do for just anyone; intending to confide in the person and to keep his or her confidences in return; and intending to spend time with the person when one can, and to 'keep in touch'"(Scanlon 2008, 132). They also include the expectations that your friend will do the same. In addition to a central core of intentions and expectations that one must have in order to count as a good friend,

66   EPISTEMIC BLAME

there are also non-obligatory intentions that are nevertheless good to have according to the normative ideal. Intending to take pleasure in the successes of one's friend, or to generally hope that things go well for them, might be two such examples.

According to this framework, a judgment of blameworthiness is a judgment that someone with whom you stand in some relationship has intentions, expectations, or attitudes that in some way fall short of the normative ideal of that relationship—or as Scanlon puts it, intentions and attitudes that "impair their relations with others" (Scanlon 2008, 131) (such a judgment need not be explicitly recognized as such by the judger). A *blame* response consists in a modification to the intentions and attitudes you have toward that person, in a way that is somehow appropriately or fittingly connected to your judgment that they are blameworthy.[2] Lani might judge that her friendship with Lee has been impaired because Lee failed, without any excuse, to keep a promise to Lani. A fitting response to this judgment might be for Lani to intend to place less confidence in Lee's word in the future; depending on the severity of the breach of confidence, it might be fitting to stop intending to feel pleasure at Lee's successes in the future, for example, or to cut off relations altogether. Such a combination of judgments, and modifications to intentions and attitudes as a result, is what Lani's blame response consists in.

The framework leaves room for negative emotions which are often associated with blame, such as feelings of indignation and resentment. But it is distinctive in the centrality it gives to modifications to our intentions and expectations as opposed to negative emotions. Feelings of indignation and resentment (and other emotions) are of course a regular part of what happens when we blame, but for Scanlon they are not central. Indeed, Scanlon advertises as an advantage of his account that it can accommodate the coolness of certain examples of our blaming practices. As we have discussed in some detail already (Chapter 2, section 1), we seem sometimes to blame others simply by deciding not to make certain plans with them, or by cutting off relations. While heated emotional responses need not accompany such attitudes and behaviors, according to Scanlon they can nevertheless be genuine forms of blame. What makes them genuine—and what they have in common with negative emotional responses (when the latter function as genuine forms of blame)—is that they are ways of modifying our relations with others in a way that is somehow made fitting by a judgment of relationship impairment.

---

[2] I have left the connection between judgment of relationship impairment and relationship modification deliberately vague for now. An important challenge has recently been presented by Chislenko (2020) about how to fill this connection out more precisely. Filling it in will take special care (section 3.2). For now, what's important is the basic idea, which can be spelled out without getting into these details.

3.2 Refinements to the Relationship-Based Framework

Consider Jill, who forgets her wedding anniversary every year.[3] Her partner Susan always remembers the date, but says nothing when the time comes. She just silently registers Jill's forgetfulness each year. This year, the seventh year in a row, the anniversary comes and goes, and Jill does nothing to show recognition of the occasion to Susan. Susan blames Jill for forgetting again. But by now it has become so familiar that she makes no modifications to her intentions and expectations toward Jill. One worry we might have is that because Susan doesn't make any *changes* to her intentions and expectations, she doesn't count as blaming Jill according to Scanlon's account.

Perhaps even in a case like this, one may modify their intentions and expectations ever so slightly, in a way made fitting by the judgment that the relationship falls short of some normative ideal. Given the contextual features of the case, even very subtle adjustments may provide a plausible way of understanding what someone's blame-response consists in. But we can also simply make a minor adjustment to the way I have presented the account. In addition to focusing on modifications to intentions and expectations, we can add the plausible idea that sometimes our existing intentions and expectations simply become more *recalcitrant*, in response to judgments of relationship-impairment. Under certain circumstances (such as those of Jill), perhaps this too can be central to a blame response. It is interesting to consider the mechanisms by which our intentions and expectations might become more recalcitrant in these scenarios. Perhaps they become more recalcitrant through a kind of *reaffirmation* (whether done consciously or not), in the sense that we modify certain higher-order intentions and expectations regarding existing first-order intentions and expectations.[4] In any case, it may be true that Jill blames her partner in the above example without making any modifications to her (first-order) intentions and expectations. It is plausible that when Jill judges her partner blameworthy, she nevertheless reaffirms, or in some way maintains the intentions and expectations she originally formed in response to the impairment a number of years ago.[5]

---

[3] I have noted that the relationship-based framework is, while prominent, somewhat controversial as an account of moral blame, and that one of my aims in this book is to propose some adjustments to the framework to allay some important objections. I do this mainly in the present section. As such, this section may primarily be of interest to those with axes to grind on more general issues about the nature and ethics of (moral) blame. For those wishing to get to the *epistemic* extension of the account, skip ahead to section 3.3.

[4] Thanks to Adam Piovarchy for helpful discussion, and suggesting this possibility of higher-order intentions and expectations.

[5] A final comment on the case: if Jill really does not modify her intentions and expectations in any way, nor do her intentions and expectations become more recalcitrant, then I simply find it implausible to say that, on the moment of the seventh wedding anniversary, anything takes place that constitutes a new blame response over and above some existing stance she already takes toward her partner.

68 EPISTEMIC BLAME

A different sort of case may seem to raise another worry. Assume for the sake of argument that the normative ideal of a parent-child relationship involves children intending and doing what they can to care for elderly parents in certain ways. Knowing that no one is perfect, Ulla arranges a plan for her old age to ensure she has care even if her son fails to *fully* live up to the ideal in question. To this extent, it might seem like she judges that her son falls short of the normative ideal of the parent-child relationship, and modifies her expectations and intentions in a way made fitting by this judgment. Yet, it doesn't look like she thereby blames her son.

In response, note that the notion of a relationship as "normative ideal" is not meant to imply *perfection* on behalf of any party to that relationship. Rather, the normative ideal of the parent-child relationship specifies intentions, expectations, and attitudes characteristic of a *good* parent-child relationship—it specifies intentions, expectations, and attitudes that parties to the relationship ought in this sense to have. We can spell this out in such a way as to account for the fact that no one is perfect. It seems to follow from this that it would be inappropriate to judge that your child falls short of the normative ideal of the parent-child relationship, simply because you judge that they may not be perfectly reliable in taking care of you in your old age. For this reason, the relationship-based account does not misclassify this kind of case.[6]

Recently, Eugene Chislenko (2020) has identified an issue with what I will call the account's "fittingness requirement." The fittingness requirement concerns the connection between the account's two central components, namely the judgment and relationship modification components. Recall, according to the account, *blaming* someone involves forming a judgment of blameworthiness, and modifying your intentions and attitudes in a way that is *somehow* appropriately or fittingly connected to your judgment of relationship impairment. As Chislenko has forcefully pointed out, it is not entirely easy to see how this "somehow" should be further specified (2020, 3–10).

For instance, we could start by filling it out as follows. Let's say that, in all cases of blame, the relevant relationship modification is such that it is *judged* fitting by the blamer. Notice that this immediately leads to a seemingly fatal set of problems. First, it is psychologically unrealistic to maintain that all cases of blame involve

---

[6] Someone might continue pressing a worry in the neighbourhood. Returning to the example of friendship, aren't we allowed to be bad friends sometimes, without deserving *blame* for it? It is far from clear that it is even possible to be a good friend to all your friends most of the time (we can't keep in touch with everyone, after all). I think this worry rests on a misunderstanding. Most centrally, we should keep in mind a role for excuses or other exculpating conditions. We all have a lot going on in our lives. Of course, we sometimes fail to be "good friends," because sometimes the demands at work are too much, or we are going through a tough time personally. This is entirely consistent with the framework. There are times when someone lets you down, but they've got a perfectly good reason for it, or perhaps an excuse. Strictly speaking, on the technical understanding of *relationship impairment*, these are not really instances of relationship impairment. I think this tracks our intuitions. At a certain point, if a friend keeps letting you down, and you start wondering whether whatever else is going on in their life is enough to get them off the hook, you'll start judging them blameworthy. That is the point at which you judge them to have attitudes and intentions that impair their relations with you.

A RELATIONSHIP-BASED ACCOUNT OF EPISTEMIC BLAME 69

people judging that their responses are ones made fitting by their judgments of blameworthiness. Second, this way of filling out the fittingness requirement renders *irrational* blame impossible. That is to say, if all cases of blame involve instances of relationship modification judged fitting by the blamer, then there cannot be cases in which people find themselves blaming others (or themselves) despite their own better judgment, or, in other words, despite judging that their responses are *not* ones made fitting by a judgment of blameworthiness (perhaps because they haven't formed a judgment of blameworthiness at all). As Hannah Pickard (2013) has convincingly argued, people clearly can blame irrationally.[7] So, this approach to the fittingness requirement cannot be right (cf. Chislenko 2020).

Trying out a second approach, why not maintain that the relevant relationship modification must *itself* be a fitting response to the blamer's judgment of blameworthiness. The thought is to maintain that an objective connection of fittingness must hold between the blamer's judgment of blameworthiness and the response they manifest in light of it. This might seem to avoid the issue of psychological plausibility. After all, on this approach, the fittingness requirement can be met regardless of whether the blamer has formed a judgment about the fittingness of their response. Unfortunately, this approach seems to take us no further with respect to irrational blame. To see this, consider a slightly different form of irrational blame, which we can call "disproportionate blame." It seems perfectly possible for someone to form a judgment of blameworthiness, and then modify their relationship with that person in a way that is disproportionate to the judgment of blameworthiness—for example, perhaps they get extremely angry at a relatively minor interpersonal infraction. Intuitively, such a response is still a blame response, even though it is disproportionate. However, precisely because this person's extreme anger is disproportionate, it is not a response made fitting by the judgment of blameworthiness. So, this approach to the fittingness requirement seems fatally flawed as well: it seems to mistakenly bar such responses from counting as blame responses.

To get around this issue, I propose the following alternative approach. Rather than locating the sort of fittingness we are looking for in the blamer's view of their own responses, or in an objective relation between judgment of blameworthiness and token response, I propose locating it in an objective relation between the blamer's judgment of blameworthiness and a *type* of response, of which their token response may count as a member. Here is what I have in mind:

Scanlonian Blame*

A judgment of blameworthiness, plus a modification to one's intentions and attitudes that is a fitting *type* of response to that judgment.

---

[7] In Chapter 4, I address a closely related worry about whether blame requires any kind of judgment component (see section 4.1).

70 EPISTEMIC BLAME

This approach can handle cases of disproportionate blame. In such cases, the blamer's *token* response may not be fitting, but it may nevertheless be a token of a type of response that we would typically understand as one made fitting by a judgment of blameworthiness. For example, we might say that anger is a fitting type of response to a judgment of blameworthiness. Someone manifesting *extreme* anger in a given case, however, might be going in for too much of this fitting type of response. We can thus count disproportionate blamers *as* blaming—indeed, we can even explain why their blame is disproportionate: they count as blaming disproportionately because their token response is an unfitting instance (too extreme) of a more general class of responses that are fitting types of responses to judgments of blameworthiness.[8]

One drawback of this approach is that now we have to classify "types" of relationship modification that can be made fitting, as such, by a judgment of blameworthiness. On the face of it, this may seem daunting. But in fact, on the contrary, I think such a project is an opportunity to connect the relationship-based view of blame to a wide range of existing views in the literature about the nature of blame. It provides an opportunity to highlight the *ecumenical* dimension of the relationship-based approach.

My idea is to begin classifying "types" of relationship modification along lines that correspond to various attitudes, behaviors, or practices that other theorists have identified as candidates for spelling out the nature of blame. For example, we could understand the following as characteristic types of relationship modification:

- negative emotions
- rebuke
- protest
- pointed requests for reasons, etc.

Each of these types of response (of which there may be numerous varieties) can be understood as types of relationship modification that are fitting responses to

---

[8] One might worry that this is too vague. Here is a way of pressing that worry. What happens if a person forms one *type* of judgment of blameworthiness, and modifies their relationship in a way that may be fitting to *another* type of judgment of blameworthiness, but is not fitting to this type? If we take on the task of spelling out which types of relationship modification can count as fitting responses to which types of blameworthiness judgments, we may run head-first into the sort of counterexamples we started with: namely, ones involving a person who intuitively blames someone, but who now fails to meet the conditions of our account. To get around this worry, I suggest that any *type* of blame response can, in principle, be a fitting type of response to any type of judgment of blameworthiness. What might vary, however, is the range of strength or degree that a given type of response may take while still counting as a fitting token of that type of response to the relevant judgment of blameworthiness. In a sense, what this proposal amounts to is denying that there really is a relevant difference between putative "types" of judgments of blameworthiness, when it comes to the types of responses that can be made fitting by them. This may need to be relativized to domains of blame (i.e. moral, epistemic, etc.). Thanks to Sebastian Köhler for drawing my attention to this issue.

judgments of blameworthiness. The fact that each has been focused on as a candidate for spelling out *the* nature of blame would suggest that they are, minimally, good candidates for types of blame responses. That said, we might reasonably wonder whether they are plausibly types of *relationship modification*. So let me pause to address this question.

It is important not to forget the quasi-technical sense in which I understand "relationships" in this book. Recall, relationships are just sets of intentions, attitudes, and expectations people have concerning how to act and feel toward one another—intentions, expectations, and attitudes that are justified by a wide range of facts about parties to the relationship, depending on those involved and the kind of relationship it is. *Modifying* relationships only requires adjusting (or re-affirming) one's intentions and attitudes in response to a judgment of blameworthiness. It is plausible, for example, that protest and rebuke consist, in part, in adjustments to our intentions and attitudes in response to a judgment of blameworthiness. For instance, in certain cases at least, what it means to protest someone's wrongdoing may involve intending to maintain a certain negative stance toward them, perhaps accompanied by the sort of verbal behavior we typically associate with protest ("don't do that!"). So, it is natural to think of "protest" as a term that picks out one characteristic cluster of modifications or reaffirmations of intentions and attitudes we manifest in response to a judgment of blameworthiness. Protest is a plausible candidate for a type of relationship modification that is useful for present purposes.

Similar stories can likely be told about negative emotions and pointed requests for reasons. For example, as we have seen, Wallace argues that there is a constitutive connection between negative emotions widely associated with blame—reactive attitudes, such as indignation and resentment—and holding others to relationship-constituting expectations (Wallace 1994; 2011). On his view, being susceptible to these reactive attitudes under the right circumstances just is a unique way of holding others to relationship-constituting expectations. If something like this is on the right track, then forming such attitudes amounts to a way of registering—perhaps modifying, but minimally re-affirming (however implicitly)—certain intentions and attitudes that are constitutive of one's relations with another.

The proposed way of adjusting the relationship-based account not only explains why the account does not fall prey to an important kind of counterexample (cases of disproportionate blame), it also shows how the account can explain the appeal of so many other accounts of blame. Each has something—perhaps lots of things—going for it. But a central part of what that *is*, according to my formulation of the relationship-based account, is that the attitude or behavior is a *type* of blame-response—or, to use my terminology, it is a type of relationship modification made fitting by a judgment of blameworthiness. What unifies the wide variety of blame-responses focused on in the literature is that they are types of relationship modification made fitting by a judgment of blameworthiness.

72 EPISTEMIC BLAME

This is already a considerable degree of progress in our understanding of the fittingness requirement. But there remains another, related, worry about the relationship-based account that I think we are now well-positioned to address. This is the objection—made forcefully by Angela Smith (2013, 38)—that the account misclassifies cases of relationship modification that intuitively have nothing to do with blame, because they are in some sense too positively valanced. Smith imagines a mother who forms a judgment of blameworthiness about her son (say, he has committed a horrible crime and is blameworthy for it), but as a result, rather than modifying her relationship in a way that we might pretheoretically understand as blaming him, she modifies it in a positively valanced way, for example by resolving to love her son even more.[9]

One might think that this sort of case is already covered by my alternative approach to the fittingness requirement. That is, perhaps the account understood as such does not classify this as a case of blame because it is not a type of response made fitting by a judgment of blameworthiness. But many will balk at this suggestion. Who is to say whether the mother's resolution to love her son more is a fitting type of response to her judgment of blameworthiness? This may depend on the details of their relationship, among other things. I don't want to take a stance on the question of whether positively valanced relationship modification can be made fitting by judgments of blameworthiness. This strikes me as an interesting question for the ethics of blame: exactly *when* might this sort of thing, as opposed to a blame response, be a fitting response to a judgment of blameworthiness?

Thankfully, to ensure that the relationship-based account does not classify positively valanced responses (such as the mother's intention to love more) as blame responses, we need only make a small adjustment to my alternative formulation of the account:

Scanlonian Blame**

A judgment of blameworthiness, plus a *negatively valanced* modification to one's intentions and attitudes that is a fitting *type* of response to that judgment.

What does it take for a modification to one's intentions and attitudes to count as "negatively valanced"? For now, we can understand negatively valanced modifications to one's intentions and attitudes as modifications that manifest a negative

---

[9] The objection is of course similar to, but also importantly different from, Smith's concern about Brown's account (see Chapter 2, section 7). How are the two objections different? Notice that the mother-son case functions as a straightforward counterexample to the relationship-based account. Meanwhile, recall, treating the version of the mother-son case above as a counterexample to the Sher-based framework misses the point of that objection entirely.

evaluation of the target instance of relationship impairment.[10] One might think that, understood as such, this takes us no further in avoiding Smith-type cases after all, since perhaps the mother's intention to love her son more—despite seeming on its face to be a "positive" change in attitude—is actually negatively valanced in the sense I mean here. For instance, perhaps the mother's intention to love her son more is a change that has arisen out of a negative judgment concerning the son's relationship impairment.

However, on closer inspection, the adjustment I am proposing does enable us to make headway on Smith-type cases. While the mother's change in attitude may *arise* out of (or in other words, be "instigated by," "caused by," or "a response to") a negative evaluation of an instance of relationship impairment, it need not be construed as manifesting that negative evaluation. The way I understand the case, the mother's change in attitude is one she has taken up *despite* her negative judgments about her son, and as a way of responding to the situation, in light of certain facts about her loving relationship with him. So, it does not count as negatively valanced in my sense. However, were the mother's intention to love her son more, in some strange way, to manifest a negative evaluation of an instance of relationship impairment, then I think it may in fact best be described as a kind of blame response, perhaps an "unhealthy" one.

This tweak to the relationship-based account might seem ad hoc. To mitigate that appearance, it would be helpful if we could say something about the connection between positive and negatively valanced versions of relationship modification. What do they have in common such that all it takes for relationship modification of one sort to count as blame, is that it's a negatively valanced form of the other? Here is a proposal, drawing on a well-known distinction of Scanlon's. All forms of relationship modification done in response to judgments of blameworthiness are ways of responding to or reflecting the *meaning* of a person's actions (in a sense to be contrasted with their permissibility). As such, they are imbued with a kind of significance that merely evaluative judgments (whether positive or negative) do not have. In Smith-style cases, the relevant relationship is such that, as it happens, the way the mother chooses to react (or finds herself reacting) to her judgment of blameworthiness, is to respond in a positively valanced way—perhaps as a kind of proleptic mechanism, or something along those lines. Crucially, the fittingness of such a change in attitudes and intentions is surely constrained by specific details or features of the relationship in question. It seems plausible that few kinds of relationship are such that fitting types of responses to judgments of blameworthiness within them will often—or ever—be positively valanced. And perhaps that is exactly why it is easy to overlook the Smith-type case.

---

[10] In Chapter 7, I slightly refine this articulation, in a way that is useful for a more detailed examination of valance in the context of the ethics of epistemic blame.

74 EPISTEMIC BLAME

This proposal avoids ruling out the possibility that Smith's loving mother can fittingly respond to her blameworthy son with an intention to love him more. To that extent, it avoids controversial commitments in the ethics of blame. But the proposal does not avoid substantive commitments in the ethics of blame altogether. For one thing, the account *classifies* blame responses as types of negatively valanced responses that are made fitting by judgments of blameworthiness. Skeptics about the value or appropriateness of blame might bristle at this. I will take up a detailed defense of negatively valanced responses in the epistemic domain in Chapter 7.

Again, there are of course other worries we might have about the relationship-based framework. I will address some of the more pressing issues—a number of which seem equally important for my epistemic extension of Scanlon's basic ideas—in the next chapter. For now, a crucial question needs addressing. How can an epistemic extension of this framework so much as get off the ground? What, for starters, is the relevant *relationship* with which we might begin developing an account of epistemic blame? To extend the view, I propose making use of the notion of an "epistemic relationship."

3.3 Epistemic Blame and Epistemic Relationships

Let an epistemic relationship be a set of intentions, expectations, and attitudes people have toward one another that are oriented toward their epistemic agency in different ways. Sometimes they are oriented toward cultivating epistemic agency; other times, they are oriented toward utilizing it in more or less specialized ways. In broad outline, my view is that we should understand judgments of epistemic blameworthiness as judgments that someone has fallen short of a normatively idealized set of such intentions and expectations, against which we can measure their epistemic relationship with that person. Epistemic blame-responses can then be understood as (negatively valanced) modifications to the actual intentions and expectations that one has toward that person, in types of ways made fitting by this judgment.[11] Here is the basic idea of the account:

Epistemic Blame

A judgment of epistemic blameworthiness, plus a negatively valanced modification to one's epistemic intentions and attitudes that is a fitting type of response to that judgment.

---

[11] The account does not require that ordinary speakers have the concept of an "epistemic relationship," or the concept of an impairment of such a relationship. Rather, the contents of any blame-relevant judgment can be more specific: they can concern failures to conform belief to the evidence, assertions of falsehoods, etc. These are things that, we will see below, constitute impairments of epistemic relationships.

To begin filling this out, it is helpful to think about examples of familiar kinds of relationships that have strong epistemic dimensions. Consider the relationship between teachers and students. When all goes well, teachers typically intend to do their best to bring it about that each of their students has an adequate opportunity to learn some range of material. They also expect that each student does what they can to be in a position to learn the relevant material. Moreover, when all goes well, students typically intend to do what they can to be in a position to learn some range of material, and expect their teachers to do their best to bring it about that each student has an adequate opportunity to learn the relevant material. These are arguably intentions and expectations that teachers and students need to have in order to count, in some sense, as "good" teachers and students. Perhaps there are more supererogatory intentions and expectations that, while not obligatory, would nevertheless be good for a teacher to have—for example, an intention to show enthusiasm when students reach benchmarks in the learning process.[12]

This is useful for fixing the idea that people can have sets of intentions and expectations toward each other that are directed toward their epistemic agency in distinctive ways, and which might thereby constitute a kind of relationship in the technical Scanlonian sense. But obviously not all cases of epistemic blame involve teachers and students. We need a framework that is much more general. To develop this, I propose pushing the notion of an epistemic relationship a bit further.

The division of epistemic labor is a basic fact of human social life. We rely on one another on a near continual basis for information. This is as true for the mundane as it is for matters of great importance. I rely on the stranger sitting next to me for information about when the next bus arrives. I rely on experts for information that will help me decide whether the vaccine is safe. Importantly, I do not *merely* rely on others for information, in the way that I might rely on an old car that I fear might break down any day. Rather, other things being equal, we tend to have a certain degree of confidence in one another when it comes to our ability to run our intellectual lives. This confidence is partly constituted by a mixture of *expectations* in both the predictive and normative sense of "expectation." Other things being equal, we tend to expect, in the sense of anticipate it to be the case that, other epistemic agents will meet at least certain minimal criteria in the running of their intellectual lives (for example, they will recognize ordinary mid-sized objects when they can see them in good lighting). But we also expect, in the sense of making a kind of demand, that they will meet certain epistemic criteria in the running of their intellectual lives, sometimes in a way that outstrips our predictive expectations (Goldberg 2017; 2018, chapter 5). In my view, it is in

---

[12] In Chapter 6, I examine the epistemic dimensions of a wide range of different types of relationships. I also explore the limits on when these epistemic dimensions really amount to, or have the capacity to impact or constitutively contribute to, anything deserving the label of an "epistemic relationship."

76 EPISTEMIC BLAME

this way that members of an epistemic community stand in a relationship of mutual epistemic expectation—one that is bound up with a complex network of intentions and expectations that are oriented around our epistemic agency in very basic ways. This is what I call the General Epistemic Relationship (GER).

To help spell out the GER in more detail, I will introduce an additional technical term. This is the notion of an "intellectual act":

> **Intellectual act**: any attempt at exercising one's epistemic competence, such as: forming a belief that p (perceptually, inferentially, by memory access, etc.) through one's ability to believe true propositions (perceptual ability, inferential ability, memory ability, etc.); asserting that p through one's ability to assert true propositions; maintaining a belief that p through one's ability to maintain true beliefs that p, etc.

The unifying feature of intellectual acts is that they are the sorts of things that can be evaluated by epistemic criteria. I will remain deliberately open at this point on the question of what count as "epistemic criteria." But the sort of thing I have in mind includes the standards of *rationality, justification, reliability,* and *truth.* Beliefs can be rational and justified; acts of inquiry can be reliable; assertions can be true. And so on. This notion of an intellectual act will become important again in Chapter 5, when I consider in more detail what sorts of things can be appropriate targets of epistemic blame.[13]

I propose that the intentions and expectations that are constitutive of the *normative ideal* of the GER include the following candidates. When all goes well, for any member A, B:

- A intends, for any intellectual act X of A's, to meet epistemic criteria Y, unless A has good reason, or an excuse, for not doing so.[14]

---

[13] One might worry that building attempts at exercising competences into the very idea of an intellectual act will lead to problems down the road. For example, perhaps there are cases—ones that seem especially relevant to the topic of epistemic blame—in which someone does something that intuitively counts as an "intellectual act," but does not even *attempt* to exercise an epistemic competence. Consider a person who is so deeply committed to believing in conspiracy theories that when they form conspiracy belief p they do not in any way attempt to exercise an epistemic competence. In response, I would point out that even those embroiled in conspiracy theories typically take themselves to be following the evidence where it leads. There may be cases of genuine "epistemic akrasia," but most of the time, even those with intellectual habits that others may regard as epistemically bad, can fairly be interpreted as *attempting* to exercise basic epistemic competences. There may be interesting complications in this area; the possibility of epistemic akrasia may raise problems of its own. I set these issues to the side in the service of laying out the bigger picture. Thanks to Chris Kelp for discussion.

[14] Thanks to Susan Wolf for noting that good reasons and excuses are very different sorts of things. In a previously published paper containing some of this material (Boult 2021b), I carelessly conflated the two—that is, my formulation of the intentions and expectations constitutive of the normative ideal of the GER did not adequately differentiate ways a person can be off the hook for not meeting the relevant expectations, or having the relevant intentions.

A RELATIONSHIP-BASED ACCOUNT OF EPISTEMIC BLAME 77

- A expects, for any intellectual act X of B's, that B will meet epistemic criteria Y, unless B has good reason, or an excuse, for not doing so.
- B intends, for any intellectual act X of B's, to meet epistemic criteria Y, unless B has good reason, or an excuse, for not doing so.
- B expects, for any intellectual act X of A's, that A will meet epistemic criteria Y, unless A has good reason, or an excuse, for not doing so.

This is by no means an exhaustive list of the sorts of intentions and expectations that comprise the normative ideal of the GER. There are plausibly other intentions and expectations, perhaps most paradigmatically a standing intention to *epistemically trust* the word of others, under certain conditions, and an expectation that others will epistemically trust one's word under certain conditions.[15]

As I understand the term, epistemic trust is not identical to garden variety trust. Often, when we "trust" someone for information, this entails, among other things, that we think they do not harbor intentions to deceive or mislead. *Epistemically* trusting someone for information, however, entails that we have confidence that they are epistemically reliable—that believing what they say is a way of arriving at a favorable ratio of true to false beliefs, or knowledge, or understanding, etc.—and that we are willing to rely on them as such. Importantly, epistemic trust is not merely a matter of regarding someone as epistemically reliable. We can regard a thermometer epistemically reliable, but it sounds grandiose to construe this as a kind of "epistemic trust." A key issue in identifying a unique notion of epistemic trust is locating an attitude or disposition that goes beyond mere reliance on someone's epistemic competences, without invoking attitudes or dispositions that amount to the sort of interpersonal trust that is central to our moral lives—the kind whose betrayal licenses *resentment*. Often the latter is referred to as "affective trust" (Faulkner 2007, 882).[16] A conception of epistemic trust that does not go beyond reliance raises the question of whether it is a conception of *trust*. A conception that relies on affective trust—whether overtly or otherwise—raises the question of whether it is really about something uniquely *epistemic*. In my view, a core feature setting epistemic trust apart from both reliance and affective trust is the following. In being willing to rely on a person whom we epistemically trust, we don't merely judge them epistemically reliable; other things being equal,

---

[15] This idea is of course closely related to Kauppinen's as discussed in Chapter 2, section 2.3.3. As should already be clear, there are important differences between my approach to epistemic blame and Kauppinen's. For a start, as already noted, Kauppinen disagrees there is such a thing as epistemic blame (he frames his view as a view about holding epistemically accountable). Perhaps relatedly, Kauppinen makes no role for *judging blameworthy* (or judging that a relationship has been impaired) in his account of fitting responses to epistemic failings. Moreover, in addition to making use of the notion of epistemic trust, my account couches adjustments of epistemic trust in a more general framework of modifications to expectations and intentions that are constitutive of the GER.

[16] Here is Faulkner explicitly linking violations of affective trust with resentment: "The general reactive attitude in play here is *resentment*: in affectively trusting S to φ, A will be prone to resentment were S to show no inclination to φ" (Faulkner 2007, 882).

we also judge that they will do their best to be epistemically responsible. That is to say, they will do their best in acquiring and sharing the *relevant* epistemic goods, and will let you know when they are *not* reliable on some subject matter (Dormandy 2020; Woodard forthcoming, 10).[17] Perhaps this is why it sounds somewhat odd to epistemically trust a thermometer.

My aim here is not to develop and defend a complete view of epistemic trust. Given the massive and growing literature on trust, that would require a book in its own right. Fortunately, the foregoing is sufficient for present purposes. Even at this skeletal level, we can already make sense of a very wide range of cases. Return to THE OFFICE.[18] Jim and Dwight are engaged in a practice of living up to the intentions and expectations specified by the normative ideal of the GER. By forming (and maintaining) his conspiracy belief, in the absence of any evidence, Dwight fails to live up to the normative ideal of the GER. For example, he fails to meet an expectation of the form

- A expects, for any intellectual act X of B's, that B will meet epistemic criteria Y, unless B has good reason, or an excuse, for not doing so.

Perhaps he also reveals that he lacks an intention of the form

- B intends, for any intellectual act X of B's, to meet epistemic criteria Y, unless B has good reason, or an excuse, for not doing so.

According to my account, Jim's epistemic blame-response may amount to the judgment (however implicit) that Dwight has done something to impair the GER, plus a modification to his epistemic relationship with Dwight in a type of way made fitting by that judgment. For example, perhaps he modifies his intention to epistemically trust Dwight's word on matters in domain D under certain conditions. And as the case is described, this may of course (but need not) be accompanied by rebuke, requests for reasons, and expressions of frustration.

To illustrate the power and nuance of the relationship-based account, here is one way of specifying the sort of thing I have in mind in a bit more detail. Assume that prior to this particular incident, Jim's intentions to epistemically trust Dwight's word were broader in scope. That is to say, there were more items with respect to which he was willing to epistemically trust Dwight. In response to the incident in question—more specifically, in response to Jim's judgment that

---

[17] Katherine Dormandy uses the term "epistemic care" to get at a related idea (2020, 19). See McCraw (2015), and Carter and Simion (2020), for helpful discussions of epistemic trust and the epistemology of trust. See Faulkner and Simpson (2017) for an excellent overview of philosophical issues about trust generally.

[18] See Introduction.

A RELATIONSHIP-BASED ACCOUNT OF EPISTEMIC BLAME 79

Dwight has done something to impair the GER—the scope of Jim's intentions has narrowed.[19] There are now fewer items with respect to which Jim intends to epistemically trust the word of Dwight. Perhaps Jim simply reaffirms an existing intention with a particular scope, one that is more restricted than the normative ideal allows. Jim's negative attitudes toward Dwight in this regard simply become more recalcitrant. To represent this a bit more visually:

Let "domain D" be the domain of facts about office politics

Let "d1 – d5" specify more fine-grained sets of facts within that domain; for example,

d1 = facts about boss Michael's interests
d2 = facts about colleague Pam's interests
d3 = facts about the executive's plans to downsize
...and so on...

Let "o" represent an empty set of facts

Let's say that at time t1, a subset of Jim's intentions to epistemically trust looks like this:

- Jim t1: epistemically trusts Dwight's word concerning range < d1...dn> in domain D.

At t2, Dwight reveals his conspiracy belief to Jim. Jim forms the judgment that Dwight has done something to fall short of the normative ideal of the GER, and, as a result, his attitudes toward Dwight now look like this:

- Jim t2: epistemically trusts Dwight's word concerning range < o > in domain D.

Jim went from intending to epistemically trust Dwight's word concerning <d1...dn> to intending not to epistemically trust Dwight's word in domain D at all. This undoubtedly simplifies the sorts of changes that might occur in real-life situations, but hopefully it makes the basic point vivid. The idea is to illustrate what it means to say that Jim modifies an intention to epistemically trust that is (partially) constitutive of the GER. Such a combination of judgment and modification to intentions and expectations just is what Jim's epistemic blame consists in.

---

[19] Perhaps it is more accurate to say that *Jim* has narrowed them—however, I would like to remain as neutral as possible on the question of precisely how much voluntary control we have over our blame responses.

80 EPISTEMIC BLAME

Here is an immediate worry. Imagine that instead of his usual epistemically blameworthy self, Dwight tends to be an impeccable reasoner at all times. However, one day he swallows a pill that causes him to reason highly dogmatically and hastily on a wide range of topics, for the next week. Upon learning of Dwight's swallowing of the pill (and knowing what the pill does), Jim will of course modify his intentions and attitudes toward Dwight, in perhaps the same way as we have spelled out above. But it is certainly far from obvious that he really epistemically *blames* Dwight for swallowing the pill, at least not in the same way as our original case. Perhaps the account therefore delivers the wrong result here.[20]

In my view, the case is under-described. First, if Dwight *deliberately* took the pill, knowing full well what it will do, then I think in addition to modifying his epistemic intentions and attitudes toward Dwight, Jim will appropriately do so on the basis of judging that, by taking the pill, Dwight has done something to impair the GER. As such, his response may count as an epistemic blame response. But this seems to me like the right result.[21] However, if Dwight merely accidentally took the pill, or was somehow tricked or coerced into taking it, then, while Jim may modify his epistemic intentions and attitudes, it does not seem right to say that he can appropriately do so on the basis of judging that *Dwight* has done something to impair the GER. And so, the account does not classify Jim's modifications as a blame response. And that, too, seems like the right result. Thus, either way, the relationship-based account can accommodate such a case. I will return to this sort of concern in the bigger picture context of assessing whether the account is ultimately up to the task of meeting SIGNIFICANCE in the next chapter (4.1), and again in Chapter 5 when considering in more depth what sorts of things people can be appropriately epistemically blamed for (5.1.2).

The key lesson this objection brings out is the importance of the role for judgment in the relationship-based account. The account requires that an adjustment of one's epistemic intentions and expectations be the result of the judgment that the target of blame has done something to impair the GER. Of course, and I have pointed this out above, the blamer need not make this judgment under this description. Arguably nobody does—after all, the GER is a technical notion. It aims to capture what's theoretically interesting about the sorts of judgments that people *do* make when they seem to count as epistemically blaming someone. For example, epistemic blamers tend to judge that someone has been *intellectually irresponsible*, or *intellectually vicious*, or *reckless*, or just plain "*stupid*." Those are the sorts of things I take the notion of a judgment of GER impairment to unify. Only when an agent modifies their epistemic intentions and attitudes in a

---

[20] Thanks to Jack Lyons for raising this issue.

[21] Some might disagree with me here. Perhaps in this sort of scenario, where the epistemic shortcoming is causally connected to a practical decision (to take the pill), the sort of blame-response it would be appropriate for Jim to have is, more accurately described as a practical or even moral form of blame.

negatively valanced type of way made fitting by *this* sort of judgment do they count as epistemically blaming others.

I am trying to make sense of a very wide range of cases of epistemic blame by appealing to a very abstract specification of the GER. Note that much of the time, in real life, we can appeal to much more specific resources in filling out the nature of an individual's epistemic blame-response. The actual intentions and expectations involved in any given case will, much of the time, be impacted by more specific kinds of relationships that people have with each other. To return to the teacher-student relationship sketched earlier, perhaps a teacher's epistemically blaming their student can partly consist, for example, in modifying a supererogatory intention to show a certain degree of enthusiasm about a student's future progress, along with whatever may or may not happen at the level of the GER. Once I have developed some of the finer-grained details about our *entitlements* to have normative epistemic expectations of one another—by drawing on work by Sandy Goldberg in Chapter 6—I will be in a position to flesh these points out in more detail. It turns out that, by spelling out how expectations and intentions constitutive of different kinds of relationships can interact with the GER, we gain a principled way of explaining how epistemic blame interacts with other normative domains beyond the epistemic.

3.4 Conclusion

I have motivated the basic machinery of the relationship-based account of epistemic blame. I have also responded to some important initial concerns. The task remains to provide a fuller defense of my proposal. Most importantly, we must examine whether the relationship-based account is capable of meeting the desiderata laid out in Chapter 1. Can the account do justice to the significance of epistemic blame without positing attitudes, practices, or behaviors that seem out of place in the epistemic domain? In the next chapter, I take these tasks in turn. The result: a resolution of the puzzle of epistemic blame.

4
The Significance and Fittingness of Epistemic Blame

The central advantage of the relationship-based account of epistemic blame is that modifications to our epistemic relationships have the right kind of significance, while fitting with a natural understanding of our actual epistemic practices. Or so I will now argue.

By linking the motivational component of epistemic blame to relationship modification, the relationship-based account can tell us something deeper about the nature of epistemic blame than any of the other accounts we have considered in this book. In this chapter, I defend this claim in three main stages. First, I argue that epistemic relationship modification is a way of holding others to normative expectations. Second, I argue that epistemic relationship modification is a fitting response to epistemic failings. This already goes a long way toward showing that the relationship-based account is the preferred solution to the puzzle of epistemic blame. But I also want to ensure confidence that the account is well-motivated on independent grounds, and that it is not vulnerable to fatal objections. So, third, the chapter also advertises some further advantages of the account over Brown's, and responds to the most pressing remaining objections—including appeals to cool blame, self-blame, and blame of the dead and distant. This will complete my argument that the relationship-based account can resolve the puzzle of epistemic blame.

4.1 Significance Revisited

Epistemic relationship modification carries a significance that goes beyond merely assigning others a bad epistemic grade. Perhaps this is intuitive. Consider finding out that someone has adjusted their intention to epistemically trust your word on some domain of propositions, because they judge you irrational, dogmatic, or intellectually lazy. My guess is that this won't be a matter of trivial importance to you. If you're like me, it will be quite an unpleasant realization. Still, it would be helpful if we could say more in defense of the relationship-based account's ability to meet SIGNIFICANCE.

In Chapter 1, I connected the significance of blame to normative expectations. I said that blame responses are more significant than mere negative evaluations in

---

Epistemic Blame: The Nature and Norms of Epistemic Relationships. Cameron Boult, Oxford University Press.
© Cameron Boult 2024. DOI: 10.1093/oso/9780192890580.003.0005

the sense that they manifest a kind of holding others to normative expectations, in a way that mere negative evaluation does not entail. To show that the relationship-based account of epistemic blame meets SIGNIFICANCE, we must show that epistemic relationship-modification can function as a form of holding oneself and others to normative expectations.

The main challenge here lies in addressing the most detailed and established view about the connection between normative expectations and blame, namely Wallace's view that holding others to normative expectations is constitutively connected to susceptibility to the reactive attitudes narrowly construed (Wallace 1994; 2011). Recall, when I use the phrase "reactive attitudes narrowly construed," I mean paradigm negative emotional responses such as indignation and resentment. Epistemic relationship modification does not involve a central role for susceptibility to the reactive attitudes narrowly construed. So, if Wallace is right about the connection between normative expectations and susceptibility to these attitudes, it would seem the relationship-based account of epistemic blame cannot meet SIGNIFICANCE.

Before I address this challenge, I want to allay an immediate worry. One might be willing to agree that epistemic relationship modification is a way of holding to normative expectations, but disagree that it is a kind of *blame*. One might therefore think that addressing the present challenge is simply not going to get at the heart of whether the relationship-based account can solve the puzzle of epistemic blame. However, this rests on a misunderstanding of my strategy. I will engage directly with some important questions about the connection between relationship modification and blame shortly below. But recall that my strategy in this chapter is threefold. I do not intend the first stage alone to convince you that epistemic relationship modification is a kind of blame. Rather, I aim to build a broad case: first, by establishing that epistemic relationship modification meets SIGNIFICANCE; second, by establishing that it meets FITTINGNESS; and third, by highlighting the account's central advantages over my main competitors, and responding to some remaining objections. If by the end of all that you disagree with my conclusion, then we may have a substantive issue on our hands. But it will not do to simply point out that the first stage of this strategy does not, by itself, establish that GER modification is a kind of blame. I regard the first stage as important in its own right, so I return to that now.

In my view, Wallace is incorrect that susceptibility to the reactive attitudes narrowly construed is essential for holding to normative expectations. I am not the first to challenge Wallace on this score. Others have argued that the positive roles that Wallace associates with the reactive attitudes can be fulfilled by other attitudes, such as certain kinds of sadness, disappointment, or other non-emotional responses. Goldman (2014), Milam (2016), and Menges (2020) are notable examples. Here I aim to contribute to the picture defended by these

84 EPISTEMIC BLAME

authors. My strategy starts with observations about the role that *epistemic* expectations can play in this context.

As we are by now familiar, we seem to hold each other to normative expectations in the epistemic domain. We normatively expect doctors to know information about well-established findings relevant to their area, or lawyers to know the legal matters involved in their cases. In line with my claims about the GER, we also appear to have more general expectations concerning the basic conducting of our intellectual acts. The point is that these appear to be genuine forms of *normative* expectation, and they are not obviously moral or directly personal in nature, at least not exclusively so.

One point we can make in defense of this claim is that the expectations just enumerated do not appear to be *predictive* forms of expectation, at least not exclusively. Many will be familiar with the experience of normatively expecting a tired-looking doctor in a walk-in clinic to apply up-to-date knowledge in family medicine in a skillful differential diagnosis, even if not predictively expecting them to do so. If this is right, then anyone challenging the idea that we hold one another to normative expectations in the epistemic domain owes us an account of what sort of expectations these are, if they are neither predictive nor normative.

This is relevant for the following reason. By his own lights, Wallace at most demonstrates that being susceptible to the reactive attitudes narrowly construed is a constitutive part of holding others to *moral* expectations (Wallace 1994, chapter 2). But then, because moral expectations are not the only form of normative expectation—because epistemic expectations are also normative—this does not yet show that susceptibility to the reactive attitudes narrowly construed is the only way to hold others to normative expectations. And if susceptibility to the reactive attitudes narrowly construed is not the only way to hold others to normative expectations, this removes a core obstacle to thinking that epistemic relationship-modification can be a way of holding to normative expectations.

Rima Basu has recently developed a more expansive picture of expectations, according to which there are other kinds of expectations in addition to predictive and normative (Basu forthcoming). If a more expansive picture of expectations is correct, perhaps we cannot conclude that epistemic expectations are normative on the basis of the observation that they are *non-predictive* expectations. And so, perhaps Wallace can resist the argument just sketched, and insist that his story about holding to moral expectations exhausts the proper realm of holding to normative expectations.

According to Basu, in addition to predictive and normative expectations, we should also make room for "proleptic" and "peremptory" expectations. Proleptic expectations typically function in parent-child, or other relationships of dependence and attachment (e.g. teacher-student). They combine elements of both predictive and normative expectations, in that they are both belief-like and express demands. But they have a further dimension in virtue of serving as a kind of

THE SIGNIFICANCE AND FITTINGNESS OF EPISTEMIC BLAME   85

"expectival scaffolding" within the relevant relationship. The very presence of the demand-like properties of these expectations, when all goes well, make their predictive side *more likely to be correct* (Basu 9).

According to Basu, a paradigm example of *peremptory* expectations is that of a parent expecting their child to "be a good person." As Basu puts it, "when you expect your child to be a good person that expectation is neither predictive, prescriptive, nor proleptic. Rather, it is an expectation about objective moral requirements and such expectations can feel pretty weighty as well. After all, they are moral requirements!" (9). The basic idea is that, while bearing a resemblance to normative expectations, peremptory expectations form a class of their own insofar as they have a kind of *non-negotiable* character, perhaps stemming from a connection to deep moral commitments.

What is important for present purposes is that, even if we follow Basu and enrich our understanding of kinds of expectations along these lines, epistemic expectations of the sort I have in mind do not appear to be proleptic or peremptory. Perhaps they are sometimes proleptic, but it is doubtful they always are. After all, proleptic expectations typically function in parent-child, or other relationships of dependence and attachment. And it is just not the case that all epistemic expectations function within these kinds of relationships.

On peremptory expectations, I find it hard to see how these are not simply equivalent to normative expectations. Perhaps they are a species of normative expectation, one deserving separate classification—perhaps in virtue of having a content concerning "objective moral requirements," or functioning as imperatives. But if that is the case, then epistemic expectations are not helpfully understood as peremptory expectations. Our epistemic expectations do not seem to have a content concerning objective moral requirements, and while they perhaps sometimes function as imperatives, it is far from clear that they always or even very often do.

The upshot of all this is that, even taking on board Basu's more expansive picture of expectations, my argument from the observation that epistemic expectations are *expectations*, but not predictive ones, still needs a response. Again, anyone challenging the idea that these are normative expectations owes us an account of what sort of expectations they are, if they are neither predictive, proleptic, peremptory, or normative. So far, I have challenged Wallace on the idea that normative expectations are essentially bound up with susceptibility to the reactive attitudes narrowly construed. At most, Wallace may have established that *moral* expectations are essentially bound up with the reactive attitudes narrowly construed, but not that normative expectations more generally are. What remains is a defense of an alternative picture.

In my view, negative emotional responses are just *one* way in which we can hold one another to normative expectations. Moreover, it seems to me that the reason *why* negative emotions sometimes count as ways of holding people to normative

86 EPISTEMIC BLAME

expectations is precisely because they are a form of relationship modification. Perhaps they are (and only can be) a form of moral/personal relationship modification, though I suspect we could even argue that there are broader ways in which *moral* relationship-modification can be a way of holding others to moral expectations (I won't be defending this point here). In my view, ("mere") epistemic relationship modification (of the relevant kind) is a way of holding oneself and others to normative expectations. Why think otherwise?

One potential reason to worry about this picture is if it turns out there can be clear cases of relationship modification without blame. I briefly addressed this issue in Chapter 3, section 3.3, but the time has come to consider it in greater depth. The following case, inspired by Susan Wolf (2011), is designed to argue precisely this point:

> BOOK PUBLISHER: Susan has agreed to publish a collection of essays. She's having trouble getting the volume's introduction done and repeatedly misses the deadline agreed upon with her editor, Peter. Peter is a seasoned editor who tends not to get upset about the tardiness of his authors. It has simply become too familiar by now. However, Susan's difficulties meeting the deadline do have an impact on his relationship with her. He takes her continued procrastination to impair their relationship in certain ways. Peter also modifies his intentions and attitudes in response to this judgment. For example, he takes his knowledge of Susan's unreliability into account in considering whether to offer her a contract on other projects, in planning publication schedules, advertising budgets, and other such things.

Peter seems to modify his relationship with Susan in response to becoming aware of her tardiness. He even seems to do so as a result of judging that her tardiness impairs their relationship. But it is not clear that he blames Susan. "He may be the sort of person who doesn't go in much for blaming, at least not in relation to his authors" (Wolf 2011, 3). According to Wolf, the case reveals that "there are (in my way of talking) ways of adjusting one's attitudes—even adjusting one's attitudes to reflect an impairment—that leave the question of blame to one side" (Wolf 2011, 3).

We might infer from this case that not all forms of relationship modification count as blame, even if they are done in response to judgments that someone has in some sense let us down. And perhaps this is right. If I am going to maintain that relationship-modification is central to blame, it seems I need to do more to defend a principled limit on *which* forms of relationship modification—while not necessarily accompanied by negative emotions—are nevertheless central to blame.

Interestingly, engaging with Wolf's BOOK PUBLISHER case may lead to a better understanding of what this principled limit is. I want to argue that once the case is more clearly described, we will see that it is in fact missing an important

THE SIGNIFICANCE AND FITTINGNESS OF EPISTEMIC BLAME 87

ingredient of blame in the relationship-based framework. According to our framework, blame is a kind of relationship modification made fitting by a judgment, namely the judgment that the relationship has been *impaired*. Precisely what a "judgment of relationship impairment" involves is not always clear in Scanlon's work. Let's bring this into view with another example.

> BLACK ICE: Your friend is on their way to meet you on a cold winter's day. Sadly, they hit some black ice and slip, cracking their head on the pavement and entering a coma.

In a sense, your friend has impaired their relations with you. After all, for the time being, you can't even speak with them, let alone mutually participate in anything resembling an ideal of friendship. But obviously, in judging that this is the case, and perhaps even modifying certain intentions you have toward your friend accordingly, you do nothing we would appropriately call blaming your friend for their unfortunate encounter with the black ice. And that is because they have done nothing to impair their relations with you, in the relevant sense of "relationship impairment." Relationship impairment of the blame-relevant kind requires performing actions or having attitudes that fall short of the normative ideal of the relationship in question. Again, the normative ideal of a relationship is just the set of intentions and expectations that parties to the relationship *ought* to have, qua parties to the relationship. It is no part of the normative ideal of friendship that people avoid accidentally entering into comas. The question then, returning to the BOOK PUBLISHER case, is whether Peter takes Susan to have performed actions and have attitudes that fall short of the normative ideal of whatever relationship they stand in.

It is easy to imagine that Peter simply does not regard keeping strictly to one's deadlines as a genuine obligation constituting part of the normative ideal of his professional relationship with Susan. He plausibly regards it as something it is *good* for authors to do. But being the seasoned editor that he is, someone like Peter won't think of this as a necessary requirement. Of course, a lot hinges on just *how* far off the deadline an author happens to be. Perhaps this is one way the case is under-described. But what is important is that we can acknowledge that Peter regards Susan's procrastination as a nuisance, perhaps even one that leads him to modify certain intentions he has toward her, without maintaining that he judges their relationship to be impaired in the relevant sense. There is nothing inconsistent about this stance. So, we can agree that Peter doesn't blame Susan.

One might be tempted to tell a version of the story according to which Peter *does* regard meeting deadlines as part of the normative ideal of the relationship, and point out that it seems possible for him to modify his relations in response to a judgment that the ideal has been impaired, while feeling no negative emotional response. And so perhaps he can satisfy all the conditions of the

88   EPISTEMIC BLAME

relationship-based framework without blaming Susan. However, I think this simply begs the question in favor of the idea that negative emotions are essential to blame. In my view, if Peter really does modify his relationship in response to a judgment of relationship impairment *of the relevant kind*, then he *is* blaming Susan, despite being free of any negative emotions toward her.[1]

The point generalizes, enabling a defense of a principled limit on the kind of relationship-modification we are looking for. Only forms of relationship modification which are types of responses made fitting by the judgment that the target of blame falls short of the relevant normative ideal count as ways of holding others to normative expectations. It may be impossible to say in advance what these responses are, since that will be heavily contextually determined. But we don't need to spell out a list of responses in advance. We simply need to provide a way of avoiding cases like Wolf's BOOK PUBLISHER case (and the BLACK ICE case) without endorsing the idea that holding to normative expectations essentially requires susceptibility to the reactive attitudes narrowly construed. Judgments of relationship-impairment can do this job.

Here is an objection. Placing such a heavy burden on the role for judgment in the account leads to deep worries about the possibility of irrational blame. Can't there be cases in which a person genuinely blames someone despite realizing that they do not judge that person blameworthy? Can't we blame others while being fully aware that we shouldn't (because the target of our blame is not blameworthy)? There are a number of things to say in response to this worry. First, it is interesting to consider whether this is one issue on which the epistemic extension of the relationship-based framework is actually more plausible than the original moral version. Because we might wonder whether such cases of "irrational" blame really occur, or are at least very rare, in the epistemic domain. Think: have you ever found yourself *just epistemically blaming someone* while realizing they are an impeccable epistemic agent? That seems kind of strange.

One explanation of the difference here might have to do with the nature of epistemic failings and their connection to relationships. As I have argued, many paradigmatic kinds of epistemic failings are not direct personal harms; meanwhile, many paradigmatic kinds of moral failings are. Consider the following speculative line of thought. In cases of irrational moral blame, perhaps what is going on is that our blame in some sense "misfires"—we direct an attitude toward someone that would normally be made fitting by a judgment that they've directly harmed or wronged us, even though we realize they haven't. Perhaps this happens when our relations with a person are fraught or unhealthy, for example. I cannot establish

---

[1] Craig Agule suggested to me that it doesn't seem like a big cost to simply argue that the book publisher *does* blame Susan. I am inclined to agree. However, one advantage of my overall approach here is that it allows us to simply grant Wolf her own interpretation of the case (on which Peter doesn't blame Susan).

THE SIGNIFICANCE AND FITTINGNESS OF EPISTEMIC BLAME 89

here whether this line of thought is empirically well-supported. But the point for present purposes is simply that it seems like there is less room for such a story in the epistemic case. Many paradigm epistemic failings just aren't direct personal harms or wrongs; so, in a wide range of circumstances, human beings simply do not have to worry about responding to direct personal harms or wrongs in the epistemic domain.[2] So, perhaps it is somewhat odd to imagine a similar sort of "misfiring" in the epistemic domain. Perhaps this is why it seems odd to imagine epistemic blame in the absence of judgments of epistemic blameworthiness. Of course, I don't consider this a knock-down argument. Perhaps we can irrationally epistemically blame in this sort of way. If so, I would be keen to see a case. I suspect it will be more difficult to describe a case in which a person is epistemically blaming someone they do not regard epistemically blameworthy, as opposed to doing something else.

This last point connects with a broader one that I think also applies in the moral case: surely there needs to be *something* like a judgment of blameworthiness in cases of (irrational) blame. Otherwise, how do we differentiate between, say, irrational *blame* and just plain *anger*, or unhinged emotion directed toward someone? Even Hannah Pickard (2013), the one who pointed out that the possibility of irrational blame places constraints on accounts of the nature of blame, agrees with this point. She sketches a kind of "proto-judgment" that is supposed to be involved even in cases of irrational blame (and which differentiates them from mere anger). One way to put pressure on the objection, then, is to request further details about what this "proto judgment" really amounts to. What makes it so different from the judgment in my preferred account?

Here is another objection. How can judgments of relationship-modification do such an important job if relationship-modification itself can sometimes have the same *consequences* for people even in the absence of the relevant judgment of relationship impairment? Imagine that John is deeply prone to biased thinking about climate change. However, unbeknownst to John, these biases were inculcated in him by his parents and other close community members from an early age. Discovering these facts about John, you modify your stance in the GER with him, in the sense that you suspend your standing intention to epistemically trust his word, when it comes to the domain of propositions about climate change. However, because you realize that John simply grew up in an unfortunate epistemic environment, you don't judge that he has impaired the GER in the relevant sense required for judging him epistemically blameworthy. To put it one way, his biased thinking about climate change doesn't reveal that he falls short of the

---

[2] As I have noted, testimonial injustice and other kinds of epistemic harm seem to complicate this picture. I discuss the connection between epistemic blame and testimonial injustice in detail in Chapter 5.

90 EPISTEMIC BLAME

intentions and expectations constitutive of the normative ideal of the GER, precisely because there *is* an exculpating reason why he does not meet epistemic criteria Y in performing certain intellectual acts. In other words, John has an excuse.

The point of the objection is that it seems your modification of your intentions toward John has the same interpersonal implications for him, regardless of whether it is accompanied by a judgment of GER relationship impairment or not. But if that is the case, then it seems the proponent of the relationship-based account is in a difficult position. After all, in this case, the proponent of the relationship-based account will surely *not* want to regard these responses as ways of holding John to a normative expectation (for one thing, in this case, the proponent of the account does not want to call this a *blame* response). But why should adding a mere judgment of relationship impairment to the mix take these responses over the threshold from not counting as ways of holding someone to a normative expectation to ways of doing so, if they are the same in all other respects (that is, the same in terms of their interpersonal consequences)?

I have two responses to this worry. First, in my view, holding others to normative expectations simply is not all about consequences. To return to a larger-picture notion at the heart of Scanlon's normative ethics, I find it plausible that holding others to expectations is also about recognizing the *meaning* of their actions and attitudes. I am happy to dig in my heels and connect my view about epistemic blame with deeper elements of a non-consequentialist view of epistemic expectations. Second, it is important not to get carried away with claims about consequences in the first place. It is arguably often a contingent matter of fact that relationship modification done in response to a judgment of relationship modification *will* have wider-ranging interpersonal consequences for the target of blame than instances of relationship modification done in the absence of such a judgment (for example, when the would-be blamer judges that the target has a good excuse). Why is this? To stay focused on the epistemic case, it has something to do with the fact that when someone impairs the GER, they reveal themselves prone to epistemically fail in a wide-ranging set of circumstances. This is because typical ways of impairing the GER involve certain epistemically flawed dispositions. When someone has simply made an honest mistake, or has a good excuse for their epistemic failing, this does not mean that they are prone to epistemically fail in as wide-ranging a set of circumstances. The very reason for their exculpation will be some environmental factor that constrains the scope of likely epistemic failings for the person in question.[3]

---

[3] There is a lot to say about the varieties of exculpating conditions, and there may be exceptions to the point I am making here. See Littlejohn (forthcoming) for helpful application of Austin's seminal work on excuses and exemptions in the epistemic domain. See also Boult (2017a); Greco (2019); Madison (2018); Williamson forthcoming.

THE SIGNIFICANCE AND FITTINGNESS OF EPISTEMIC BLAME   91

Consider Bill, who is briefly visiting fake barn façade county. Suppose you are a member of the community who lives in fake barn county. When Bill passes through, completely oblivious to all the barn façades in the county, you know that he's likely to form unknowledgeable beliefs about barn façades in the area. So, you suspend your presumption of epistemic trust in Bill's word about barns. Importantly, though, you don't epistemically *blame* Bill, because you don't judge him to have impaired the GER. He has a good excuse for being presently disposed to form unknowledgeable beliefs about barn façades in the area. Correspondingly, however, it is only because Bill is in fake barn façade county that you (appropriately) suspend your presumption of epistemic trust in his word on these matters. When he leaves the county, you may once again appropriately trust his word about barns just as much as you may trust his word about many other things. So, in this scenario, the modifications you make in the absence of a judgment of GER impairment do correspond with a more attenuated set of interpersonal implications for Bill. And this is because the source of epistemic failings at issue is an unfriendly epistemic environment, which Bill merely happens to be temporarily visiting. It doesn't have anything to do with Bill's intellectual character, or quality of epistemic agency.[4]

A different sort of objection to the claim that the relationship-based account meets SIGNIFICANCE is to take a step back and critically assess the criterion of SIGNIFICANCE itself. Perhaps there is a problem, not with the idea that epistemic relationship modification (of the right kind) is a way of holding people to normative expectations, but with understanding SIGNIFICANCE in terms of normative expectations in the first place. Perhaps the significance of blame lies elsewhere than with the tight connection I have suggested it has with normative expectations. If so, and if the relationship-based account cannot do justice to whatever *that* is, then there may be an altogether different sort of reason to reject the relationship-based account (and perhaps reconsider any one of the alternative approaches to epistemic blame considered in previous chapters).

One route to take here is to connect SIGNIFICANCE to a substantive claim about what blame is. For example, Strawsonians might argue that the significance of blame just lies in its tight connection to negative emotional responses, which mere negative evaluation doesn't seem to have. Or someone like Sher might argue that it lies in a connection with *desire.* But these approaches obviously beg the question against the relationship-based framework. This is why I attempted at the outset to provide a theory-neutral approach to spelling out the significance of blame. Such an approach is needed if we are to avoid stacking the deck against (or in favor of) one or another substantive view about the nature of epistemic blame. Is there a plausible alternative theory-neutral approach to understanding the significance of

---

[4] Thanks to Daniel Buckley for discussion.

92   EPISTEMIC BLAME

blame, one that I have overlooked and which might somehow undermine my view that the relationship-based framework can meet SIGNIFICANCE?

One option might be to stick with something like Hieronymi's (2004) notions of "sting, force, and depth." The project of accounting for blame's significance would then be a matter of showing that a given response has the requisite sting, force, and depth. In my view, these notions are simply too metaphorical to be of much use in advancing debate here. Another option is to focus on certain conditions on appropriate blame, such as those I identified earlier as going hand in hand with blame's significance. For instance, I pointed out that, according to many, one condition on appropriate blame is that the blamer must have a certain kind of *standing*, while something similar does not seem true of mere negative evaluators. Perhaps we can somehow cash out blame's significance in terms of this fact. I am not entirely sure how this approach would go. But rather than attempting to flesh it out, I will point out that the relationship-based account can accommodate the significance of blame understood as such. This is because the relationship-based account can readily make sense of standing to epistemically blame. Properties of a person's standing to blame can be readily explained in terms of properties of the relationship (or lack thereof) that holds between blamer and target of blame (Scanlon 2008, 166–98). I explore how this works in the epistemic case in Chapter 6.

In short, these alternative approaches to theory-neutral ways of cashing out SIGNIFICANCE either lack promise, or do not pose any threat to relationship-based account of epistemic blame. A different worry at this point, however, is that I myself have failed to articulate SIGNIFICANCE in a theory-neutral way. Perhaps by articulating SIGNIFICANCE in terms of a connection to normative expectations, I have somehow stacked the deck in favor of the relationship-based account. In response, I think it is fairly clear that this is not the case. First of all, the idea of connecting SIGNIFICANCE to normative expectations is inspired by Wallace, someone who has written extensively *against* a relationship-based approach to (moral) blame, and who is one of the staunchest defenders of a Strawsonian approach to blame. If anything, then, we might have expected my approach to SIGNIFICANCE to favor an emotion-based approach to epistemic blame. Still, while it may sound dialectically odd, just because the idea was inspired by an opponent of my account, this does not entail that it doesn't somehow stack the deck in my account's favor. Perhaps unbeknownst to Wallace, this is in fact the case.

One reason you might think I have stacked the deck in favor of my account is because the notion of a normative expectation is a core constituent of the account itself. But this would be hasty. My account takes as an explicit *starting point* an independently plausible idea about the nature of blame—namely, that it has something essential to do with normative expectations. The notion of a normative expectation is simply a natural way of capturing the idea that blamers are *exercised* and *engaged* in a way that goes beyond mere negative evaluation. Moreover, while it is true that normative expectations play *a* role in my approach to blame, they are not the central theoretical unit (as *desire* frustration is in Sher's account, for example; and as *reactive attitudes* are in the emotion-based account). Rather, the central theoretical unit of the relationship-based account is the notion of a relationship, and relationship impairment. To be sure, normative expectations are *part* of what my notion of a relationship boils down to. But they don't exhaust it. As we know by now, relationships as I understand them are constituted by sets of intentions, expectations, and attitudes people have concerning how to act and feel toward one another—intentions, expectations, and attitudes that are justified by a wide range of facts about parties to the relationship, depending on those involved and the kind of relationship it is. I also added in Chapter 3 that, strictly speaking, relationships consist in actual dispositions people have toward each other (in addition to their *intentions*, for example), as well as the *reasons* why they have those intentions and dispositions. But I bracketed these additional two points for the sake of presenting the basic idea of the account. All of this is to say that understanding the significance of blame in terms of normative expectations does not stack the deck in favor of my approach to blame, because it doesn't come anywhere near to being the central theoretical unit that is doing the bulk of work for the account. This is a markedly different situation than the one facing the alternative ways of cashing out the significance of blame I have considered, which quite clearly stack the deck in favor of one substantive approach to blame or another.

4.2 Fittingness Revisited

Is GER modification a fitting response to epistemic failings? Importantly, to have a bearing on the question of whether the relationship-based account of epistemic blame is a viable account of *epistemic* blame, we need to show that GER modification is a fitting response to epistemic failings in the technical ("target-based" sense) laid out in Chapter 1. We need to show that GER modification can be rendered legitimate by epistemic failings, *independently of practical considerations*. We must treat the relationship-based account with the same critical eye as we treated, for example, the emotion-based account.[5] Recall, in Chapter 2, one of the main objections I leveled against emotion-based approaches to epistemic blame is that it seems negative emotional responses, such as indignation and resentment, are not really fitting responses to epistemic failings, so long as those

---

[5] Note, the desire-based account obviously must satisfy this desideratum as well. But I took it as fairly straightforward that the desire-based account can do so. The fact that it makes a central role for desires *about epistemic norm violation* means that it can readily meet FITTINGNESS. The main issue with the desire-based account was its inability to meet SIGNIFICANCE.

94   EPISTEMIC BLAME

failings are considered *independently of practical considerations* (including moral ones). I took this to imply that putative cases of "epistemic blame" *qua* negative emotional response may just be cases of moral blame (which, perhaps, simply happen to involve epistemic considerations in a contingent way). Thus, if we are to show that putative cases of epistemic blame qua epistemic relationship-modification really are cases of *epistemic* blame, we must show that the relationship-based account is not vulnerable to the same objection.

There is good reason to think that this can be established. For a start, it is of course worth emphasizing that the *kind* of relationship modification at the heart of the account is a kind of epistemic relationship modification. That is to say, it is a kind of modification to intentions and expectations that members of an epistemic community have which are distinctively oriented toward their epistemic agency as such. On the face of it, it is perhaps unclear why practical or moral considerations would be needed to make modifications to an epistemic relationship appropriate. For example, modifying one's presumption of epistemic trust toward another person on a subject matter they seem to be prone to think dogmatically about, is something it can easily seem appropriate to do, for reasons that do not obviously have anything immediately to do with practical considerations. In contrast with alternative approaches to epistemic blame, the relationship-based account is poised to articulate the motivational component distinctive of epistemic blame in a way that is tailor made for the epistemic domain. This is because it is relatively easy to import the idea of relationship-modification to the epistemic domain. We simply have to focus on modifications to people's intentions and expectations that are oriented toward epistemic agency in the way characteristic of an epistemic relationship.

That said, it is also plausible that the intentions and expectations we have toward one another, oriented toward our epistemic agency in the way characteristic of an epistemic relationship, do not float utterly free of practical considerations. Indeed, it is plausible that the very reason—in a causal-historical sense—people stand in epistemic relationships with one another is that epistemic relationships are *useful* (arguably indispensable) for getting around in the world. And that is a paradigmatically practical consideration. Does this mean that epistemic relationship modification is necessarily bound up in a problematic way with practical considerations after all? I don't think so. The issue once again boils down to the complexity of what it means for something to be "independent of practical considerations."

Consider Edward Craig's (1990) story about the *point* or *function* of epistemic concepts like justification and knowledge within an information-gathering and distributing economy such as ours. On Craig's account, very roughly, when we say that someone knows that p, we "flag" that person as a "reliable informant" (1990, 11–17). But what exactly is a "reliable informant"? How reliable does someone have to be? One hundred per cent reliable? A bit less? If reliable informants had to be 100 per cent reliable in order to count as such, it is perhaps unclear how *useful* the concept of knowledge would be. Arguably, hardly anyone meets the standard of one hundred per cent reliability. Given the importance of being able to make decisions on the basis of what people believe and say, we often need to rely on others even when they are not one hundred per cent reliable. So, it is plausible that the notion of a reliable informant took the shape it has—i.e. a fallibilistic shape— precisely in light of pressures of *expedience*. So, someone like Craig might insist that the concept of knowledge took shape in light of pressures of expedience. In this spirit, we could say that one way epistemic evaluations (such as knowledge ascriptions) "involve practical considerations" is simply insofar as various ecological and social forces shaped the concept of knowledge, and other epistemic goods. There is an etiological sense in which epistemic evaluations have a practical dimension.[6]

Embracing this point does not imply that the relevant evaluations are not epistemic. First, consider an analogous story for moral concepts. Assume for the sake of argument that we can also reverse-engineer moral concepts. Plausibly, *epistemic* considerations played an important role in the shaping of our moral concepts. For example, the question of whether a person is aware of what they are doing, or in some sense ought to have been aware of what they are doing, plays an important role in fixing our judgments about whether they are responsible for what they are doing. A concept of moral obligation that did not discriminate between knowers and non-knowers in this way would have a seriously attenuated utility. But no one has ever appealed to this idea to challenge the notion of a distinctly moral domain. Epistemic factors may have played a role in shaping moral concepts, but we can employ moral concepts in our moral evaluations now, at a given time t, in a distinctively moral way.

My point is that an etiological understanding of the way certain epistemic evaluations "involve practical considerations" leaves wide open a clear distinction between epistemic and practical/moral evaluation. Elements of the epistemic domain (i.e. epistemic concepts involved in our epistemic evaluations) may have taken shape in light of practical pressures. But this is compatible with the idea that, here and now, token applications of those epistemic concepts through our epistemic evaluations are importantly different from token applications of moral or practical concepts through other sorts of evaluations.

In my view, something along these lines is true of epistemic blame as I understand it. That is to say, even though we plausibly came to have epistemic relationships for practical reasons (in a global, causal-historical sense), and certain concepts bound up with my understanding of epistemic relationships—such as epistemic trust, and epistemic agency—may themselves have correspondingly

---

[6] See Hannon (2019) for an excellent recent discussion of the function of the concept of knowledge, partly inspired by the early work of Craig.

96 EPISTEMIC BLAME

been shaped by practical pressures, this does not entail that we cannot epistemically blame each other—in the sense of modifying our epistemic relationships in response to epistemic failings—quite independently of the question of whether those failings themselves are bound up with practical considerations.

Even if human beings evolved to be the kind of creatures who have a standing intention to epistemically trust other members of the epistemic community—say, because it helped us get around in the world—this does not entail that practical considerations must play a role in every appropriate instance of someone modifying their standing intention to epistemically trust the word of another. There is a real sense—what I have called the "target-based" sense (Chapter 1, section 1.5.2)— in which we (at least sometimes) make modifications to these epistemically oriented intentions independently of the practical factors that causally influenced us to be the sorts of beings who have such standing intentions.

Notice the difference here between my account of epistemic blame and the emotion-based account. It is not plausible that we could make the same maneuver with the latter account. It seems quite obvious that when we appear to *resent* others for their epistemic failings, what we resent them for are the practical/ personal dimensions of those failings. It is just much more plausible that this sort of response is *itself* a manifestation of a concern for practical (moral) reasons, as opposed to a practice we have that has merely been shaped by evolutionary forces, for example. To put it another way, the disvalue of epistemic failings simply does not seem sufficient to render resentment or indignation legitimate. Meanwhile the disvalue of epistemic failings does seem sufficient to render legitimate a modification to one's intention to epistemically trust another person, under the right circumstances. But this leads to my next point.

My claims about the connections between the causal-historical origin of a practice and token instances of behaviors constituting that practice may be true as far as they go. But what about specific cases? Earlier, when evaluating the Bold Approach to the negative emotion view of epistemic blame, I argued that negative emotions such as indignation and resentment more plausibly target the moral or practical dimensions of certain cases of putatively epistemically blameworthy conduct, as opposed to epistemic dimensions of that conduct. I said, for example, that while it may be true that—from an epistemic point of view—the political leader should know better about climate change, it is also true that, as someone in such an important position of power, they should—from a moral point of view— be properly informed and clear-headed about the issue. I also said that, when someone hastily and mistakenly tells you that the nearest gas station is fairly close by, they may very well commit the epistemic blunders of not thinking carefully about how far away it is, and asserting something inaccurate. But, at least when it is $-30°C$ outside, they *also* commit a moral blunder: they put you at significant risk of harm. My point was that moral considerations—as opposed to epistemic ones—are what generate intuitions about the appropriateness of negative emotional responses in these cases. Might the same be true about epistemic relationship-modification?

For instance, when someone hastily and mistakenly tells you that the nearest gas station is fairly close by, what makes it appropriate for you to suspend your presumption of epistemic trust in this person's word on some domain of propositions? Is it because they have committed the epistemic blunder of not thinking carefully about how far away it is, and asserting something inaccurate? Or is it because it is −30°C outside, and they have put you at significant risk of harm? My view is that, regardless of what might be empirically true of different individuals' reactions in real-world cases, the epistemic blunder itself in this sort of example *can* make the suspension of a presumption of epistemic trust on the relevant domain of propositions legitimate. Again, the disvalue of this epistemic failing strikes me as sufficient, under the right circumstances, to render legitimate a modification to one's intention to epistemically trust another—and it does so whether it is −30°C outside, or whether the temperature is such that the speaker does not put you at serious risk of harm through a careless assertion.

Still, it bears emphasis that in a wide range of cases, epistemic failings just are bound up with practical and moral ones too. Indeed, the precise aim I have when arguing that a given account of epistemic blame can meet FITTINGNESS needs to be kept clearly in mind. When going on about how a given type of epistemic failing is sufficient to render legitimate a given type of response, independently of practical considerations, it can easily sound as though I am trying to argue that these normative domains always stand in stark isolation from one another. This is not my intention. My intention is to make clear that there is a distinctively epistemic dimension to our complex ways of responding to one another for actions and attitudes. Sometimes this dimension shows up in isolation. But often it is also part of a complex mix of considerations and responses. In my view, it is important not to lose sight of the constituent components involved in this complex mix.

One reason I think this is important is simply because the epistemic dimension of our blaming practices is *there*. Losing sight of it means losing sight of an element of who we are as social and norm-abiding creatures. But I also think it is important insofar as downstream consequences hang in the balance. Perhaps most centrally, failure to recognize the epistemic dimension of our complex ways of responding to one another for actions and attitudes renders invisible further normative issues: among other things, going forward I will be arguing in detail that recognizing *epistemic* blame as a kind of *blame* response gives rise to unique issues about standing, as well as issues about the role and value of this practice in our social and political lives. I mean "unique" in the sense that these issues take on their own character in the epistemic domain, generating novel puzzles. They cannot be resolved simply by applying existing moral analogues—to my mind, this is a natural corollary of my claim that they do not simply reduce to issues in moral philosophy.

98 EPISTEMIC BLAME

The point of arguing that epistemic blame is something that can be appropriately manifested independently of practical considerations is not to suggest that this is how it typically works. Rather it is to demonstrate that epistemic blame is a unique component of our social and normative lives. I will be arguing that the relationship-based account is especially well positioned not merely to accommodate epistemic blame's interaction with other normative domains. It can also go a considerable way toward structuring our understanding of that interaction. Initial observations about this come up in the next section, but especially in Chapter 6, section 6.5, I will be arguing that this, too, is an important result in its own right.

4.3 Defending the Relationship-Based Account

We are well on our way to establishing the relationship-based account of epistemic blame's ability to offer a compelling solution to the puzzle of epistemic blame. I have now argued that the account is well positioned to meet both SIGNIFICANCE and FITTINGNESS. But I said above that we must also ensure confidence that the account is independently well motivated, and is not vulnerable to obviously fatal objections. In this section and the next, I turn to these tasks. I start with some comments on further advantages of the relationship-based account, advantages independent of its ability to solve the puzzle of epistemic blame.

4.3.1 Further Advantages of the Account

For those sympathetic to the idea that desires about norm violation are not necessary components of epistemic blame, the relationship-based account will be attractive for the reason that it remains silent on whether a desire about norm violation is necessary for epistemic blame. Modifications to epistemic relationships do not necessarily require the manifestation of any such desire (though of course they might). However, while I have criticized Brown's appeal to desires about bad believing, it is nevertheless plausible that desires about bad believing play a role in *many* instances of epistemic blame. If an account of epistemic blame can explain why such desires seem present in some cases of epistemic blame, but not others, that would be a strong mark in favor of the account. The relationship-based account is well positioned in this regard.

On my view, some (perhaps many) cases of epistemic blame involve a desire, or other emotional response, because we *generally* want to have well-functioning epistemic relationships with each other. Epistemic relationships are useful things. But the relationship-based account can also explain why some cases of epistemic blame may intuitively lack desire (recall ROOMMATE RIVALS, section 2.6). In such cases, the blamer may all things considered be happy to have their epistemic relationship with the target of blame impaired in the relevant way (they may lack a desire to not have it impaired). This is not to say that the blamer thereby opts out of that relationship, or that they were never in it to begin with. It is only to say that, in such cases, they lack the desire that their flawed epistemic relationship be any different than it is.

The relationship-based account also has resources available to explain the *variable strength* of epistemic blame. The fact that each of us partakes in many different kinds of relationship can partly explain the differences we see in strengths of token instances of epistemic blame. Such differences may partly correspond to differences in the intentions and expectations that comprise other kinds of relationships we stand in, but which have the capacity to interact with the GER in different ways. For example, a scientist might be open to a stronger epistemic blame response (involving more consequential changes in one's intentions) than a layperson for failing to conform their beliefs to the evidence, because of their role as an expert in the epistemic community. When a scientist is lazy and misses some important bit of evidence, this may say something about how they view their role in the scientific community, and perhaps the role of that community in the broader epistemic community. It may say something about them that seems particularly epistemically bad. So, a strong epistemic blame response can be fitting.

Another, perhaps closely related advantage of the account is its ability to provide a structured understanding of how epistemic blame interacts with other kinds of blame altogether. Consider the difference between how you might blame your physiotherapist for failing to know the most up-to-date best practices in their area of physiotherapy, with how you might blame a pub quiz teammate—one who *claimed* to know lots about physiotherapy—when they fail to supply the relevant epistemic goods during a physiotherapy-themed pub quiz. We might think of each example as involving some degree of epistemic blame (surely one more than the other). But intuitively—perhaps in addition to being somehow "stronger"—it seems it would be appropriate for your blame toward your physiotherapist to have a different character altogether.

To be clear, there are *two* related observations that need accounting for here. On one hand, it seems there can be differences in the degree to which we *epistemically blame* someone for an epistemic failing—this is what I mean by "strength" of epistemic blame. On the other hand, it seems token responses to epistemic failings can differ in how they combine epistemic blame with other (non-epistemic) types of blame response, such as moral or professional. In the remainder of this book, when I refer to epistemic blame's "interaction" with other normative domains, and the idea that the intentions and expectations constitutive of other relationships can "impact" the GER, I will have both of these dimensions in mind—that is to say, I will be referring to how epistemic blame's strength can modulate as a result of various factors, and how epistemic blame can combine with other forms of blame as a result of those factors. I will specify which dimension in particular I am focusing on where appropriate.

The relationship-based account of epistemic blame is well positioned to do justice to these observations. Real-world cases of epistemic blame will include dimensions that result from the fact that people stand in many different kinds of relationships with each other. Your professional relationship with your physio-therapist is arguably partially comprised of certain normative expectations that you are entitled to have of them, which concern epistemic matters and which may thereby have an impact on the epistemic relationship you have with your phys-iotherapist. A more detailed investigation of how this works will have to wait till Chapter 6, section 6.5, when I explore our entitlements to expect certain kinds of epistemic conduct and outcomes from one another, in virtue of different relation-ships we may stand in.

For now, note that it is not quite clear how an account that puts frustrated desires about norm violations at center stage is really in a position to do anything as nuanced as this. If all cases of epistemic blame are essentially manifestations of a standing desire that an epistemic norm not be violated, how exactly can we explain the difference between what a patient does when she epistemically blames her physiotherapist, and what the pub quiz participant does when he epistemically blames his teammate for an amateur epistemic blunder? Is this really just a matter of differences in *strength* of the desire that an epistemic norm not have been violated? (What if the pub quiz participant *really* wants to win the pub quiz?) Perhaps, but we'd need an account of how this works. Meanwhile, the finer-grained properties with which the relationship-based account underpins token instances of epistemic blame automatically enable a more nuanced explanation of this difference. After all, the intentions and expectations specified by normative ideals of different relationships have different contents. Instances of epistemic blame in each of these kinds of relationship will naturally reflect these differences, perhaps in virtue of being combined with other forms of blame.

In my view, an underappreciated virtue of the relationship-based framework in general is its ability to explain, not just blame's *varied* nature, but also its *fineness of grain.* This is one of the payoffs of thinking about blame in terms of relation-ships. The project of articulating blame's nature typically presupposes the idea that there is something that all instances of blame have in common. While there are surely many forms that blame can take, the thought is that something unifies them, marking them out as members of a class of response. If an account can accommodate this variety while nevertheless identifying a unifying feature, this is one reason to think that the account is on to something. In addition to the varieties of blame, I suggest that blame responses have a kind of fineness of grain, lending them a further form of variety that has not been fully appreciated in the literature. By "fineness of grain," I mean simply that token instances of blame often seem tailored to the interpersonal situations in which they arise. When I blame my brother for not returning my calls, my blame response is different from when I blame my romantic partner for not returning my calls, or when I blame my co-worker for the same. In each case, in addition to having a different phenomenology, the behaviors, dispositions, intentions, etc., that I manifest as a response to the judgment that I've been wronged, often seem uniquely tailored to the facts of the interpersonal situation.

In contrast, notice that when I simply *judge* that my brother has violated some moral rule—a rule requiring one to keep their promises, for instance—that judgment arguably has pretty much the same sorts of properties as the one I make when I judge that my *partner* has violated the promise-keeping rule, or that my co-worker has done so, and so on. What will likely vary, however—and considerably so—is the *reaction* I have to the judgment in each case. This strikes me as a central and salient feature of our blaming practices, one calling out for explanation.

By tying our understanding of the nature of blame to our relationships with one another, the relationship-based framework is ideally suited to provide such an explanation. How so? On the relationship-based approach, blame just *is* a kind of relationship modification. It follows naturally from this that unique features of the interpersonal situation will be reflected in—and partially constitutive of—a given blame response. This is another way of saying that the contours of a given blame response are in a sense tailored to the interpersonal situation in which it arises.

One might challenge the idea that blame *itself* is in fact tailored to specific interpersonal circumstances. One might insist, rather, that if anything is tailored to specific interpersonal circumstances, it's simply an individual's reactions *downstream* of their blame response. The thought is that blame responses themselves are more or less the same across individuals—whether they are just kinds of emotion, forms of protest, or what have you. But the way an individual reacts to their blame, or allows blame to guide subsequent action, of course may be uniquely tailored to their interpersonal situation.

This is one way of interpreting things. But it strikes me as unduly restrictive. It seems unduly restrictive to isolate a single form of response from the various actions that it is natural to think of *as* examples of blame. Especially given the wide range of authors who consider it a desideratum in our theorizing about blame to accommodate blame's variety, I suggest that the proponent of the restrictive interpretation has the burden of proof, not the other way around.

Can other accounts accommodate blame's fineness of grain? Perhaps. I am simply pointing out another source of independent motivation for the relationship-based framework, one that hasn't been given enough attention—namely, the obvious ease with which it accounts for this important phenomenon.

4.3.2 Objections and Replies

Despite my account's advantages, there are no doubt some lingering and important worries a critic might have. For a start, some may be wary of an account of epistemic blame that seems to rely on ideas at the heart of anything as controversial as the relationship-based approach to moral blame. I want to begin this discussion of possible remaining objections by making a general dialectical point in this regard.

The dialectical point is that, as I think should be fairly clear by now, I am not *basing* my account on the relationship-based approach to moral blame. It is more accurate to say that my account is inspired by some key ideas of Scanlon's, and that it can perhaps even function as a defeasible *defense* of the fruitfulness of those ideas, as opposed to presupposing their truth.[7] If a few simple ideas can be used to account for a wide range of phenomena—as I have tried to argue they can in this case, by extending the account to the epistemic domain—that strikes me as a mark in support of those ideas. Thus, I do not consider my account hostage to the truth of Scanlon's account. If anything, I see it as providing further support for that account, from a source of independent motivation. However, I don't want to make too much of this point, nor accede that the Scanlonian framework is, or at least should be, all that controversial. On this latter note, here are a couple of responses to some remaining potential worries about the account.

(i) Cool Blame

Perhaps the most prominent objection to the relationship-based approach in the moral domain—due in independent ways to R.J. Wallace (2011) and Susan Wolf (2011)—is that the approach "leaves the *blame* out of blame." That is to say, according to people like Wallace and Wolf, reactive attitudes such as indignation and resentment are simply an essential part of blame. The point is essentially another way of framing the issue addressed above about the connection between holding people to normative expectations and susceptibility to the reactive attitudes narrowly construed. I have already challenged the connection maintained by people like Wallace. But a few more details are in order.

First, it's important to note that I need not take a stand on whether moral blame is essentially connected to negative emotions. In fact, I think this point reveals one reason why an extension of the relationship-based approach to blame to the *epistemic* domain is particularly promising. While reactive attitudes such as indignation and resentment may or may not be integral to moral blame, I have argued at length that they do not seem integral to epistemic blame (Chapter 2). We can and should account for SIGNIFICANCE without appealing to negative

---

[7] I very much doubt Scanlon himself would agree with everything I've said in interpreting his account.

emotions. Moreover, it must be remembered that, at least in the moral domain, the framework *can* allow negative emotional responses to play a role in certain kinds of blame. Forming certain reactive attitudes under certain circumstances may constitute, or at least be part of, certain *ways* of modifying our relationships with one another. But relationship modification can be done in many ways.

Finally, it is worth recalling that by making negative emotional responses essential to blame, theorists such as Wallace and Wolf may put themselves in an equally difficult position of accounting for other kinds of cases, such as cases of affectless blame (cf. Fricker 2016, 170; Sher 2006, 88).

(ii) Self-Blame

It seems we can blame our*selves* for certain wrongdoings. We might think that an account that understands blame in terms of relationship modification is going to have problems in this regard. In particular, it seems the account will require positing that people can have relationships with themselves, and that there are ways we can impair this relationship, as well as modify it in response to judgments of impairment. While at first this might sound a bit strange, on reflection it's not at all implausible. I suggest, along with Scanlon (2008, 155) that one *does* have a relationship with oneself, perhaps even in the ordinary sense of that term. We tend to rely on ourselves, believe in ourselves, know ourselves, hate ourselves, love ourselves, etc. These are all things that arguably figure essentially in our relationships with *others*, things that make those relationships the sorts of things that they are.

Importantly, this claim is even more plausible when we recall the technical sense in which I am using the term "relationship." In the framework, roughly speaking, relationships are just certain sets of intentions and expectations people have toward one another (with the properties specified in Chapter 3, section 3.1). To accommodate the idea of a relationship with oneself, we simply have to allow that there can be certain intentions and expectations that one can have toward oneself—intentions and expectations concerning how one will act toward oneself, and concerning the feelings one has for oneself. This is a familiar idea. When one blames oneself, on this picture, one judges that one falls short of some normative ideal (one let oneself down, say) and modifies one's understanding of one's relationship with oneself in a type of way made fitting by that judgment (for example, perhaps one places less trust in one's ability to follow through in the future, and perhaps this is accompanied by guilt or anger, etc.).

What might an intuitive case of epistemic self-blame look like? There are many possible examples. But here is one that I happen to personally relate to:

CHESS BLUNDER: Cameron and Sebastian are adversaries in chess. They play daily on chess.com. Sebastian is a fair bit more advanced than Cameron—his rating hovers close to 1500 while Cameron is relatively inexperienced and is yet

104 EPISTEMIC BLAME

to break 1400. Cameron has dreams of one day reaching the benchmark of Sebastian's rating, and maybe even going beyond. Unfortunately, he is pretty prone to blundering. Every time he blunders, he is quite deeply engaged by his judgment that he has epistemically failed. He says to himself, "I'm such an idiot!" and so on.

This strikes me as a natural example of epistemic self-blame. On the relationship-based account, we can cash it out as follows: when Cameron blunders, he judges that he falls short of some normative ideal (perhaps an epistemic dimension of the relationship he has with himself in his efforts at improving at chess—he judges that he's let himself down in this regard, say) and modifies (or reaffirms) his intentions toward himself in a negatively valanced type of way made fitting by that judgment. Perhaps he places less epistemic trust in his ability to spot blunders before making a move, and resolves to be even more careful in future; perhaps he modifies his willingness to take on games with other more advanced players for the time being, and so on (all of this may of course be accompanied by a distinctive feeling of frustration).

(iii) On Being a "Fitting Response" to Relationship Impairment

It seems fair to request an explanation of which modifications to our relationships count as *fitting* (types of) responses to judgments of relationship impairment, and why that is the case. In addition to Chislenko's worries from last chapter about what it is that relationship modifications in general are supposed to be made fitting *by*, we might also wonder how we're supposed to tell what makes a response "fitting" in the first place. Some might argue that this talk of fittingness is rather vague, and thereby too easily deployed in unmotivated ways.

The account ultimately relies, in part, on a shared grasp of the sorts of things we typically associate with blame and relationship impairment. In this regard, it is no different from my most sophisticated competitor, Brown's Sher-based account. According to Sher, blame is a *characteristic* set of dispositions to feel and behave, unified by a belief-desire pair. The sorts of dispositions Sher has in mind are just those we "ordinarily associate with blame" (Sher 2006, 93–114). Neither Sher nor Scanlon are in the business of giving a reductive analysis of blame. The primary contributions of both of their accounts are their explanations of what *unifies* a diverse range of phenomena in our practice of responding to one another for moral failings. In Sher's case, it is a belief-desire pair. In Scanlon's, it is the modification of intentions and expectations in response to the judgment that one's relationship has been impaired.

It is also worth pointing out that we may want to embrace a somewhat revisionary approach to the concept of blame (Scanlon 2008, 211). Perhaps some things that get counted as blame on our account do not seem intuitively quite like blame; this may simply be a cost proponents of the relationship-based framework should be willing to take on, in light of theoretical advantages the account has otherwise. In such cases, it is open to for one to admit that perhaps we don't tend to think of them quite fully as blame-responses, but argue that we should. Scanlon himself has done much to highlight the theoretical advantages of his own account. He explores issues such as moral luck, moral standing, and the relationship between blame and control (Scanlon 2008, 123–213). This book is in part an exploration of a further theoretical advantage, namely the applicability of its central ideas to the epistemic domain.

Finally, note that I will return in detail to this issue in Chapter 7. In sections 7.5 and 7.6, I take up the question of whether other, more *positively valanced* forms of relationship modification might be more fitting or beneficial (or both) as ways of responding to people for their epistemically blameworthy conduct.

(iv) Blaming the Dead and the Distant

Some have objected to the relationship-based framework by pointing out that it seems we can appropriately blame people with whom we do not stand in any personal sort of relationship (Sher 2013, 50–55; Wallace 2011, 360). Opponents of the framework have taken this as evidence that the notion of a relationship is not doing any real theoretical work for the account. Consider reading in the Sunday paper about a gruesome series of murders, and that the courts have found person X guilty of committing them. You might blame person X for the gruesome murders, even though you only just heard about the existence of person X. Or consider learning about the atrocities committed by a dictator in a distant country. You don't stand in any obvious sort of relationship with the dictator, but you might blame them for the atrocities. Relatedly, Sher has argued that we can appropriately blame dead people in the distant past (Sher 2013). Call these cases of "impersonal blame." How can the relationship-based framework account for them?

There are two main things to say in response here. The first is to emphasize the importance of the distinction between blaming and judging blameworthy. When reacting to these sorts of cases, one must not mistake the intuitiveness of the idea that the Sunday morning paper reader of course judges the murderer blamewor-*thy*, with the idea that the Sunday morning paper reader actually *blames* the murderer. I find this especially salient when thinking about culpable dead people from the distant past, such as Leopold II. Some may find it more intuitive to say that they judge such people blameworthy (perhaps extremely so) than that they actively blame them for their horrible deeds.

Still, for those who disagree, a second point can be made. Even if it is true that we sometimes appropriately blame the distant and the dead, this does not show that the notion of a relationship is doing no theoretical work for the account. One way to see this is to consider the following. Note that, related to the points I just made above (section 4.3.1), the nature of our responses in cases of impersonal

106 EPISTEMIC BLAME

blame intuitively differ in character in comparison with the sorts of responses we have to impairments to our personal relationships. For example, whatever the Sunday morning paper reader's response amounts to, intuitively it will have a different character from the sort of response they would have toward a good friend for betraying an important secret. It is also plausible that whatever my response to the dictator in a distant country amounts to, it will be very different in character in comparison with the response of someone who is currently suffering under the reign of that dictator. If we can appropriately blame perfect strangers for wrongdoings—even ones as grave as murder—arguably we do so in a some-what more detached or abstract kind of way. Meanwhile, when we blame our good friends for betraying our trust, for example, this typically consists in, or is accompanied by, much more specific sorts of emotions, behaviors, and attitudes—things that have a more direct connection to the lived reality of our daily lives. The notion of a relationship does important theoretical work for the relationship-based framework insofar as can help explain the difference in char-acter between these different kinds of responses. For example, we can say that impersonal blame consists in a modification to attitudes that comprise some very thin notion of a relationship one stands in with the blamee. For example, we might say that all members of the moral community stand in this comparatively thin relationship insofar as they are fellow rational beings capable of showing concern for the moral justifiability of their actions and attitudes (Scanlon calls this the "moral relationship" (2008, 39–40)). Meanwhile, blame within personal relationships involves modifications to the very sorts of inten-tions, expectations, and attitudes that make such relationships more intimate and personal.

An opponent might double down and maintain that this "thin" notion of a relationship enabling the account to accommodate impersonal blame is not doing any real theoretical work. Why not simply understand such cases in terms of violations of moral obligations or norms? One answer, I think, comes down to the issue at the heart of this book. *If* we are to understand the Sunday morning paper reader's response as a genuine *blame* response, then it must consist of something beyond a judgement that the murderer has culpably violated some moral norm. The blamer must be engaged by such a judgment in some way. Now, as we have seen, there are different ways of attempting to account for that engagement. But by understanding the Sunday morning paper reader's response in terms of a judg-ment that the murderer has done something that has some *significance* for him—for example, insofar as they are fellow rational beings capable of showing concern for the moral justifiability of their actions and attitudes—and a modification to his attitudes toward that person accordingly, we can begin to get some fruitful traction on the kind of engagement that is characteristic of blame. And this is all I really have in mind when I connect blame to relationships. Moreover, by emphasizing, as I have earlier, that there are of course different kinds of relationships, we can get traction on the difference between the degree or kind of engagement that is characteristic of different kinds of blame.

All of this said, I am really only committed to defending my *epistemic* extension of the relationship-based framework. And, much like the "leaves the blame out of blame" objection, the present worry strikes me as less weighty when it comes to my epistemic extension. Perhaps this is because I am more confident readers will share my intuition that our epistemic blame responses toward very distant or dead people—if we ever appropriately have them—are in some sense different in kind from our epistemic blame responses toward people who occupy some more significant role in the GER.

4.4 Conclusion

This chapter completes my resolution of the puzzle of epistemic blame. In addition to arguing that the relationship-based account meets SIGNIFICANCE and FITTINGNESS, I have advertised independent considerations in favor of the account, and addressed some lingering worries. In the next three chapters, I turn my attention to some important new questions that have now become visible, concerning the ethics and value of epistemic blame.

5

Blameworthy Belief, Assertion, and Other Epistemic Harms

In the remaining three chapters, I turn my attention to three issues in the ethics of epistemic blame. The first of these concerns the scope of appropriate epistemic blame. In Chapter 3, I pointed out that people are typically regarded as appropriate targets of epistemic blame for things like dogmatism, wishful thinking, and other forms of biased cognition (under the right circumstances). What would a complete list of behaviors and attitudes for which people can be epistemically blameworthy look like?

I address this question, first by taking a step back and thinking about whether our starting assumption—namely, that people can be epistemically blameworthy for things like dogmatism and wishful thinking—is itself mistaken. One concern here is the well-worn question of whether people can be blameworthy for actions and attitudes that are in some sense outside of their control. I argue that the relationship-based account is well-positioned to address this issue. I then turn my attention toward *assertion*, *testimonial injustice*, and other forms of *epistemic harm*, such as epistemic exploitation and gaslighting. Important challenges arise when examining whether epistemic blameworthiness is the right concept to apply to failings in each of these cases. My primary aim is to argue that epistemic relationships are a useful tool for illuminating the nature of a wide variety of failings, and illustrating their connection to epistemic blame.

5.1 Bad Thinking

My canonical examples have been things like dogmatism, wishful thinking, and certain forms of biased reasoning. One feature these examples have in common is that they all seem like paradigm instances of "bad thinking." I've largely taken for granted the idea that, if anything we do is epistemically blameworthy, then bad thinking is a paradigm case. But perhaps I shouldn't be so quick.

The main worry I wish to examine here is whether the plausibility of this idea rests on an ambiguity. Take dogmatic thinking. Typical cases of dogmatic thinking involve a mix of importantly different things. Minimally, they involve a doxastic state component—belief, disbelief, suspension, or credal states. But they also

Epistemic Blame: The Nature and Norms of Epistemic Relationships. Cameron Boult, Oxford University Press.
© Cameron Boult 2024. DOI: 10.1093/oso/9780192890580.003.0006

BLAMEWORTHY BELIEF, ASSERTION, AND OTHER EPISTEMIC HARMS   109

involve what I will call "acts of inquiry"—the gathering of evidence, avoidance of evidence, weighting and interpretation of evidence, and so on. Consider a case:

> RADICAL EXTERNALIST: For as long as she can remember, Angelika has believed that internalism about epistemic justification is false. Early in undergrad, her intro epistemology professor did a great job expounding the problems for internalism; but she didn't spend much time on the problems of externalism (the professor was a dogmatic externalist herself). Angelika formed the belief that internalism can't possibly be right. From that point onward, she has found herself avoiding talks by internalistically minded scholars, avoiding reading the latest best articles defending the view, and seeking out work defending externalism. Whenever confronted with evidence that supports internalism, she interprets it uncharitably. When weighing evidence for and against, she tends to focus her mind more carefully and favorably on the evidence that supports externalism.

Angelika has formed a belief and maintained it in the face of available counterevidence, by actively avoiding that counterevidence, and digging in her heels and explaining it away in an epistemically problematic fashion. In my view, we need *both* of these components to capture what's involved in dogmatic thinking.

What interests me here is the potential issue this may raise for our understanding of the scope of appropriate epistemic blame. A skeptic of epistemic blameworthiness might suggest that our intuitions about whether a dogmatic thinker could be epistemically blameworthy depend on the separability of these two components in a problematic way. After all, when pumping intuitions about *blameworthiness*, it might seem like we don't want to focus too much on the doxastic state component: many find it implausible that people can be appropriately blamed for that which is outside their voluntary control (and many find it plausible that doxastic states are outside our voluntary control—more on this soon). So perhaps acts of inquiry can help here. After all, *acts* of inquiry seem like something we have (more) control over. However, because we're pumping intuitions about *epistemic* blameworthiness, we might want to avoid focusing too much on acts of inquiry, since it may be unclear whether an *epistemic* form of blame is a fitting response to such acts. We might worry that suggesting as much threatens to broaden the scope of epistemic blame in problematic ways (call this the problem of "epistemic bloat").[1] Perhaps a slight of hand is at work: we avoid each of these sources of concern by directing the mind toward one component or the

---

[1] I will explain this point in more detail shortly. The name is inspired by the phrase "cognitive bloat," which has been used to refer to an analogous issue facing defenders of the so-called "extended mind" hypothesis.

110 EPISTEMIC BLAME

other, in ways that allow us to retain the illusion that dogmatic thinking can be epistemically blameworthy.

I am not convinced that this is a real problem. First, I am not convinced that worries about voluntary control undermine the idea that people can be blameworthy for doxastic states. Second, I think we can make sense of the idea that acts of inquiry can be epistemically blameworthy, without proving too much. If I am right, then even if there is an ambiguity in our understanding of the target of epistemic blame in bad thinking, this is unproblematic because epistemic blame can be appropriately directed toward both components.

5.1.1 Doxastic Control

One potentially salient difference between the epistemic and moral domains—one that might give us pause for thought about whether people can be blameworthy for their doxastic states—centers on the notion of control. Consider some well-known observations about differences in the kind of control we have over our doxastic states in comparison with the kind we have over our actions. Imagine being offered $1,000,000 to raise your arm, or to flip a light switch. Under normal circumstances you'd be able to earn this desirable sum of money. But now imagine trying to form a belief that the Liberals won a majority government in the 2021 Canadian federal election, just because you are being offered $1,000,000. Even when such a reward is on offer, one cannot simply believe that p so long as it goes against one's evidence.[2]

Many are impressed by the idea that it would be inappropriate to blame someone for something that was outside their control. Showing that something was outside your control is a paradigm *exculpating* defense. If our doxastic states are outside our control, how could we be appropriately blamed for them? This is a longstanding issue, and there is a lot to say. For a start, we can argue about the nature of doxastic control. Most agree that we do not have "basic voluntary control" over our beliefs (Alston 1988). But perhaps we have a kind of indirect control over our doxastic states, such as by making decisions about who to associate with, or what bodies of evidence to consider (Alston 1988; Peels 2016; Rettler 2018).[3] Perhaps doxastic control simply amounts to a kind of reasons-responsiveness (Hieronymi 2008; McHugh 2017; Mitova 2011; Ryan 2003; Shah

---

[2] And it is not merely a matter of going *against* one's evidence. McHugh argues that we are incapable of forming beliefs for which we take ourselves to have no supporting evidence, or even insufficient evidence (McHugh 2012, 69).

[3] Rik Peels has developed the most detailed defense of the "indirect-control view." Peels argues against direct-control, compatibilist, and reasons-responsiveness views, maintaining instead that responsibility for beliefs is grounded in the "influence" we have over them. "The basic idea here is that we cannot choose our beliefs, but that we can choose to do or refrain from doing certain things that make a difference to what we believe, even though we hardly ever foresee to which specific beliefs it will make a difference" (2016, 9).

BLAMEWORTHY BELIEF, ASSERTION, AND OTHER EPISTEMIC HARMS   111

2002; Steup 2008).[4] If it turns out we *do* have a kind of control over our doxastic states—even if not basic voluntary control—then perhaps we can be appropriately blamed for them.

We can also challenge the more basic assumption that blame implies control. For example, some have appealed to the fact that there seem to be a number of areas, outside epistemology, where blame appropriately applies in the absence of control (Adams 1985; Owens 2000; Ryan 2003). Others have argued that while blame implies some kind of *ability*, this falls short of the claim that blame implies control (Chuard and Southwood 2009).

As with our central puzzle of epistemic blame, my preferred take on this issue is that the connections between blame and control force us to get clear, among other things, on what blame *is*. If blame is one sort of thing—say, a manifestation of emotional responses like indignation and resentment—then perhaps it really is hard to see how blame could be appropriate in the absence of control. But if blame is something else—for example, a certain kind of relationship modification, as I've argued—then perhaps it's not. In my view, when we ground our understanding of blame in terms of our relationships with one another, it is not hard to see how blame can be appropriate in the absence of control. Consider the fact that, often times, attitudes and actions that we do not (seem to) have voluntary control over can nevertheless express a great deal about how we regard one another. They often imply a great deal about our attitudes, intentions, and expectations toward one another. As Angela Smith has pointed out, sometimes things we do that are not under our direct voluntary control say *more* about who we are, and the regard we have for others, than things we do have control over. Smith discusses a variety of responses that she calls "involuntary responses," which, she argues, are an important indication of a person's underlying values and "moral commitments"—of "who they are." Her interest in these responses is that, "As a number of philosophers have pointed out, their alleged 'passivity,' far from undermining their attributability to persons, may actually be the strongest mark of their genuineness and sincerity" (Smith 2005, 242).[5] The sorts of responses Smith has in mind include things like *noticing, neglecting, "what occurs to us,"* and a variety of other reactions, such as jealousy, contempt, and regret.

To illustrate this in a bit more detail, consider *noticing*.[6] Smith points out that the significance of what someone notices is most vivid in the context of personal relationships. We are all familiar with moments in friendships or partnerships

---

[4] Reasons-responsiveness views of doxastic control move away from thinking of control in volitional terms altogether. Instead, they think of doxastic control in terms of a kind of rational sensitivity. One exercises doxastic agency by manifesting a responsiveness to epistemic reasons. One can be said to exercise "doxastic control" through successful exercises of one's doxastic agency. See Fischer and Ravizza (1998) for an influential modal approach to the notion of reasons-responsiveness.

[5] Smith points to the work of Robert Adams (1985), Jonathan Bennett (1974), Harry Frankfurt (1988), and Bernard Williams (1973) as inspiration for this idea.

[6] It's worth pointing out that "noticing" has a strong epistemic component, which fits nicely with my aim in this section of connecting Smith's approach to involuntary responses to our doxastic lives.

112 EPISTEMIC BLAME

when a friend or partner's unreflective patterns of awareness—for example, their failure to notice something about what food you dislike, or what music you love—reveals a great deal about our place in that person's overall "emotional and evaluative outlook" (Smith 2005, 243). A similar phenomenon is also recognizable in the narrower moral domain:

> If I do not notice when my music is too loud, when my advice is unwelcome, or when my assistance might be helpful to others, these again can be described as "involuntary" failings; nevertheless, these failings are commonly taken to be an appropriate basis for moral criticism. These forms of moral insensitivity provide at least some indication that I do not judge your needs and interests to be important, or at least that I do not take them very seriously.   (Smith 2005, 244)

When others are entitled to complain or criticize us for these failings, it is not pertinent to point out that we have no voluntary control over what occurs to us.

A person's beliefs and other doxastic states fit comfortably on the list of involuntary responses. What we are disposed to believe, under certain circumstances (given our evidence, background beliefs, and so on), often says much about who we are, at least from the perspective of our epistemic agency. If I am disposed to believe things about Prince Harry's love life simply on the basis of some trashy tabloids I read, this says something about my intellectual character. Think of all the terms, familiar from virtue epistemology, that suggest as much. We often refer to each other as *open-minded, gullible, conscientious, curious,* and so on. Importantly, the doxastic dispositions implied by these terms express features of our deeper evaluative commitments, and they do so irrespectively of any voluntary control we may or may not have over them.

Adjustments to our expectations and intentions toward one another, in light of our epistemic conduct, can be apt because of what a person's epistemic conduct and doxastic states say about a person—about their intellectual character—and what this in turn *means* for others, insofar as they stand in certain relationships with that person (including, of course, the General Epistemic Relationship, or GER as I called it in Chapter 3). Adjustments to our expectations and intentions toward one another—the kind that count as a sort of relationship modification made fitting by a judgment that one's epistemic relationship with another falls short of the normative ideal of that relationship—is what epistemic blame *consists in* on my account. So epistemic blame can be an appropriate response to a person for being in certain doxastic states in the circumstances, even if (or maybe even partially *because*) these are attitudes over which that person has no immediate voluntary control. Thus, the fact that belief is a paradigm example of a state over which agents do not have immediate voluntary control provides no reason to worry about whether people can be blameworthy for their doxastic states. The relationship-based account of epistemic blame has resources for handling, and, in my view, ultimately deflating worries about epistemic blameworthiness that stem from the putative connection between blame and control.[7]

One might object that this argument trades on an ambiguity about different kinds of responsibility. Perhaps we are responsible for our involuntary responses, but the kind of responsibility we have is not relevant to the question of whether we can be appropriately *blamed* for these responses. Smith herself frames her discussion of involuntary responses in terms of "responsibility in the most basic sense" (2005, 237). She uses the label "attributability," where attributability-responsibility is what it takes to be *open* to moral appraisal (whether positive or negative). Smith differentiates this from a "stronger sense of responsibility" which indicates an assessment of blameworthiness, pointing out that the stronger sense *presupposes* her more basic sense. One thing it is important to note in this context is that Smith's use of "attributability" is not equivalent to Gary Watson's (1996) well-known use, which he *contrasts* with accountability, or openness to blame. Call what Watson has in mind "mere-attributability." I do not take Smith's discussion simply to be about the appropriateness of mere-attributability judgments for involuntary responses. Indeed, the observations above about *noticing* directly suggest we can be criticized and perhaps blamed for involuntary responses, though Smith happens to refrain from making substantive commitments about what degree or kinds of criticism can be appropriate (271). She does argue that we can be *answerable* for our involuntary responses—requests for reasons and demands for justifications can be appropriate. I take all of this to motivate my point in this section, which is that certain forms of epistemic relationship modification can be appropriately made in response to involuntary responses.[8]

There is much more to say about this issue. But it is also something that *any* account of epistemic blame needs something to say about, perhaps more pressingly so, depending on whether I am right that some attitudes (like indignation and resentment) seem to have a tighter connection to considerations about control than relationship modification.

5.1.2 Acts of Inquiry and Epistemic Bloat

What about the other worry about bad thinking? The worry is that including acts of inquiry within the scope of appropriate epistemic blame threatens to prove too much, or lead to what I called epistemic bloat. What is the basis of this worry?

---

[7] Of course, there are limits to this point. Not everything I do, over which I lack voluntary control, is something I am open to blame for. But this fits naturally with the obvious point that, not everything I do is open to interpretation as a way of impairing my relationships with other people.

[8] Thanks to Sebastian Schmidt for discussion.

114   EPISTEMIC BLAME

The basis of the worry has to do with the motivation for thinking that acts of inquiry *can* be appropriate targets of epistemic blame. Recall that I avoided articulating the concept of epistemic blame as a kind of "blame for belief." Instead, I articulated the concept as a kind of blame for epistemic failings, done from the perspective of promoting epistemic goods like truth and knowledge. Understood as such, an act of inquiry seems like a fitting target of epistemic blame, since acts of inquiry can be assessed from the perspective of promoting epistemic goods. The issue, however, is about how far we are willing to take this idea. Consider a couple of cases.[9]

> BAD NIGHT'S SLEEP: Sam has a big conference tomorrow. He is presenting his latest paper, and there is also a great line-up of talks in his area. This evening, it's the conference banquet and Sam is having a blast. Unfortunately, he ends up drinking way too much and has an awful night's sleep. As a result, he misses two important talks in the morning, and has a hard time paying attention to the one he does catch. Worst of all, he does a horrible job presenting his paper.

> MISSED BREAKFAST: Mesfin has a tendency to hit the snooze button. On mornings before Intro Biology, he often ends up hitting snooze a few too many times, leading to a mad dash effort to get to class on time. Mesfin is a breakfast person, but the mad dash leaves no time for food. The missed meal has a big impact on his concentration. Mesfin's hectic morning routine ends up leading to all kinds of missed epistemic goods over the course of the semester.

Both cases involve people who have done something that leads to a suboptimal performance in the promotion of epistemic goods. It seems these cases can be assessed from that perspective. But do we really want to say that failing to get a good night's sleep, or missing breakfast, are things for which we can be *epistemically* blameworthy? That doesn't sound right.

Happily, the relationship-based account of epistemic blame can make good sense of what is going on here. As should be clear by now, when it comes to the appropriateness of epistemic blame, these cases are missing an important ingredient. At least on a natural reading of what is going on, they are not cases of someone impairing the epistemic relationship. Failing to get a good night's sleep does not seem like a way of showing that you fall short of the normative ideal of the GER. On my view, impairing the GER is a necessary condition on being epistemically blameworthy. So, these agents don't count as epistemically blameworthy according to my account. As with worries about doxastic voluntarism, it may appear as though there is a worry in the general vicinity here. But once we get

---

[9] Thanks to Elise Woodard for discussion. Notice that this issue is closely related to the worry I addressed in Chapter 3 about Dwight and the pill (is Dwight epistemically blameworthy for *taking the pill*?). In this section I develop my response to this issue in more depth.

clearer about the nature of epistemic blame and blameworthiness, we can see that there is no real issue.

Of course, this raises questions about which actions and attitudes, exactly, are capable of impairing the GER. Consider the many ways a person can put themselves in a position to lose out on epistemic goods they ought to have (evidence about who the killer is, for example). We can do so through forms of bad thinking, such as hasty reasoning or dogmatism. And those seem like ways of impairing the GER. But we can also do so by taking drugs, or—to stick with our original example—by getting a bad night's sleep. While getting a bad night's sleep may fall outside the scope of the class of actions and attitudes that can impair the GER, we might worry about whether there are certain borderline cases, threatening the idea that there is really a principled distinction to be found here. For instance, imagine you are a detective on a case, and you have the belief that taking LSD helps you solve cases (as it happens, this belief is unjustified and false). Just before investigating the scene of a crime you take some LSD. We might think that this action sits somewhere on a hazy line between bad thinking and reckless sleeping.[10]

Discussion of this issue leads quickly into difficult philosophy of action questions. Detailed examination would take us too far afield. But the following response should suffice for present purposes. Recall from Chapter 3 the important role that *intellectual acts* play in the core intentions and expectations specified by the normative ideal of the GER. Here again is a list of some basic candidates:

- A intends, for any intellectual act X of A's, to meet epistemic criteria Y, unless A has good reason, or an excuse, for not doing so.
- A expects, for any intellectual act X of B's, that B will meet epistemic criteria Y, unless B has good reason, or an excuse, for not doing so.
- B intends, for any intellectual act X of B's, to meet epistemic criteria Y, unless B has good reason, or an excuse, for not doing so.
- B expects, for any intellectual act X of A's, that A will meet epistemic criteria Y, unless A has good reason, or an excuse, for not doing so.

One way of framing the present issue is simply by focusing on the role of intellectual acts in the normative ideal of the GER. Recall, intellectual acts just are the sorts of things that can be evaluated by epistemic criteria. Paradigm

---

[10] If the detective is culpable for having an unjustified false belief about the cognitive effects of LSD, we might think the case is just an instance of bad thinking. But notice a couple of additional features of the case. First, the decision to take LSD also leads to the downstream loss of many epistemic goods, and to that extent resembles reckless sleeping. Second, the detective's bad thinking is also somehow constitutively bound up with the downstream loss of epistemic goods, in a way that sets it apart from reckless sleeping. So, I see it as sitting somewhat hazily between bad thinking and reckless sleeping. Of course, some may disagree that the case needs any kind of special treatment. I would take that to be good news for my project here. Thanks to Adam Carter for drawing my attention to the LSD-taking detective version of the issue.

116 EPISTEMIC BLAME

epistemic criteria include the standards of rationality, justification, and reliability. We have seen that the formation and maintenance of doxastic states, the making of assertions, and the carrying out of acts of inquiry are all things that can be evaluated by epistemic criteria.

Getting a bad night's sleep is not an intellectual act. It is not even a kind of action, but rather an unfolding event comprised of a series of "smaller" actions and attitudes (and things external to one's agency). Actions can be nested within higher-level actions. At a certain level of description, all of our actions involve intellectual acts, even if they are not intellectual acts themselves (this is often simply because of the role that belief and intention play in action). When it comes to getting a bad night's sleep, there may well have been actions and attitudes involved that can be evaluated by epistemic criteria. So, perhaps depending on how we further fill out the case, someone's "failure to get a good night's sleep" may be a kind of proximate target of appropriate epistemic blame. But the proper target will be the action or attitude more directly connected to intentions and expectations that show the person to have fallen short of the normative ideal of the GER—intentions and expectations directed toward intellectual acts. To be sure, there is a haziness to all this. But questions about epistemic blameworthiness are themselves hazy. So I take that to be a feature, and not a defect of the approach.

The relationship-based framework can accommodate a variety of intuitions people might have about these sorts of cases, depending on how certain details get filled in. Perhaps we can spell out cases in such a way that the subject really does seem to be doing something epistemically irresponsible. The extent to which that seems right will simultaneously track the extent to which it seems correct to say that the person does something to impair the GER, and so may count as epistemically blameworthy. A virtue of the framework is its ability to broaden the boundaries where it seems appropriate, but in a principled way.

To return briefly to the original worry about bad thinking—namely, that our sense that people can be blameworthy for bad thinking trades illicitly on an ambiguity in the role that doxastic states and acts of inquiry play in bad thinking—we can see now why this is not a real problem. Even if there is an ambiguity in our understanding of the target of epistemic blame in bad thinking, this is unproblematic because epistemic blame can be appropriately directed toward both components.

5.2 Assertion

You overhear someone on the bus to work assert that there is no evidence of the efficacy of vaccines in fighting pandemics. The hairs on your arms stand up, your heart rate increases, you glare in their general direction. You judge this person morally blameworthy for making a reckless and false assertion on a matter of importance. Perhaps you judge them epistemically blameworthy for their assertion too. Indeed, the epistemic credentials of the person's views on vaccine efficacy may even be directly relevant to the question of whether the person is morally blameworthy for their assertion.[11] It is worth pausing to examine this issue in its own right: can assertions be epistemically blameworthy?

This is an important question, not least because assertion has long been a central topic in contemporary epistemology. Epistemologists routinely discuss assertions as appropriate targets for epistemic criticism and blame (Brown 2011; DeRose 2002; Gerken 2011; Kelp and Simion 2017; Lackey 2011; Williamson 1996, 2000). In Chapter 1, I used the epistemic norms debates—a central topic of which is the "epistemic norm of assertion"—as a way of motivating the importance of epistemic blame. If it turns out assertions are not appropriate targets of epistemic blame, that would seem to be an important result.

Here is a more specific example of what hangs on this. If it turns out that people cannot be epistemically blameworthy for their assertions, a key heuristic often deployed in assessing candidate norms of assertion may fail. This heuristic relies on an intuitive connection between norm violation and openness to blame. Using the heuristic, a candidate view about the epistemic norm of assertion—say, that it's *knowledge*—is challenged by showing that one can assert without knowledge, but be entirely blameless. The thought is that this is evidence that knowledge is *not* the epistemic norm of assertion (so, presumably something else is). There is a lot to say about this line of argument, but Kauppinen makes an observation relevant for present purposes (2018, 11–15). According to Kauppinen, if it turns out the user of this heuristic is appealing (perhaps unwittingly) to intuitions about *moral* blameworthiness, it is hard to see how we can draw conclusions about the *epistemic* norm of assertion. For example, just because someone is morally blameless for asserting without knowledge, it doesn't follow that they haven't violated an epistemic norm. Kauppinen argues that this sort of inattention to blame's nature indeed affects the literature: many appeals to blame in the assertion literature misfire because they are invocations of a moral response, supporting conclusions only about moral norm violations. Users of this heuristic might respond to Kauppinen, then, by claiming that assertions in the relevant cases are indeed *epistemically* blameworthy or blameless, not just morally blameworthy or blameless. Of course, for that to work, we need to know whether people can be epistemically blameworthy for their assertions.

One way to challenge the idea that assertions can be epistemically blameworthy is to acknowledge that the man on the bus is epistemically blameworthy for

---

[11] This is another way of putting the idea that there is an "epistemic condition" on moral responsibility—that is, the idea that non-culpable ignorance can function as an exculpating factor. I do not endorse substantive claims about the epistemic condition here, I simply mention it because some may find it a helpful way of motivating an examination of the epistemic dimension of blameworthy assertion.

something, but to insist that he's not epistemically blameworthy for his *assertion*. For instance, someone might argue that he's epistemically blameworthy for the doxastic attitudes that this assertion *expresses* (perhaps along with whatever acts of inquiry were involved in acquiring and maintaining that attitude). If that is the case, then we have no need to expand our conception of the scope of epistemic blameworthiness beyond our canonical cases.

I agree that the man on the bus may be epistemically blameworthy for the doxastic state(s) his assertion expresses. But it strikes me as unduly restrictive to stop there. After all, the man's assertion is something that can be assessed from the point of view of promoting epistemic goods like truth and knowledge. For example, those around him may be influenced in such a way that they lose out on epistemic goods (let's say he's a father of three, an uncle of six, and a grandfather of nine). But we've already seen that being evaluable from the perspective of promoting epistemic goods is not enough to get something on the list of appropriate targets of epistemic blame. The test for determining whether assertions belong on that list, of course, is to consider whether assertions can amount to ways of impairing the GER. And I think the answer is *yes*. In recklessly and falsely asserting that p, a person may show that they have expectations, attitudes, and intentions that fall short of the normative ideal of the GER. This is because assertions are a kind of intellectual act. In addition to being evaluable from the perspective of promoting epistemic goods, assertions are also the sort of thing that can be evaluated by epistemic criteria. Assertions can be irrational, unjustified, and false. There seem(s) to be (an) *epistemic* norm(s) governing assertion, as the debates noted earlier discuss in detail. Thus, on my view, asserting badly can be a way of impairing the GER. Asserting badly is something for which people can be appropriately epistemically blamed.

Note that another interesting, and important, category of seemingly blameworthy assertion counts as epistemically blameworthy on this picture. Sometimes people carelessly, or misleadingly, assert things (whether true or false), even though they do not *believe* what they say. Sometimes people bullshit. Perhaps some cases of people saying things they don't really believe aren't quite full-blown assertions. Either way, a range of speech acts in this vicinity—I will group them under the heading *bullshit*—seem like ways of falling short of the normative ideal of the GER.[12] The bullshitter's speech act can be evaluated by epistemic criteria. Bullshitters may be entirely aware that they have no idea whether what they assert is true, and so lack belief and therefore knowledge of (and justification for) what they assert. Here's a useful example, taken from Cassam:

---

[12] The seminal work on bullshit is of course Frankfurt's *On Bullshit*. But the topic has taken on a life of its own. See Cassam 2021 for a helpful overview of a variety of analyses of the concept of bullshit. The connection between bullshit and epistemic blame would likely be a fruitful one to explore elsewhere.

BLAMEWORTHY BELIEF, ASSERTION, AND OTHER EPISTEMIC HARMS 119

TRADE DEFICIT: At a fundraising dinner President Trump described a meeting with Canadian Prime Minister Justin Trudeau. An issue that came up in the meeting was whether the U.S. had a trade deficit with Canada. Trudeau insisted that this was not the case. Trump insisted that it was. Trump bragged at the dinner that he had no idea at the time whether what he told Trudeau was true, but that he had repeated his claim several times. (Cassam 2021, 51)[13]

On just about any plausible account of the epistemic norm of assertion (whether it's a knowledge-, truth-, belief-, or reasonable belief-norm), Trump's assertion that the USA has a trade deficit with Canada does not comply with the norm, and to that extent is unjustified. So, it too seems like an appropriate target of epistemic blame. Notice that diagnosing the appearance of epistemically blameworthy assertion in terms of the *doxastic states* that assertions express does not seem able to explain why this sort of case is epistemically blameworthy.

Consider cases that introduce complexities of a different sort, such as Jennifer Lackey's (2008, 48) creationist teacher case. In Lackey's example, a teacher asserts something true and well-founded (namely, that humans evolved from apes), but does not believe this herself (because she's a creationist). Lackey is interested in whether others can come to *know* on the basis of such an assertion. Incidentally, she thinks they can, and so argues that so-called "transmission theories" of testimony are false (cf. Carter and Nickel 2014). What's interesting for our purposes is how to appropriately react to this sort of assertion. Its content is true and well-founded, so should the assertion be considered epistemically blame-*less* (in a non-trivial sense)? Note again, the expressed-doxastic-state view seems incapable of delivering this answer. After all, the teacher does *not* have the relevant (well-founded) belief. We might even think that lacking such a well-founded belief is an epistemic failing.

Perhaps it is unclear whether the assertion itself is epistemically blameless. One might argue that there is a kind of *incoherence* between the teacher's assertion and her beliefs, and that this incoherence renders the assertion blameworthy. It seems to me that this depends on how we fill out further details of the case. If the teacher asserts that humans evolved from apes because she believes that this is profes-sionally required of her, I do not see this as criticizably incoherent. Perhaps it's simply a conflict between her private and professional life. For those who find the idea that the assertion is (non-trivially) blameless attractive, the GER can help explain why. The assertion is accurate and well-founded, so it does nothing to reveal that the teacher falls short of the normative ideal of the GER. Perhaps it even shows that she's committed not to let her personal beliefs obstruct knowledge-acquisition opportunities for her students. That arguably puts her in

---

[13] The example based on a report in the *Washington Post* in March 2018.

120 EPISTEMIC BLAME

good standing with the normative ideal of the GER. We would have to know more about her doxastic states and how she acquired and maintains them in order to determine whether the teacher is epistemically blameworthy in such a case. And that seems like the right result.

The teacher example brings to center stage another important question that we can ask about assertion, one that applies equally to all sorts of epistemic failings, but somehow seems especially pressing in the case of assertion because of its communicative function. How do facts about a bad asserter's *professional role*, or other social roles (institutional, personal, political, etc.) impact their blameworthiness? Consider: other things being equal, it seems worse for a teacher to incorrectly assert that p (to her students) than it does for a person on the street to incorrectly assert that p. One thing to consider here is whether there really is a difference between these cases from the *epistemic* point of view—or whether the relevant differences can only be seen from some other normative perspective.

In my view, this sort of question highlights the need for a better grasp of the interconnections between epistemic relationships and other more specific kinds of relationship. I take up a detailed discussion of this in the next chapter (6.5).

5.3 Testimonial Injustice

We have now examined bad thinking and blameworthy assertion, concluding that they have a place on our list of appropriate targets of epistemic blame. To my mind, this accords with standard practice in much of the literature. What I want to do next is consider whether there are grounds to take things further, perhaps into somewhat revisionary territory. I want to explore what can be said in support of the idea that the scope of epistemic blameworthiness extends beyond doxastic states and assertion, to a seemingly entirely different sort of failing, one that clearly has something to do with the epistemic domain, but in a less straightforward way: testimonial injustice.

Testimonial injustice is by now a mainstream topic in epistemology. As Miranda Fricker explains in her pioneering work, testimonial injustice occurs when a speaker suffers a *credibility deficit* as a result of the effect that prejudicial stereotyping has had on the hearer's uptake of their testimony. A speaker suffers a credibility deficit when the credibility she is afforded by a hearer is less than she otherwise would have been afforded, absent the operation of prejudicial stereotyping (Fricker 2007, 17).[14] Different types of harm can attend testimonial

---

[14] A number of authors have recently challenged Fricker's claim that testimonial injustice only occurs when someone suffers a credibility *deficit*. For example, Wright (2018), Davis (2016), Lackey (2021), and Luzzi (2016) have argued in different ways that testimonial injustice can also occur in cases of credibility *excess*. I come back to this important development in section 5.6.1, when I discuss a range of epistemic harms connected to testimonial injustice. In addition to *testimonial* injustice, there has of

BLAMEWORTHY BELIEF, ASSERTION, AND OTHER EPISTEMIC HARMS 121

injustice, including both practical and epistemic harms. In paradigm cases, a victim of testimonial injustice is harmed in their capacity as a *knower*—or, put differently, their status as an epistemic agent is unjustly impugned.[15] This underpins the sense in which testimonial injustice is a distinctively *epistemic* kind of injustice. Additionally, there are "secondary" harms that may—but do not necessarily—attend cases of testimonial injustice, such as practical consequences of suffering a credibility deficit, or downstream epistemic consequences, such as losing confidence in one's beliefs and thereby losing opportunities for knowledge.

Here are two well-known paradigm cases:

> **MR RIPLEY:** In *The Talented Mr Ripley*, Herbert Greenleaf does not believe Margery Sherwood's testimony regarding her fiancé's disappearance. Margery is entirely correct about her fiancé. But, because Herbert is a man of 1950s America, he fails to see Sherwood's testimony as reliable. He dismisses her claims that the fiancé has been killed.

> **MOCKINGBIRD:** In *To Kill A Mockingbird*, Tom Robinson is a Black man accused of beating and raping Mayella Ewell, a white woman. Robinson's lawyer, Atticus Finch, has mounted a compelling defense making it clear to any relatively unprejudiced person in the courtroom that Robinson is entirely innocent. But the jury sees him as a lying Black man with no self-control. They convict him.

Is Herbert blameworthy for perpetrating testimonial injustice? What about the Maycomb jury?[16] The idea that testimonial injustice is a form of harm or wrongdoing is uncontroversial. But getting into questions about the *culpability* of perpetrators for committing these harms or wrongs tends to be more complicated. Fricker herself has argued that while Herbert Greenleaf's treatment of Marge is of course a form of wrongdoing, he is nevertheless blameless for it. Meanwhile, the jurors in MOCKINGBIRD are culpable for their wrongful treatment of Tom Robinson. The basic difference, according to Fricker, is that the jurors had reasons accessible to them as a basis upon which to critically reflect on their reaction to the testimony of Robinson. Namely, they had access to clear evidence that Robinson wasn't guilty, as well as the persuasive arguments of Finch. Meanwhile, according

---

course been a good deal of discussion about other kinds of epistemic injustice, including hermeneutical injustice (Fricker 2007; Hänel 2020; Jackson 2019; Medina 2012a, 2012b; Pohlhaus 2012). I will not be discussing hermeneutical injustice in this chapter.

[15] There is live debate about the nature of this harm. For example, some maintain it is best understood as a kind of "epistemic objectification" (Fricker 2007, 132–3; McGlynn 2020, 2021); others argue it should be understood as a kind of "epistemic othering" (Medina 2012b, 203–4; Pohlhaus 2014, 102–4).

[16] Concerns have been raised about how this case involves perceived *lying* as opposed to mere lack of credibility, and whether this is consistent with the idea of *epistemic* injustice. For the purposes of this section, I am assuming that in perceiving Robinson as lying *without self-control* that the jury does accord him a credibility deficit of the sort found in paradigmatic forms of testimonial injustice.

122 EPISTEMIC BLAME

to Fricker, nearly any male in Greenleaf's position in 1950s America would have perceived Margery as he did. Mr Greenleaf would have had to perform a significant feat of epistemic excellence to see things differently.

Not everyone agrees with Fricker's assessment of the comparative culpability of these agents. For example, Adam Piovarchy (2021b) argues that according to two of the most prominent accounts of responsibility in the literature—namely, *control* accounts and certain *attributionist*[17] accounts—*none* of these perpetrators of testimonial injustice count as blameworthy for their wrongdoings. At the heart of his argument is the observation that "testimonial injustice differs to more common forms of wrongdoing in that it is neither an action nor an omission, but a *perception*" (2021b, 1). Because the mechanisms at work in testimonial injustice, by their very nature, go undetected by the perpetrator, according to Piovarchy, careful reflection on paradigm cases reveals that perpetrators of testimonial injustice are not morally blameworthy for their testimonial injustices.[18]

The question of moral blameworthiness for testimonial injustice is clearly a complex issue in its own right. It would seem to require making substantive commitments about the nature of moral responsibility and blameworthiness, about what follows from those commitments in particular cases, and getting clearer on crucial details about things like the reasons available to the agents in question, what was within their control, and so on.[19] In light of all this, my strategy in this section will be as follows. Assuming that a hearer in a given case is in some way blameworthy for testimonial injustice, in what way, if any, are they *epistemically* blameworthy for this testimonial injustice? And what might hang on this?

This is also complicated. On one hand, testimonial injustice is deeply bound up with a kind of belief about a speaker, or at least a way of *perceiving* them—one that can be proportioned to the evidence to greater or lesser degrees and so is clearly evaluable by epistemic criteria. But "according a speaker a credibility deficit" may also be understood in broader terms, perhaps involving dispositions to *treat* them in certain ways, for example, by not listening to them, or patronizing them, etc. And it is not clear that such dispositions, strictly speaking, are evaluable by

---

[17] Piovarchy focuses on Talbert's (2008) prominent form of attributionism (2021b, fn 11).

[18] Piovarchy does argue that other sorts of response are entirely appropriate. He argues that we can account for our inclination not to let perpetrators of epistemic injustice off the hook in terms of holding them attributability-responsible. As he puts it: "even if completely excused, the fact is the Maycomb jurors are very racist. They hold offensively false beliefs about the equality of persons, and they are indifferent towards or endorse the suffering of black people" (Piovarchy 2021b, 17). The idea is that our ability to judge them *racist*, *offensive*, and *indifferent* in this way is enough to "assuage worries that excusing them means negative attitudes are unwarranted altogether" (2021b, 17). Piovarchy also says we may be entitled to *argue* with the jurors, engage in *social activism*, and *protest* their decision. He adds that we might even be *justified* in blaming them, even if blame is inappropriate (that is to say, justified by all-things-considered consequences of doing so).

[19] Ishani Maitra argues there are at least two ways prejudice in testimonial injustice can be sourced in epistemically culpable activity. In addition to failures to be responsive to evidence one *has*, some prejudices are the result of failures to *gather* evidence in a culpable way (Maitra 2010, 4). This may raise complications for Fricker's view about the blameworthiness of hearers in her paradigm cases.

BLAMEWORTHY BELIEF, ASSERTION, AND OTHER EPISTEMIC HARMS   123

epistemic criteria. If not, then it may be unclear whether acts of testimonial injustice are strictly speaking intellectual acts at all. Perhaps acts of testimonial injustice cannot be ways of impairing the GER. By my account, then, perhaps they should be barred from our list of things for which people can be epistemically blameworthy.

Next section, I will take as my starting point the idea that perpetrators of testimonial injustice can be epistemically blameworthy in at least one fairly straightforward sense. Perpetrators of testimonial injustice can be epistemically blameworthy when they culpably irrationally believe things about the credibility of someone. Doing so is simply a kind of bad thinking, one that happens to be about the credibility of a speaker. But precisely because this bad thinking concerns the *credibility of a speaker*, I think the epistemic blameworthiness of testimonial injustice can consist in *more* than just bad thinking. As just indicated, testimonial injustice goes beyond forming credibility judgments, or perceiving speakers in certain ways: it also involves dispositions to treat speakers as more or less credible. Whether or not a perception of speaker credibility fits the hearer's total evidence, the sheer act of treating someone as less credible than they are strikes me as a way of impairing the GER. I want to develop an account on which testimonial injustice can impair epistemic relationships in at least *two* ways. The first is when testimonial injustice embodies a kind of culpable irrationality. The second, is when it embodies a *deficiency of normative expectation* of a speaker. As we will see, the latter kind of relationship impairment inverts the typical form of epistemic relationship impairment we have so far considered. Notice that a feature of human relationships in general seems to be that we can impair them not just by falling short of others' expectations, but also by revealing certain deficiencies in our own normative expectations of others.[20] A father might have deficient normative expectations concerning his daughter's aspirations of having a fulfilling career (and instead normatively expect her to aspire to be a great stay-at-home mother, for example), thereby impairing their relationship in significant ways. I will argue that recognizing this form of impairment in epistemic relationships can help us make sense of cases of testimonial injustice that do *not* involve culpable irrationality, and can also be put to work to illuminate a wide variety of epistemic harms.

5.3.1 Testimonial Injustice and Deficient Normative Expectations

It seems clear that some cases of testimonial injustice are epistemically blameworthy simply because the credibility judgments involved are culpably irrational.

---

[20] Thanks to Sebastian Köhler for discussion of this point.

124 EPISTEMIC BLAME

I will stipulate that there can be hearers in cases otherwise like MR RIPLEY, for example, who should have known better than to perceive or treat Margery as lacking credibility. Consider:

> MR RIPLEY*: Herbert Greenleaf* does not believe Margery Sherwood*'s testimony regarding her fiancé's disappearance. Margery* is entirely correct about her fiancé. But, because Herbert* is culpably irrational in his beliefs about the credibility of women, he fails to see Sherwood*'s testimony as reliable. He dismisses her claims that the fiancé has been killed.

My interest is not so much in defending the claim that people can be epistemically blameworthy for being culpably irrational in their credibility judgments, but rather in showing that it is not *enough* in accounting for what goes epistemically wrong in cases of testimonial injustice. There is a further epistemic dimension to testimonial injustice than bad thinking.

In Chapter 3, we focused on the epistemic expectations that a *blamer* may have of a target of blame. This fits naturally with the predominance of theorists taking wishful thinking, dogmatism, and other forms of biased cognition as paradigm examples of conduct for which people can be appropriate targets of epistemic blame. They are forms of epistemic conduct that fall short of the normative ideal of the GER, in the sense that they are forms of conduct that fall short of the would-be *blamer's* epistemic expectations. But notice that we can also focus on the epistemic expectations of the *target of blame* themself in illuminating ways.

Sticking with MR RIPLEY*, in addition to asking questions about whether Herbert* meets our epistemic expectations in performing his intellectual acts, we can also examine his epistemic expectations of *Marge*. Generally speaking, in addition to falling short of expectations in our *intellectual acts*, there is plenty of room for an epistemic agent to fall short, or somehow be deficient, *in their epistemic expectations* of others. For instance, by not taking Marge*'s word seriously, perhaps Herbert* reveals that he lacks (to an extent that falls short of some normative ideal) an expectation of the form

- A expects, for any intellectual act X of B's, that B will meet epistemic criteria Y, unless B has good reason, or an excuse, for not doing so.

Herbert* has a standing prejudicial belief that women are irrational, which seems like another way of saying that he does *not* expect that, for any intellectual act X of B, that B will meet epistemic criteria Y, unless B has good reason not to.[21] I want to argue that what's going on here is (at least in part) a failure of normative

---

[21] This of course assumes that, once suitably spelled out, Y includes a role for rationality, which is plausible.

expectation, and that this failure of expectation is an important part of what the harm attending epistemic injustice in this sort of case amounts to. That is to say, it is part of what it means for Herbert* to "harm the speaker in their capacity as a knower," as Fricker puts it. Of course, Fricker would add that, in order to count as an instance of epistemic injustice, this failure of expectation must be the result of *prejudice* on behalf of the hearer. Indeed, for a number of reasons, my point here will take some careful handling.

For a start, we might worry that this proposal simply trades on an ambiguity in the notion of an "expectation." We have identified the sorts of expectations that partially constitute the GER as *normative* expectations, not predictive ones (though, we acknowledged, when all goes well, the latter typically accompany the former, as a result of the connection between normative expectations and established social practice). Testimonial injustice clearly seems to involve a lack of *predictive* expectation that the speaker will meet certain epistemic criteria in their intellectual acts.[22] It might seem less clear that testimonial injustice involves a certain absence of *normative* expectation of the speaker. However, I will argue now that testimonial injustice typically does involve a certain absence of normative expectation.

Start with the plausible thought that holding others to normative expectations regarding their credibility comes in degrees. We can normatively expect people to be credible to a greater or lesser degree. The degree of credibility we normatively expect of someone reporting in a newspaper may differ from the degree of credibility we normatively expect of a child reporting on her day at school.[23] Granting this, the idea that paradigm perpetrators of testimonial injustice lack the relevant normative expectations becomes more plausible. This is because, on this assumption, all we need commit ourselves to is the idea that paradigm perpetrators of testimonial injustice have a deficiency in the *degree* of credibility that they normatively expect from a speaker—not that they lack normative expectations regarding the speaker's credibility altogether. This strikes me as compelling in at least two ways. First, it is clear that paradigm perpetrators of testimonial injustice have a normative expectation that the speaker be credible to at least *some* degree— for instance, they don't judge the speaker capable of just any nonsense. But second, it is also plausible that perpetrators of testimonial injustice do not expect *enough* of the speaker.

As I just noted, predictive expectation typically accompanies normative expectation, given the connection between normative expectation and established social

---

[22] I take this to be constitutively connected to what it is to assign someone a credibility deficit, given that testimonial injustice does not involve inaccurately perceiving someone as *insincere*, or *deceitful*, but rather as epistemically *incompetent*.

[23] Note also that "credible" is a gradable adjective. It makes perfect senses to refer to someone as "a very credible source," for example. How exactly to cash out the notion of "degrees of credibility" is something I will leave for another time. A workable account may focus on degrees of reliability.

126   EPISTEMIC BLAME

practice. When I'm in Canada, I normatively expect people to drive on the right-hand side of the road, I normatively expect people to avoid getting into fistfights on the bus, and for restaurants to serve untainted food. I also tend to predictively expect all of these things as well, other things being equal. Flipping this observation on its head, we might think the *absence* of a predictive expectation is thus defeasible evidence of the absence of a corresponding normative expectation. Of course, one can have normative expectations in the absence of corresponding predictive ones. In Chapter 4, I used the example of normatively expecting a tired-looking walk-in clinic doctor to apply up-to-date knowledge of family medicine in a skillful differential diagnosis, even if not predictively expecting them to do so. Still, given that predictive expectations often do accompany normative expectations (and note that this is true of the GER, at least when all goes well), the absence of a predictive expectation (of the appropriate degree) takes us some way toward our target.

Building on this, another form of defeasible evidence of the absence of a normative expectation in cases of testimonial injustice is a lack of disposition on the part of the hearer to criticize, (epistemically) blame, or manifest any of the sorts of attitudes and behaviors that are arguably constitutive of what it *is* to hold someone to a normative expectation. If someone judges a person to lack property X, but does none of these things as a result, this is defeasible evidence that they do not normatively expect that person to have property X.

Perpetrators of testimonial injustice judge the speaker to lack credibility; but, at least in the sorts of paradigm cases discussed so far, we don't see them manifesting any of the sorts of behaviors constitutively connected to holding others to normative expectations in response to this judgment. For instance, paradigm perpetrators of testimonial injustice don't seem to modify attitudes or intentions toward the speaker as a *result* of judging them to lack credibility (in the way we might modify our attitudes toward someone for asserting a falsehood when we think they should know better). Perpetrators of testimonial injustice *already* have a set of attitudes and dispositions that both lead to and reflect (and indicate to others) their judgment of the speaker's lack of credibility.

This is suggestive. But it does not yet establish that paradigm perpetrators of testimonial injustice lack the relevant normative expectations concerning speaker credibility. After all, there are at least two ways of explaining why they do not manifest any of the behaviors I've suggested are constitutively connected to holding others to normative expectations. One is to maintain that paradigm perpetrators of testimonial injustice *do* hold the speaker to appropriate normative expectations of credibility—perhaps just as they hold any other member of the epistemic community to such expectations—but they do not show a tendency to criticize the speaker for lacking credibility because they do not regard doing so worth their time, or think it's somehow beneath them to bother with criticism. This may have some plausibility. But an alternative explanation, of course, is that the absence of a tendency to criticize, epistemically blame, or manifest other

BLAMEWORTHY BELIEF, ASSERTION, AND OTHER EPISTEMIC HARMS 127

behaviors constitutively connected to holding someone to a normative expectation, simply is an indication that paradigm perpetrators of testimonial injustice do
not hold their victims to appropriate normative expectations of credibility.

One argument in support of this latter explanation is that it is both simpler and
fits well with independently plausible ideas about testimonial injustice. It is
simpler in the sense that it does not require positing an additional psychological
claim about paradigm perpetrators of testimonial injustice: namely, that they
judge criticizing or blaming the speaker somehow beneath them, or not worth
their time. For my own part, I have no idea whether that's true, and I am not aware
of any studies corroborating this. Meanwhile, we already know that hearers in an
epistemic community tend to have *some* degree of normative expectation of
speaker-credibility in testimonial exchanges. Moreover, consider some standard
claims about speakers in paradigm cases of testimonial injustice (helpfully summarized by Ishani Maitra):

- "Testimonial injustice undermines a capacity of the speaker's that is essential
  to human value, namely, the capacity to impart knowledge" (Maitra 2010, 3;
  cf. Fricker 2007, 44).
- "Given this connection between imparting knowledge and human value, the
  speaker who is thus undermined is also symbolically degraded qua human
  being" (Maitra 2010, 3).
- "Further, testimonial injustice involves treating a speaker as a mere source of
  information, rather than as a subject of knowledge, and as such, (epistemically) objectifies the speaker in a morally problematic manner" (Maitra 2010,
  3; cf. McGlynn 2021).[24]

In my view, a natural way of understanding "undermining a capacity essential to
human value," "degrading the person qua human being in the process," and
"treating them as a mere source of information" is in terms of a deficiency of
normative expectation, and not merely a lack of *predictive* expectation that a
speaker will meet certain epistemic criteria in performing their intellectual acts.
Perhaps one way to diminish someone's epistemic agency is by not *predictively*
expecting that they will meet certain epistemic criteria in performing their
intellectual acts. But, to my mind, a deeper way of diminishing someone's
epistemic agency—one that seems more commensurate with the problem of
testimonial injustice—is by not even according them the sort of respect inherent
in *normatively* expecting them to meet certain epistemic criteria in performing
their intellectual acts. To make this vivid, consider switching the normative
expectations we have concerning the credibility of a child reporting on her day
at school with the kind we have of a typical news reporter: it seems clear this would

---

[24] See fn15 for alternatives to the "objectification" paradigm.

128   EPISTEMIC BLAME

be deeply demeaning to the reporter. Normative expectations imply judgments of competence and ability, and that is what seems lacking in paradigm cases of testimonial injustice.

The interesting point for present purposes is that, taking all of this on board, we can deploy the relationship-based account of epistemic blame to make sense of testimonial injustice in a richer way than simply understanding it as a kind of bad thinking. Return to MR RIPLEY*. On the picture being developed here, were Marge* to epistemically blame Herbert*, her response might consist in judging that he impairs the GER in at least *two* ways, and a modification to (or reaffirmation of) her intentions and attitudes toward Herbert* in a negatively valanced type of way made fitting by that judgment. First, her response might consist in the sorts of modifications we have discussed at length in Chapter 3—the kind made fitting by standard judgments of culpable irrationality, or bad thinking more generally. But second, she might also reaffirm her intention not to assume that Herbert* will normatively expect of her that she will meet epistemic criteria Y for some range of intellectual acts. She might modify or reaffirm her (un)willingness to enter into other kinds of (epistemic) relations with Herbert* as a result. And all of that seems entirely appropriate.

The responses at issue in this account are not moral blame responses. They are distinctively epistemic insofar as the judgment and corresponding attitude adjustments are distinctively epistemic. They are oriented toward epistemic agency in distinctive ways. Despite not being moral responses, they nevertheless have a kind of significance—they are weightier than mere epistemic grading, for example—in that they consist in modifications to a *relationship* that is central to human cooperation. They amount to ways of holding perpetrators of testimonial injustice to normative expectations.

Before continuing, let's take stock and summarize the argument I am proposing here:

Argument from Deficient Expectations

i.   People can be appropriate targets of epistemic blame when, without good reason, or an excuse, they fail to expect of others that they will meet certain epistemic criteria when they engage in intellectual acts.

ii.   According a knower a credibility deficit as a result of prejudicial stereotyping can be a way of failing to expect of them that they will meet certain epistemic criteria when they engage in intellectual acts.

iii.   (One kind of) testimonial injustice just is a kind of credibility deficit as a result of prejudicial stereotyping.

iv.   Thus, perpetrators of (this kind of) testimonial injustice can be appropriate targets of epistemic blame, and in a way that goes beyond blame for bad thinking.

One might object that there is a foundational or conceptual problem with thinking about how to appropriately respond to perpetrators of testimonial injustice by appealing to an epistemic as opposed to moral response. Perhaps because testimonial injustice is often attended by significant practical and moral, as well as epistemic harms, intuitions about not letting perpetrators off the hook can only be accounted for by appeal to moral blame. In response, recall that I do not claim that perpetrators of testimonial injustice cannot be appropriate targets of moral blame. I find it plausible that they often are. What I have aimed to do so far, rather, is open up conceptual space for the idea that they can also be epistemically blameworthy, and in a way that is importantly different from standard cases of bad thinking, bad inquiry, and bad assertion.

5.3.2 Contaminated Evidence Cases

I said earlier that this proposal can help us make sense of cases of testimonial injustice that do not involve culpable irrationality, and can also be put to work to illuminate a wide variety of epistemic harms. I will now explain what I have mind, starting in this section with the first point.

Sandy Goldberg has recently argued that there can be no "distinctly epistemic answer" to the following question: "suppose someone tells you something. Under what conditions do you owe it to her to accept what she's said?" (Goldberg 2022, 375). Goldberg is concerned with the conditions under which we ought to accept the say-so of another person (who is entitled to our attention); and he denies that a story can be told about these conditions which only relies on epistemic considerations. According to Goldberg, there is a fundamental "normative clash" between ethics and epistemology, in that there can be cases in which one does everything one *epistemically* ought to do in this regard, while violating ethical norms or norms of justice (in virtue of not giving a speaker what they are owed).

As it happens, I think the proposal I have just developed poses a challenge for Goldberg's claim that there is no epistemic answer to his question. It does so by entailing claims about the deficiency of epistemic expectations that can occur in cases of testimonial injustice. I will briefly outline some of Goldberg's key ideas, and then explain what I have in mind.

According to Goldberg, epistemic answers to the question of what a speaker is owed turn on claims about the epistemic condition of either the speaker, or a hearer, in a given conversational context. We might argue, roughly, for example, that if a speaker *speaks from knowledge* (or meets some other suitable epistemic condition), then they are owed acceptance. Goldberg convincingly argues that there are clear-cut false-positives to this proposal, which I will not rehearse here. Alternatively, focusing on the epistemic condition of the hearer, we might argue that, so long as the hearer's total evidence supports the proposition that the

130   EPISTEMIC BLAME

speaker speaks from knowledge (or meets some other suitable epistemic condition), then the hearer is owed acceptance. Goldberg argues that it generates both false-positives and false-negatives, the latter of which he regards as more important. I will focus on false-negatives here.

The central idea behind Goldberg's challenge to hearer-based epistemic answers to his question is the following. There are cases in which someone speaks from knowledge (or meets some other suitable epistemic condition), but the hearer's total evidence regarding that person's credibility *misleadingly* suggests that they are not to be believed. And so, in failing to accept the speaker's word, the hearer fails to give the speaker what they are owed—despite complying with evidential norms. According to Goldberg, we can *only* appeal to moral or other norms of justice to explain what is going wrong in such cases.

Goldberg calls these cases of "contaminated evidence," and compellingly shows how common they are.[25] Cases of contaminated evidence have been discussed at length by critical race theorists and feminist epistemologists for decades (Collins 2000; Davis 2016; Dotson 2011; Medina 2012a; Mills 1997, 2007, 2013; Tuana 2006). They are none other than the effects of systemic racism, misogyny, and other prejudices, on the epistemic environments of the socially privileged (Goldberg 2022, 388–9).[26] Goldberg—and the pioneering work he draws on—makes a compelling case for the possibility of contaminated evidence, as well as the consequences it can have for non-culpable compliance with narrowly evidential norms. So, I will not defend the possibility of contaminated evidence further. Instead, I will get to my main point: even if Goldberg's challenge from contaminated evidence goes through, this does not yet show there is no epistemic answer to the question of what a speaker is owed.

My basic idea is that, even in cases of contaminated evidence, it can nevertheless transpire that a hearer manifests a *deficiency of normative epistemic expectation* of the speaker, where this constitutes an epistemic answer to how speakers are wronged in such cases (one that is consistent with the idea that they are morally wronged). I have just argued at length that paradigm cases of testimonial injustice are attended by a deficiency of epistemic normative expectation. What I add here is that, whether or not such cases involve hearers whose credibility judgments are fitting responses to their total evidence is irrelevant. Testimonial injustice can involve a kind of epistemic wronging, even if the credibility judgment is evidentially well-supported. In effect, the proposal I've been developing provides resources beyond *evidential* considerations, for filling out an epistemic answer to Goldberg's question. Hearers can epistemically wrong speakers via credibility

---

[25] Fricker seems to regard the original *Mr Ripley* as a case of contaminated evidence.

[26] One important distinction to draw is between factors leading to the *acquisition* of corrupt, *misleading* evidence (e.g. Mills 2007), and factors leading to the conspicuous *absence* of *non*-misleading evidence (e.g. Dotson 2011). I will not focus on this distinction here because in-depth discussion would take me too far afield.

judgments that impair the GER, not (only) by falling short of *others'* epistemic expectations, but through deficiencies in their own epistemic expectations. My claim that testimonial injustice has an epistemic dimension beyond bad thinking is a reflection of this idea.

You might agree that cases of contaminated evidence involve, in some sense, a "deficiency" of normative expectation, but balk at the claim that hearers in such cases are *blameworthy* for that lack of expectation. After all, hearers in cases of contaminated evidence do not fall afoul of narrowly evidential norms in disbelieving the speaker, so it seems they are not epistemically blameworthy in *that* regard. But if their total body of evidence is contaminated in this way, is it not equally plausible that they are blameless for any deficiency of normative expectation with regard to the speaker? Whatever epistemic expectations they have will no doubt have been deeply shaped, in part, by their evidential environment.

This challenge might even be developed into a kind of dilemma for my general account of epistemic blame for testimonial injustice. Either a case of testimonial injustice does not involve contaminated evidence, and so the hearer violates evidential norms in their credibility judgment—and so is epistemically blameworthy for *that* reason, as opposed to any complicated story about deficiency of normative expectation. Or, the case does involve contaminated evidence, and so the hearer does not violate evidential norms in their credibility judgment—and is therefore blameless, including for any deficiency of normative expectation. Either way, perhaps perpetrators of testimonial injustice can only be epistemically blameworthy to the extent that they manifest bad thinking in their credibility judgments.

Perhaps the most I can do with my framework is argue that, in cases of contaminated evidence, even if the hearer is not epistemically *blameworthy*, they nevertheless fail to give a speaker what they are *epistemically* owed, in the sense that they have a deficiency of normative epistemic expectation of the speaker. To my mind, this is still an "epistemic" account of what speakers are owed, one that Goldberg does not consider. More controversially, however, I want to float the following proposal.

The normative epistemic expectations we ought to have—and can perhaps even be (epistemically) blameworthy for *not* having—can diverge in important ways from our available evidence. Notice I have not made any claims about who would be within their rights to blame the hearers in contaminated evidence cases. One way to allay "internalist" worries about the appropriateness of (epistemic) blame in these cases is to grant that perhaps not just *any* other member of the epistemic community—say, another member of the hearer's privileged group—would be within their rights to blame the hearer. Perhaps the hearer is epistemically blameworthy in an attenuated sense, such that *members of the wronged group* would be within their rights to epistemically blame the hearer.

132 EPISTEMIC BLAME

It is important not to lose sight of what this entails on my view of the nature of epistemic blame. It means that, when a hearer disbelieves a member of the group who spoke from knowledge, members of the victimized group would be within their rights to judge that the hearer has impaired the GER, and to reaffirm their intention not to assume that the hearer will believe them when they speak from knowledge in the future. On the relationship-based account, epistemic blame can consist in this sort of epistemic relationship modification.

All of this speaks to an additional difference between narrowly evidential considerations and claims about normative expectations. To return to a recurring theme in this book, the latter are *interpersonal* in a way that narrowly evidential norms are not. The harms that can attend a failure of normative epistemic expectation have a different kind of structure and significance (for different people). This is (partly) why I find it plausible that a speaker could be appropriately epistemically blamed for falling short of them, despite complying with their available evidence.

This is significant because it may provide a way to resist Goldberg's conclusion that there is a fundamental normative clash between ethics and (all of) epistemology. As it happens, I do not have an interest in defending one view or another about normative clash. I have put this proposal forward simply in the service of providing one example of what hangs on my claim that perpetrators of testimonial injustice can be epistemically blameworthy.

5.4 Epistemic Relationships and Other Forms of Epistemic Harm

The discussion so far leads naturally to a more general insight: perhaps there is room here to deepen our understanding of a variety of epistemic harms with the resources of the relationship-based account of epistemic blame. That is to say, perhaps other forms of testimonial injustice, as well as different forms of epistemic harm altogether, can be illuminated through the lens of impairments to the GER. I want to take things a bit further and explore the idea that there is room to deepen our understanding of a *wide range* of epistemic harms with the resources of the relationship-based account of epistemic blame. More specifically, I want to examine whether other forms of testimonial injustice, as well as different forms of epistemic harm altogether, have a place on our list of things for which people can be appropriately epistemically blamed. Importantly, even if we don't reach a conclusive answer to this question, examining these epistemic harms through the lens of impairments to the GER is an interesting project in its own right.

I'll start with cases of testimonial injustice through credibility *excess* rather than deficit. I'll then move on to a discussion of what Nora Berenstain (2016) has recently called "epistemic exploitation," and also touch briefly on gaslighting.

5.4.1 Testimonial Injustice through Credibility Excess

Emmalon Davis (2016) argues—against Fricker's early position on this matter—that some forms of testimonial injustice involve an excess of credibility, not a deficit. She identifies cases of "typecasting," and treating members of marginalized groups as "tokens" or "spokespersons," as examples of testimonial injustice through credibility excess. Let's look at her argument in more detail.[27]

Start with the following two cases:

> DRYER SHEETS: A male shopper walks up to another shopper in a discount retailer and asks where he can find dryer sheets. "I don't know...I don't work here," the shopper responds. Somewhat baffled, the man replies, "I know you don't work here, but you're a woman!"
>
> MATH HELP: A group of American high-school students struggle to complete a difficult algebra question during their lunch period. After several failed attempts to solve the problem among themselves, the students decide to seek outside help. The students have heard that Asian-Americans are particularly good at math, so they ask an Asian-American student seated nearby for help with the problem.
>
> (Davis 2016, 487)

According to Davis, these cases illustrate what she calls "identity-prejudicial credibility excess" (PCE) (2016, 487). In a similar way to Fricker's cases of credibility deficit, the credibility of speakers here is being assessed on the basis of prejudicial stereotypes that are associated with the speakers' *social identity*. However, in these cases, rather than resulting in the speaker being perceived as *less* credible than they ought to be, the speaker is accorded an *excess* of credibility. As Davis puts it:

> In cases of PCE, hearers assume that features of their target's social identity—as indicated by a target's racialized, gendered, and so on, appearance—are reliable indicators of what sort of knowledge the target possesses. Because the underlying prejudicial stereotypes are epistemically unreliable, resulting credibility assessments are often unmerited. (2016, 487)

A standard form of PCE occurs when a person is "typecast," and regarded as possessing knowledge of topics that are stereotypically associated with their social group. As Uma Narayan observes, targets of typecasting are "often expected to be

---

[27] In what follows, I focus on her discussion of typecasting, partly for sake of space, but also because I think it provides a straightforward and clear way to get at Davis's central ideas.

134   EPISTEMIC BLAME

virtual encyclopedias of information" (Narayan 1997, 132). In other words, targets of PCE are perceived to be exceedingly knowledgeable, in some cases even experts. Partly for this reason, Davis argues that the distinctive harm involved in cases of PCE is not adequately captured through Fricker's objectification model of epistemic harm (Fricker 2007, 132–3; McGlynn 2020, 2021). It is implausible that speakers in these cases are treated as *mere* sources of information. After all, in these cases of testimonial injustice, speakers are harmed via an overly inflated judgment of epistemic competence on behalf of the hearer. Davis suggests that a better model for understanding the nature of the harm attending this form of testimonial injustice is Gaile Pohlhaus *epistemic othering* model (Medina 2012b, 203–4; Pohlhaus 2014, 102–4).

I wish to remain neutral on whether the epistemic objectification model, or epistemic othering model of epistemic harm, is more suitable for capturing the distinctive harm of testimonial injustice through credibility excess. My concern here is the fact that, whatever the harm consists in exactly, it may seem unclear how to understand its relation to the form of epistemic relationship impairment I have so far been discussing. Taking Davis's work on board, one worry that comes into view is that my account of the connection between cases of testimonial injustice involving credibility deficit and impairments of the GER does not seem to apply to this important form of testimonial injustice. Cases of testimonial injustice involving credibility excess do not seem to involve an inappropriate *absence* or deficiency of the relevant normative expectations. So, what does this form of impairment to the GER consist in, exactly?[28]

While it does not seem right to say that perpetrators of testimonial injustice through credibility excess *lack* a normative expectation of credibility, there is a closely related way of impairing the GER which does seem plausible here— namely, impairing by normatively expecting *too much*. Interestingly, in Davis's own analysis of her cases, she is nearly explicit that this is a key feature of what's going on. First, a couple of points she makes regarding stereotyping generally are important to note. Cases of PCE involve what's known as "positive stereotyping," which might be one reason the idea that they are examples of injustice may seem at first somewhat puzzling. But as Davis notes,

---

[28]   To be clear, a central worry here is the following. If my analysis of one sort of testimonial injustice is completely inapt when it comes to other sorts, this may be a reason to doubt that it was an apt analysis of the first sort as well. Consider: surely the varieties of testimonial injustice have something important in common such that they all count as instances of *testimonial injustice*. It would seem to be a mark in favor of an account of what the harms of testimonial injustice(s) is/are if it can explain what's going on among these varieties in a unified, rather than piecemeal and ad hoc way. Conversely, the more piecemeal and ad hoc our analysis of the harms of varieties of testimonial injustice is, the less it has going for it. So, my aim is to show that we can provide such a unified analysis, not only of some important varieties of testimonial injustice, but also other related sorts of epistemic harms which have been discussed recently in the literature, using the framework of impairments of the GER.

BLAMEWORTHY BELIEF, ASSERTION, AND OTHER EPISTEMIC HARMS   135

> [p]ositive stereotyping is primarily *prescriptive* (suggesting how group members *ought* to act) rather than descriptive (suggesting how group members act) (Heilman 2001; Fiske and Stevens 1993). Thus, though prescriptive stereotyping need not be inherently disparaging, research suggests that such associations can negatively affect the attention received by members of stereotyped groups.
>
> (Davis 2016, 487, italics added)

Offering examples of ways that positively stereotyped individuals can be negatively affected as a result of the prescriptive nature of positive stereotyping, Davis cites a range of results from the empirical literature:

> [T]hey may be punished more harshly than nonstereotyped individual for not succeeding at stereotyped activities (Ho, Driscoll, and Loosbrock 1998); and their performances in stereotyped areas may be compromised due to increased anxiety about failure.
>
> (Baumeister, Hamilton, and Tice 1985; Cheryan and Bodenhausen 2000)

These examples concern positive stereotypes generally. I suggest that a connection between positive stereotyping and an (unfair or otherwise inappropriate) increase in normative expectation is already visible here. But what about cases of PCE? According to Davis:

> The harms stemming from this practice are abundant. First, tagging marginalized individuals as spokespersons perpetuates the myth that the members of nondominant social groups share one monolithic experience. Second, targets are placed under tremendous pressure to deliver on behalf of their entire constituency. Indeed, targets may experience anxiety, embarrassment, or even anger at having their social identity made into a public spectacle. Alternatively, the target may fear public shaming or ridicule if she does not possess (and transfer) the knowledge prejudicially attributed.   (Davis 2016, 492)

There is an even clearer connection here between the harms Davis claims attend cases of PCE and an (unfair or otherwise inappropriate) increase in normative expectations on behalf of hearers perpetrating this form of testimonial injustice. A particularly natural way of seeing the plausibility of Davis's claim that according someone a credibility excess can amount to a kind of injustice, is precisely through the *prescriptive* nature of stereotyping, and the connection it thereby has to an inappropriately inflated normative expectation of credibility. When Davis notes that "targets of PCE are perceived to be exceedingly knowledgeable—experts even" (488), she is not highlighting a descriptive attitude that hearers take toward targets of PCE, she is highlighting a prescriptive one.

136 EPISTEMIC BLAME

All of this lends support to my suggestion that, while cases of testimonial injustice via credibility excess do not involve the same sort of epistemic relationship impairment as cases involving credibility deficit, there is a natural way of understanding how they impair the GER nonetheless. They involve excessive normative expectation. The fact that testimonial injustice through credibility excess involves a different form of epistemic relationship impairment in comparison with testimonial injustice through credibility deficit is hardly surprising. We should expect these two varieties of testimonial injustice to impair our epistemic relations in different ways. It is an attractive feature of the present proposal that it can accommodate these differences in a natural and unified way.

It is also worth noting that, just as deficient normative expectations can impair human relationships more generally, so too can excessive ones. To my mind, this is even easier to see than the former point. Consider a variation on the father example from earlier, where this time the father normatively expects too much of his daughter's aspirations of having a successful career. It is not difficult to imagine this impairing their relationship in significant ways.

5.4.2 Epistemic Exploitation

Nora Berenstain's (2016) discussion of "epistemic exploitation" stands in a close relation to (overlaps with) the kind of testimonial injustice just discussed.[29] According to Berenstain, epistemic exploitation occurs when a member of a privileged group expects a member of a marginalized group to perform epistemic labor for them without compensation. Typically, this happens when a person in a privileged social position demands information or explanation regarding issues of social justice surrounding the very power dynamic at issue between their social group and the social group of the marginalized person. Paradigm examples of this include when a man asks a woman to explain to him why some action or attitude is sexist; or when a white person asks a person of color to explain to her why some action or attitude is racist. Here's a case from Berenstain:

> Suppose Amina, a Black woman, is out with a white male acquaintance, Ben, when a white woman approaches her, reaches out to touch her hair, and exclaims how soft it is. Amina tells the white woman not to touch her hair. The white woman, offended, says "I was just trying to give you a compliment," and leaves angrily. Ben then asks why Amina was "so rude" to the woman who was "just being nice." (Berenstain 2016, 576)

---

[29] Davis discusses "epistemic exploitation" in her work on testimonial injustice through credibility excess, and regards the latter as an essential component of the former.

Similar to Davis, Berenstain is concerned with developing an account of the nature of the distinctive epistemic harm that attends epistemic exploitation. Among numerous observations she makes, one interesting point concerns the "double bind" that epistemic exploitation puts its victims in. Amina can either engage in the coerced labor of explaining why the white woman's action was racist and justifying her response to it, or, by refusing to explain herself, she can risk being seen as confirming the misogynistic controlling image of the Angry Black Woman (2016, 576). As with my discussion of Davis, I will not get into the details of Berenstain's claims in this regard, though they are well worth exploring elsewhere. Instead, I will focus on the question of how this phenomenon fits within my framework of epistemic relationship impairment.

Perhaps unsurprisingly, there is ample room here to understand this phenomenon in terms of an improper *excess* of normative expectation—perhaps to an even greater degree than cases of testimonial injustice through credibility excess. My suggestion is that cases of epistemic exploitation constitute GER impairment in the form of the hearer manifesting normative epistemic expectations of the speaker that are again improperly demanding. But it's important to identify the precise way in which this excessive expectation manifests itself. After all, it may not be entirely clear whether, for example, simply by requesting information and explanation from someone, a hearer manifests an inappropriate excess of *epistemic* normative expectation of the speaker. Perhaps they do make an appropriate judgement about the speaker's epistemic competence, but simply have some (perhaps excessive) non-epistemic normative expectation that the speaker will provide them with information.

Importantly, this concern misses the mark, because it fails to address a central feature of how epistemic exploitation works. As both Berenstain and Davis explain, an *essential* feature of epistemic exploitation is the implicit assumption that the speaker, qua member of marginalized group, possesses an expertise on the matters they are being requested to explain. Epistemic exploitation does not merely consist in a member of a privileged social group asking a speaker to do uncompensated epistemic work. Rather, epistemic exploitation occurs when a member of a privileged group asks a speaker to do uncompensated epistemic work *because* they are a member of a marginalized group—one who, because of an identity prejudice in the hearer, is expected to possess an expertise on the relevant topic. Importantly, this is an expertise that they should not (both morally and epistemically speaking) be expected to have, not *simply* as members of the marginalized group, let alone as ordinary epistemic agents.

Thus, the key to seeing the role for excessive normative expectation in epistemic exploitation is focusing on the way that epistemic exploitation overlaps with testimonial injustice as credibility excess. The demands placed on the speaker are unreasonable (and the practice thereby epistemically unreliable) in part because they stem from the assumption that, simply as a member of marginalized

138 EPISTEMIC BLAME

group X, the speaker possesses an expertise on a topic that members of group X are stereotypically assumed to have. As above, the claim here is not that this is exclusively what the epistemic harm—let alone moral or other forms of harm—epistemic exploitation amounts to. It is rather a claim about the kind of epistemic relationship impairment that this phenomenon plausibly consists in, and which underlies at least part of the distinctive harm that attends it.

5.4.3 Gaslighting

There are surely other epistemic harms worth investigating in this context. For instance, an increasing amount of work examines *gaslighting*, both in its connection to epistemic injustice (Ivy 2017) and as a form of epistemic harm in its own right (Abramson 2014; Ivy 2019; Kirk-Giannini 2022). According to Ivy, gaslighting occurs when a speaker is accorded a credibility *deficit*, and this is accompanied by the additional act of trying (whether consciously, intentionally, or otherwise) to undermine the speaker's confidence in their own epistemic reliability. Insofar as gaslighting involves a credibility deficit, there may be room to understand gaslighting within the framework of epistemic relationship impairment, in this case in the form of a deficiency of appropriate epistemic expectation.

Recently, Kirk-Giannini (2022) has helpfully characterized the literature on gaslighting in terms of *intentionalist* versus *non-intentionalist* accounts. The key disagreement concerns whether gaslighting must be intentional. Abramson (2014), Spear (2023, 2020), and Stark (2019) are notable examples of intentionalists, while Ivy (2017) and Podosky (2021) are notable examples of non-intentionalists. Kirk-Giannini also points out that, partly in virtue of maintaining that gaslighting need not be intentional, non-intentionalists tend to constitutively connect gaslighting to epistemic injustice (in different ways) (Kirk-Gianni 2022, 752).

Kirk-Giannini's own proposal should be considered in this context, in that he identifies gaslighting simply with a characteristic *dilemma* faced by the victim: whether to reject the testimony of the gaslighter, or to doubt one's own basic epistemic competence in some domain. Kirk-Giannini characterizes his proposal as "purely epistemic," rejecting an essential connection with both intentional action and epistemic injustice (though he argues that the account helps *explain* the pervasive connection between gaslighting, epistemic injustice, and differentials in social power). He argues that the "dilemmatic account" is useful in its capacity to explain the characteristic harms of gaslighting, while also making it easier to identify real-world cases. It can be difficult to say whether prejudice or intention was at play in a given instance, so, by regarding such questions as inessential, the account may play a simplifying role.

What is relevant for present purposes is that if Kirk-Giannini is right, it may be unclear whether epistemic relationship impairment is a useful lens through which to examine gaslighting per se. After all, on his account, gaslighting would seem to

BLAMEWORTHY BELIEF, ASSERTION, AND OTHER EPISTEMIC HARMS   139

require neither a deficiency nor excess of normative epistemic expectation on behalf of the gaslighter. This is for the simple reason that it does not identify the defining mark of gaslighting in terms of features of the *gaslighter*. Still, as Kirk-Giannini acknowledges, there are likely many forms of gaslighting. So, it may be the case that, perhaps especially when prejudices and asymmetries of social power are involved, certain forms of gaslighting are bound up with epistemic relationship impairment in a way that could be useful to explore further.[30]

Our discussion has revealed two forms of epistemic relationship impairment in connection with at least four forms of epistemic harm. Our model extends naturally across cases by making room for impairments consisting in improperly expecting too little of an epistemic agent, and impairments consisting in excessive normative expectation. The result is a unified framework for understanding—at least in part—the nature of the epistemic harms that attend a wide variety of phenomena increasingly discussed in the social epistemology literature, as well as their connection to epistemic blame.[31] These epistemic harms are ways of impairing our epistemic relationships. Given the importance and growing focus on the role of these harms in our social and political lives—including, for example, Goldberg's work on what speakers are owed—the concept of epistemic relationships may have an important role to play in future social epistemology.

5.5 Conclusion

This completes my discussion of the relationship between epistemic blame, belief, assertion, inquiry, testimonial injustice, and other epistemic harms. The aim has been to sharpen our understanding of the scope of our epistemic blaming practices. I have done so in a way that vindicates some prominent ideas in contemporary epistemology. But I have also explored ways of expanding the status quo. My analysis of testimonial injustice as a kind of inverted epistemic relationship impairment—one involving a deficiency or excess of normative expectations—and my claim that this constitutes a kind of epistemic blameworthiness, is a fairly revisionary approach to epistemic blameworthiness. However, I have argued that it enables us to make sense of cases of testimonial injustice that do not involve irrational credibility judgments. I have also argued that epistemic relationships illuminate a wide range of epistemic harms in useful ways.

---

[30] There may also be room to develop an account of how epistemic relationship is involved in gaslighting by focusing on the causal impact on the speaker.

[31] I say "at least in part" because, as I hope is clear, I see my proposal as consistent with other views about the nature of these harms. I do not see my proposal as competing with Fricker's objectification model, or Pohlhaus othering model, for example. Epistemic relationship impairments through excessive or deficient normative expectation may amount to forms of epistemic objectification, or epistemic othering, or something else. My aim has simply been to argue that epistemic relationship impairment is an important dimension of these epistemic harms.

6

Standing

In addition to asking questions about who the appropriate *targets* of epistemic blame are, we can also ask questions about who the appropriate *epistemic blamers* are. This takes us directly into the growing literature on standing to blame.

According to many, not just anyone can justifiably blame anyone else, even if the target of blame is blameworthy. A prominent idea is that one needs to meet certain conditions on standing that make blame an appropriate thing for one to do. I mentioned the so-called "non-complicity" and "non-hypocrisy" conditions in Chapter 1. It would be helpful to have an understanding of how each of these conditions operates in the epistemic domain. I consider the complicity and non-hypocrisy conditions in section 6.6. My primary focus in this chapter is the so-called "business condition" on standing to blame, which raises especially interesting questions in the epistemic domain. According to the business condition, a person's standing to blame is constrained in some important sense by the extent to which the target of blame's wrongdoing is that person's *business*. I am interested in an apparent tension between the business condition on standing to blame and the fact that it is not always clear *whose* business a particular epistemic failing is, and why. The relationship-based account of epistemic blame is well positioned to make sense of this apparent tension. But careful attention to the issue is fruitful for a number of reasons. First, it provides a useful angle for exploring fundamental questions about what *entitles* us to the normative expectations that partially constitute our epistemic relationships. Second, it allows us to revisit in greater depth some questions that arose earlier surrounding epistemic blame's interaction with other normative domains.

6.1 Standing to Blame: The Business Condition

At its core, "standing" identifies a normative dimension of our blaming practices, one concerning features of the *blamer* as opposed to the blamed:

> It seems uncontroversial to think that when blame is properly wielded, not only is the wrongdoer deserving of blame, but the blamer also stands in the appropriate relations with the wrongdoer and the wrong done. We might say that in

Epistemic Blame: The Nature and Norms of Epistemic Relationships. Cameron Boult, Oxford University Press.
© Cameron Boult 2024. DOI: 10.1093/oso/9780192890580.003.0007

order to properly blame another, it is not enough that the blamed is blameworthy; the blamer must have the "standing" to blame the wrongdoer.

(McKiernan 2016, 145)

A number of standing conditions have been the focus of active discussion in recent years. According to a representative way of dividing up the terrain, we can distinguish between the following conditions:

- **The business condition**: appropriate blame excludes meddling in others' business.[1]

- **The warrant condition**: appropriate blame requires that one knows, or is otherwise sufficiently epistemically well-situated, vis-à-vis the question of the wrongdoer's blameworthiness.[2]

- **The non-complicity condition**: appropriate blame somehow excludes the blamer's involvement in, or responsibility for, the relevant wrongdoing.[3]

- **The non-hypocrisy condition**: appropriate blame somehow excludes the blamer's being guilty of "doing the same thing."[4]

Some authors see the terrain as more complex. For example, Coates and Tognazzini (2014) add a "moral fragility" condition, stating that, if it is the case that person A *would have* done the same thing as person B (under the relevant circumstances), then A lacks the standing to blame B for doing that thing.[5]

Even sticking with the list above, the idea of standing is somewhat controversial. Some are skeptical of standing, preferring to explain the appearance of a distinct normative phenomenon in terms of other conditions on appropriate blame (Bell 2013; Dover 2019; King 2019). Much of what I have to say in this chapter presupposes that it is worth engaging with questions about standing. Perhaps this is consistent with a variety of stances on whether the normativity of standing reduces to something else. The complete standing skeptic may not be convinced by everything I say about standing in what follows. But this need not impact the interest of my more general discussion of entitlements to expect, and the interaction of types of relationships. I happen to find standing a useful point of departure for getting into those larger issues.

There are times when it would seem presumptuous or meddling to blame someone you do not know for a wrongdoing that does not directly harm or affect

---

[1] See Seim (2019), Radzik (2011, 2012), and King (2020).

[2] See Friedman (2013), Coates (2016), Kelp (2020), and Todd (2019).

[3] See Coates and Tognazzini (2014), Engen (2020), Cornell and Sepinwall (2020), and Cohen (2006).

[4] See Fritz and Miller (2018, 2019), Piovarchy (2020, 2023), Lippert-Rasmussen (2020), Tierney (2021), and Rossi (2018, 2020).

[5] See also Piovarchy (2023) for discussion of "subjunctive wrongdoing."

142 EPISTEMIC BLAME

you, or others close to you. I am at a party and I see a man I have never met making belittling comments to his partner. According to Angela Smith, "Since I do not know this person, or his wife, an explicit reproach on my part would be presumptuous and meddling, even if critical attitudes toward him are perfectly warranted" (Smith 2007, 478). Whether it is appropriate for me to express blame toward someone else seems to depend in part on whether their wrongdoing is my business. It seems to depend on whether, or to what extent, their wrongdoing affects me or others close to me.[6] In my view, the question of whether someone's wrongdoing is my business does not merely constrain the appropriateness of *expressing* blame. It can also constrain the mere adoption of a blaming-attitude or blame-response more broadly. As Smith puts it, "While we may not need any special authority to morally disapprove of another person on the basis of her objectionable attitudes or behavior, it seems that specific sorts of anger, resentment, and disappointment are open only to those directly wronged by the person in question" (2007, 479).

There is some debate about whether the business condition really is a condition on standing to *blame*, as opposed to a condition on the expression of blame, or anything blame-related at all. In recent work, Patrick Todd (2017) has argued that the business condition is *not* a condition on standing to blame, but rather that it is a condition on standing to express blame (publicly) (cf. Bell 2013).[7] I have three

---

[6] Here I identify the question of whether another person's wrongdoing is your business as being a matter of whether their wrongdoing has "affected you, or others close to you." This is a somewhat vague analysis. Unfortunately, precisely what it takes for one person's wrongdoing to count as another person's "business" has not been spelled out very clearly in the literature. For example, in a paper-length critique of standing conditions, Macalester Bell simply analyzes the notion of "business" as follows: "Y's wrongdoing is X's business. That is, X has an *identifiable stake* in Y's wrongdoing. Let's call this the Business Condition" (Bell 2013, 264). Coates and Tognazzini understand business in terms of an *impact* on the blamer's life. For example, discussing a case meant to illicit intuitions about the business condition, they invite the reader to compare themselves with a wrongdoer's *parents* in the following way: "Because of their close relationship, Jennifer's failure has a significant impact on her parents' lives; she has (perhaps) wasted thousands of dollars of their money. By contrast, her failure has little or no impact on our lives" (2013b, 21). Todd appears to leave the notion of "business" unanalyzed, but does imply that it has something to do with the "nature of the relationships involved" and "severity of the wrongdoing" (2017, 3). He also claims that intuitions about this notion can most easily be solicited by thinking about the "context of intimate relationships (e.g. between parents and children, and romantic partners)" (2017, 2). In her defense of something akin to the business condition, Angela Smith doesn't use the term "business," but she links the closely related idea of *meddlesomeness* to considerations about whether one *knows* the wrongdoer: "If I am not a stranger, but close friends with one or both of these people, by contrast, I may have legitimate standing to express criticism in such a case" (2007, 478). As we can see in the quote above, she does link meddlesomeness to the question of whether the blamer was "directly wronged" by the wrongdoer: "it seems that specific sorts of anger, resentment, and disappointment are open only to those directly wronged by the person in question" (2007, 479). But it may be a mistake to think of this as substantively different from an analysis that focuses primarily on the notion of a relationship. In this chapter, I take the notions of *direct harm, having a stake*, and *standing in the right relation* as an interlinked cluster of ideas which all get at the same basic concept of something being one's "business." For the purposes of this chapter, a more precise analysis of the concept is unnecessary.

[7] We can also ask whether the business condition is about a blamer's standing with "morality itself" so to speak (standing with the rules of morality), or rather with some individual or set of individuals,

things to say in response to Todd. First, the business condition is considerably more plausible if we take it as regulating the strength or kind of blame that is appropriate in a particular case, as opposed to functioning like an on-off switch. On the strength or kind-regulating model, the question of whether someone's wrongdoing is your business is a matter of degree, and the strength or kind of blame that may be appropriate covaries in certain ways with the extent to which their wrongdoing is your business (along with other conditions). On the on-off switch model, either someone's wrongdoing is your business or it is not, and the question of whether it would be appropriate to blame them is a "yes" or "no" question, as opposed to one of degree. My point is that the former model is more plausible.[8]

Second, the business condition gains further plausibility if we emphasize an additional distinction beyond that of *expressions* of blame and blame itself. This is the by-now familiar distinction between blame and *negative evaluation* (including judgments of blameworthiness). While it is entirely plausible that we can appropriately negatively evaluate others for wrongdoings that are not our business, it is much less clear whether, or to what degree, *blame*-responses are appropriate responses to those doings. This is because, as is also by now familiar, blamers are *engaged* by their negative evaluations in a way that makes it less obvious that blame is an appropriate response to a wrongdoing that is not the blamer's business. To put this in the language of normative expectation, there may be important limits on the ways we can rightly *hold someone to a normative expectation* for doing something that is not our business—as we will see in discussing the epistemic case, this has to do with questions about when we are *entitled* to normatively expect things of others.

Finally, according to a number of different ways of understanding the nature of blame—including approaches ranging from the work of Strawson and Wallace to my preferred Scanlonian view—there are fairly natural explanations of why we should (predictively) *expect* there to be a business condition on standing to blame (and not just to express blame). I'll return to this point below.[9]

6.2 The Business Condition and Epistemology

The business condition raises an important question about epistemic blame, given that epistemic blame is a response directed toward someone for an *epistemic*

---

when specifying what is inappropriate about their blame. Another question, not discussed by Todd, is whether what's flawed about meddlesome blame is *prudential* as opposed to *moral* in nature (Seim 2019). For the purposes of this chapter, these considerations should not matter.

[8] A different, but related strategy could be to think of the business condition in terms of pro tanto reasons. If someone's wrongdoing is not your business, this gives you a pro tanto reason to refrain from blaming—one that can be overridden by other considerations. See Coates (2020) for this formulation of the condition.

[9] See Radzik (2011; 2012) and Seim (2019) for other defenses of the business condition.

144 EPISTEMIC BLAME

failing. How can an epistemic failing be the business of anyone other than the person who epistemically failed? Of course, I think the idea of an epistemic relationship provides a very natural framework for understanding how one person's epistemic failing can be another's business—and I will elaborate on this in a moment. But it is worth pausing to highlight the fact that the way cases have typically been presented in the literature often leaves wide open the question of whose business the epistemic failing would be, and *why*. Discussions of epistemic blame often involve highly abstract descriptions of cases in which someone is guilty of an epistemic failing, and it is said that "we" may blame them for it. Consider Brown, using the somewhat artificial example of Maud the clairvoyant as a paradigm target of epistemic blame:

> For instance, when we blame Maud for dogmatically believing against the evidence that the President is in New York, the frustrated desire that she not believe badly leads to negative feelings such as our anger with her.   (2020a, 11)

And recall a quote from earlier, where, in the context of discussing the connection between epistemic blame and doxastic control, Connor McHugh says:

> We blame and even resent people, when, for example, they form foolish or hasty beliefs on matters of importance, and when they fail to believe what they should. [. . .] [W]e often claim that people should not hold or should give up certain beliefs because they are unsupported by evidence; we blame people who hold such beliefs.   (2012, 66)

In his book-length study of epistemic responsibility, Rik Peels says:

> It seems that we also hold each other responsible for our beliefs in more mundane situations. The following sentences can plausibly be interpreted as evidencing this: "Laurence had no right to think that I lied to him," "Julia shouldn't have believed that demagogue so readily," and "Henry ought to believe that he will pass the exams." We can also think of such expressions as "The prime minister should have known about the fraud" and "You shouldn't have known about the surprise party," for statements like these can be understood as saying that someone should (not) have held certain true beliefs about some matter.
>
> (2016, 3)

Peels uses the language of "holding responsible." But it is clear from the rest of his book that he takes this to imply the appropriateness of *blame* (under certain conditions). Importantly, except perhaps for the first example, Peels's examples leave out any details that would allow us to determine who exactly might have the standing to blame, and why. The assumption seems to be that someone *could* have the standing to blame these people under certain conditions. And perhaps that is true enough. But it is interesting to dig deeper and get a better sense of the extent to which this can be the case, and what makes it so.[10]

Of course, some epistemic failings might seem in an obvious sense to be the business of certain individuals. For example, as I mentioned at the beginning of this book, sometimes the epistemic failings of one person lead to the practical harm of another. Stephen is applying for a job. Terri, the person interviewing him, happens to have biased beliefs about the work ethic of members of the marginalized social group that Stephen identifies with. Stephen doesn't get the job. If he somehow learns that the reason he didn't get the job was largely because Terri formed unjustified beliefs about his work ethic, Stephen might blame Terri for her epistemic failing, and it seems he would meet the business condition in doing so.

Cases of someone's epistemic failure leading to a practical harm—a harm done either to yourself or someone close to you—are common. But two closely related points need emphasizing. First, it is not clear that the features of the case that make it seem like Terri's unjustified beliefs are Stephen's *business*, are specifically epistemic features of the case. Second, the tension I am interested in is that between the business condition, and the idea that there are times when it would be appropriate for one person to epistemically blame another and at least one of two things is true: either (i) no practical harm has been done; or (ii) the practical harm is not itself what licenses the blame response, or is not the only feature of the case that makes a blame response fitting. These are the sorts of cases that proponents of epistemic blame—including myself—argue we need a distinct kind of blame to accommodate. We can, and should, say more about the seeming tension between the business condition and epistemic blame than simply pointing out that epistemic failings can lead to practical harms.

6.3 More Motivation for the Relationship-Based Account

The above considerations provide further reason to think that some accounts of moral blame will be better than others as models upon which to build an account of epistemic blame. Recall that what is arguably the most prominent approach to moral blame—the emotion-based account—understands blame in terms of negative emotional responses, such as indignation, resentment, and guilt (in the case of self-blame). These are particularly heated kinds of response that we can have to wrongdoings, and, as I have discussed, they seem to be heated in a way that is uniquely fitting to wrongdoings that *directly harm or wrong* either ourselves, or others (Chapter 1, section 1.6.2; Chapter 2, section 2.4). To revisit this point, and to make it vivid for present purposes, here again is R.J. Wallace:

---

[10] These are just three, in my view fairly representative, quotes from the literature.

146   EPISTEMIC BLAME

> To resent someone is to feel not merely that they have acted wrongly, but that they have wronged us in particular, violating the norms that constitute relations of mutual regard. Likewise, we are prone to guilt when we take it that we have wronged someone else in our dealings with them. Even indignation, which is available to us when we are not ourselves directly party to an interaction that violates the relationship-constituting norms of morality, has an implicitly relational structure. To feel indignation is to be exercised on behalf of another person, on account of a wrong that has been visited on that person in particular.
>
> (2011, 369)

The idea that there is a tension between the business condition and epistemic blame is, it turns out, another way of putting a point made earlier in this book: namely, that epistemic failings often do not seem to function as directly personal harms. It simply seems quite implausible to think of many paradigmatic sorts of epistemic failings as the sort of thing that directly harm others—for example in the way that breaking a promise, or stealing someone's bike can directly harm them.[11] And this provides yet another way of supporting the conclusion that we should *not* understand the nature of epistemic blame on the model of negative emotional responses. This is significant in its own right, since, as we saw in Chapter 2, a wide range of epistemologists seem to assume such an account in their discussions of epistemic blame. But it is also important to keep in mind the additional observation—also made in Chapters 1 and 2—that, even if not functioning as direct personal harms, epistemic failings do nevertheless have a characteristic interpersonal significance. It is this feature of epistemic failings that is key to understanding, and explaining away, the apparent tension between the business condition and epistemic blame.[12]

It will come as no surprise that I think the relationship-based approach is ideally suited to explaining away the apparent tension between the business condition and epistemic blame. The way I have proposed capturing the idea that epistemic failings are *interpersonal*, and thus that they can be the business of others—even if not functioning as directly personal harms—is in terms of the

---

[11] Again, I remain open to the possibility that some epistemic failings can be direct personal harms—epistemic injustice and other forms of epistemic harm may be a case in point. I discussed my take on the relationship between these things and epistemic blame in detail in Chapter 5.

[12] Although I presented serious worries for Jessica Brown's (2020a) conative approach to epistemic blame in Chapter 2, section 7, it is worth noting that there seems to be no in principle reason why her account cannot fit with the observation that epistemic failings do not function as direct personal harms. Recall, according to Brown, epistemic blame is the manifestation of dispositions such as reproach, rebuke, and pointed requests for reasons, out of the frustration of one's desire that someone not have violated an epistemic norm. Epistemic blame, understood as such, seems consistent with the idea that epistemic blame is a response to wrongdoings that may lack the kind of direct personal significance characteristic of violations of relationship-specific norms (the opposite sort of thing that Wallace just explained resentment and indignation are fitting responses to). In my view, this is a mark in Brown's favor.

idea that they impair our epistemic relationships with one another. As I have argued at length, our epistemic relationships consist in intentions, expectations, and attitudes oriented toward one another's epistemic agency in distinctive ways. A natural idea is to understand what it is for someone's epistemic failing to count as another person's business in terms of the idea that it falls short of the normative ideal of this relationship.

Return again to THE OFFICE from the Introduction, and discussed in detail in Chapter 3. We have seen that when Dwight reveals his conspiracy belief, he falls short of a normative expectation of Jim's. To that extent, I am proposing, he does something that is Jim's business. Of course, it is Jim's business in a fairly thin or impersonal sense of the term. It is not Jim's business in the same way as when Dwight steals one of Jim's clients, for example. But this is as it should be. Again, many paradigmatic epistemic failings do not function as directly personal harms.

One reason the Dwight example is useful, in my view, is that it illustrates how, even in very mundane cases, one person's epistemic conduct can be the business of another. But it remains plausible that different types of epistemic failing, in different contexts, will correspond to richer ways of falling short of various members of the epistemic community's normative expectations. This may correspond nicely with different strengths of epistemic blame that can be appropriate across individuals and circumstances, as well as ways epistemic blame can interact with other kinds of blame.

For now, note that while this basic idea may sound suggestive and perhaps even promising, we of course need to tread carefully. For a start, notice that in order for Dwight's epistemic failing to be something it seems appropriate for Jim to epistemically blame him for, it is not enough that Dwight falls short of any old epistemic expectations that Jim has of Dwight. After all, people may irrationally expect anything they wish of anyone else. Crucially, Jim's expectations had better be ones he has legitimate claim to, or is in other words *entitled* to. If the relationship-based account has any hope of addressing the seeming tension between the business condition and epistemic blame, we need an account of what *entitles* us to have the normative expectations that partly constitute our epistemic relationships. I turn now to take up this project, and then address a couple of other worries we might have about my proposal.

6.4 Entitlements to Expect: The General Epistemic Relationship

First, a word on how I understand the project at hand. One might think it is synonymous with the project of explaining how *epistemic normativity* itself gets a "grip" on us, so to speak. Pretty much everyone agrees that our intellectual conduct can be evaluated by epistemic standards. But there is widespread

148 EPISTEMIC BLAME

disagreement about how to understand the normative status of those standards. We touched on this in Chapter 1, when discussing the "authority" of epistemic normativity (section 1.4). Those who take epistemic standards to have a special normative force, or grip on us, need a story about what it is in virtue of which they have that force or grip. To put it one way, they need an answer to the question, "why comply with epistemic standards?" Call this the project of *grounding* epistemic normativity.

This is obviously a big project. My point here is that my current task, while perhaps related, is not synonymous with this project. The reason for this is fairly straightforward. Even if we had an account of what grounds epistemic normativity, we would not thereby have an answer to the question of what entitles us to epistemic expectations. An account of what grounds epistemic normativity explains why you ought to comply with epistemic standards. Such an account need not yet explain why *other people* are entitled to expect anything from you, including whether you comply with those standards.[13] Of course, an account of what grounds epistemic normativity might be useful to have on hand when developing an account of entitlements to epistemically expect. But since the grounding project is daunting in its own right, my strategy is to avoid getting into it altogether. I will leave it an open question how my more direct approach to entitlements to epistemically expect interacts with the grounding project.

There is considerable support in both ethics and epistemology for the idea that epistemic expectations, in some form—including in the very general way proposed in my account of epistemic blame—are legitimate things for people to have of one another. The literature on culpable ignorance and moral responsibility is one place where support for this idea can be found.[14] The literature on normative defeaters to knowledge and justified belief is another very different place where support can be found.[15] Sandy Goldberg's recent work on normative expectations is perhaps most clearly aligned with my preferred approach here, so I will rely on some of his ideas in what follows.[16]

Goldberg (2017, 2018) has argued at length in defense of the idea that people are entitled to have epistemic expectations of one another, sometimes in virtue of certain social practices—such as professional, or institutional ones—but also simply in virtue of the fact that we are members of an epistemic community.

---

[13] Of course, on some conceptions of the "grounding project," such an explanation might come for free. It depends on how you approach the grounding project. See Chrisman (2022), Chapter 7 for helpful discussion of social and non-social approaches, which strike me as the most likely candidates.

[14] See Moody-Adams (1994, 291), Rosen (2003, 79), and FitzPatrick (2008, 603, 612).

[15] See Pollock (1986, 192), Meeker (2004, 162–3), Senor (2007, 207), Record (2013, 3, 8), and Miller and Record (2013, 122, 124).

[16] Goldberg himself points out that "there would appear to be some agreement among ethicists and epistemologists who think about related matters, to the effect that people are entitled to certain epistemic expectations regarding others" (Goldberg 2017, 5). He provides a helpful list of numerous authors in this regard, including those just mentioned, but also adds Montmarquet (1992, 336–7) and (1999, 845).

As part of his argument, Goldberg deploys the notion of a "practice generated entitlement." Many of our social practices involve mutual expectations in such a way that an absence of entitlements to those expectations would undermine the practice itself. According to Goldberg, if such a practice is *legitimate*, then participants are entitled to those expectations. For clarity, I will break practice generated entitlements down into two components:[17]

> **Enabling condition**: the absence of an entitlement to the expectation X amongst participants of practice Y would undermine practice Y.
>
> **Legitimacy condition**: practice Y is a legitimate practice.

When both of these conditions are met by a given expectation, participants to a practice are *entitled* to have that expectation. The basic idea is that we are entitled to expect in ways that are necessary for whatever legitimate practices we are engaged in.

Perhaps the clearest examples of what Goldberg has in mind involve social practices that structure our professional relationships, such as the doctor-patient relationship. That one's family doctor is knowledgeable about treatment protocols for familiar conditions is plausibly an expectation one is entitled to have of one's family doctor. How come? According to Goldberg, to call into question such an entitlement would go a long way toward calling into question the very practice of relying on doctors. Other things being equal, if you are not entitled to expect your family doctor to be reasonably informed about how to keep you healthy, it is far from clear why you would rely on your family doctor to keep you healthy. In other words, this expectation appears to meet the *enabling* condition. Moreover, other things being equal, our practice of relying on doctors to keep us healthy appears to be legitimate. It is just one example among many of the division of labor and expertise that benefits human communities in innumerable ways. If the practice is legitimate, then these expectations meet the *legitimacy* condition. If they meet both conditions, then we are entitled to these expectations.

Although this example involves an expectation that is epistemic in its contents (medical knowledge), it is just one instance of a much more general phenomenon. There are many practice-based entitlements beyond the domain of epistemology—for example, it seems we are entitled to expect that others drive on the correct side of the road, and refrain from mindlessly scrolling their phone while walking in public.

How should we understand entitlements to expect that are not grounded in professional relationships? Here Goldberg points out something I have already assumed—namely, that we have a practice of relying on one another's say-so in a

---

[17] Goldberg does not break things down in this way. I introduce these terms because I find them helpful for illustrating the basic structure of a practice generated entitlement to expect.

150 EPISTEMIC BLAME

pervasive way for purposes of information-exchange and co-ordination. Call this the practice of mutual epistemic interdependence. Goldberg observes that engaging in the practice of mutual epistemic interdependence is *practically rational* for the parties involved. This is hard to deny. Living a life without the high level of epistemic dependence we have on one another would be incredibly cumbersome and even dangerous. To be clear, the point is not that it is practically rational for members of the epistemic community to rely on one another's say-so on just any given matter, and under any circumstances. Goldberg's focus is the more constrained practice of epistemically relying on others—epistemically trusting their word, for example—within contextually determined domains of propositions, and only when no defeaters are present. The big picture aim is to derive certain entitlements to epistemically expect from the practical rationality of this practice.[18]

The practice of relying on the word of others seems to imply that we are entitled to have epistemic expectations of those upon whom we rely. In relying on the word of Bill about where the nearest gas station is, I implicitly reveal that I take myself to be entitled to expect that, other things being equal, Bill's word on the nearest gas station is worth heeding, and by extension, that Bill's basic intellectual conduct meets certain standards—including a standard imploring Bill to refrain from asserting where the nearest gas station is, if he does not know where it is.[19] Why else would I bother asking Bill where the nearest gas station is? It seems that a wholesale calling into question of one's entitlements to epistemically expect of other members of the epistemic community would essentially amount to calling into question the very practice of mutual epistemic interdependence. That is to

---

[18] One might worry that connecting my approach to epistemic blame with Goldberg's approach to explaining entitlements to epistemically expect undermines my ambitions of arguing that the relationship-based account meets FITTINGNESS. That is to say, one might worry that it undermines my view that epistemic blame (qua epistemic relationship modification) is something that can be appropriately done independently of practical considerations. After all, Goldberg appears to be arguing that our entitlements to the very expectations at the heart of my account rest on their role in a practice that it is *practically rational* for us to engage in. The reason this is *not* at odds with my ambitions is that it is simply an instance of the "genealogical sense" in which our epistemic concepts and practices can be dependent on practical considerations. Recall, in Chapter 4, section 2, I said: even if human beings evolved to be the kind of creatures who have a standing intention to epistemically trust other members of the epistemic community—say, because it helped us get around in the world—this does not entail that practical considerations must play a role in every appropriate instance of someone modifying their standing intention to epistemically trust the word of another. Again, there is real sense—what I have called the "target-based" sense (Chapter 1, section 1.5.2)—in which we (at least sometimes) make modifications to these epistemically oriented intentions independently of the practical factors that causally influenced us to be the sorts of beings who have such standing intentions.

[19] Bear in mind that I am not committing myself to a view about what these epistemic standards are. This is reflected in my use of a variable "Y" in spelling out some examples of the intentions and expectations constitutive of the normative ideal of the GER. Filling the details out is beyond the scope of this chapter. One important, and likely complex, question is how practical stakes may have an impact on exactly which epistemic criteria we are entitled to expect others to meet. For example, might we be entitled to expect more as the stakes go up? This strikes me as plausible, but I will not pursue the matter here. See Chapter 1, section 1.6.2 for my discussion of the relevance of pragmatic encroachment for my project.

say, our epistemic expectations of one another appear to meet the *enabling* condition vis-à-vis our general practice of epistemic interdependence. Moreover, since it is practically rational for the participants involved (arguably indispensable for finite creatures such as ourselves), and so long as the practice is free of any other objectionable features, the practice of epistemic interdependence would seem to be legitimate. If so, these expectations also meet the legitimacy condition. If they meet both the enabling and legitimacy conditions, then we are entitled to these epistemic expectations (Goldberg 2017, 18–19).

There is of course more to say about the very idea of a practice generated entitlement, and various assumptions at play in this argument for the claim that members of an epistemic community have an entitlement to expect of one another that they will meet certain epistemic criteria in conducting their intellectual lives. For example, Brown (2020b) has recently challenged Goldberg's argument and claimed that the fact that it is practically rational for someone to be engaged in any given practice at most grounds certain *predictive* expectations regarding that practice, not normative expectations. This is an important concern, so let's pause to consider the details.

According to Brown, it can be practically rational to have a practice of relying on Kant's daily walk in coming to know what time it is—perhaps because Kant is extremely reliable in taking his walk at a certain time of day (Brown 2020b, 3610). But this of course does not mean you are entitled to *normatively* expect Kant to walk at the same time every day. If Kant one day decides he doesn't want to walk at this particular time, that is up to him. At most, insofar as you really are practically rational in relying on Kant in this way (again, say, because he is highly reliable in taking his walks at the same time each day), this corresponds with an entitlement to *predictively* expect that he will continue to walk at the same time every day.

This may be a worry for Goldberg, and myself, because what we want to explain is why we have entitlements to *normatively* expect one another to meet epistemic criteria in the basic running of our intellectual lives. Without such an explanation, I cannot account for the idea that we are entitled to epistemically blame one another under certain conditions, let alone the more specific idea that some epistemic failings are indeed our *business*.

I agree with Brown that nobody has (or had) an entitlement to normatively expect Kant to walk at the same time every day, at least not just in virtue of the fact that it may have been practically rational to rely on Kant in this way. But I am not convinced that this poses a serious problem for Goldberg or myself. In my view, it simply forces us to emphasize an important point in the background of Goldberg's discussion of practice-based entitlements to expect. I have in mind a constraint that Goldberg—and I, following him—endorses regarding the notion of a "social practice." In addition to a practice being something that it is not irrational for participants to partake in, a practice in the sense Goldberg is interested in also needs to be "widely (mutually) acknowledged, with standards that are recognized and not challenged" (Goldberg 2018, 175). This is a very natural idea. I cannot simply decide on a certain daily routine and thereby normatively expect others to comply with whatever the daily routine involves. For a practice to generate entitlements to normatively expect things of people, that practice must itself be widely mutually acknowledged, and be governed by standards that are recognized and not challenged.

Brown's Kant example falls short of these latter criteria. It is not a legitimate social *practice* in the sense relevant to practice generated entitlements. And I think this is why it is intuitive that the person who relies on Kant for keeping time does not have an entitlement to normatively expect that Kant take his walk at the same time every day, even though it might be practically rational for the person to so rely on Kant.

Goldberg is aware of a pressing question here. At what point are these additional constraints met by a given practice? At what point does an evolved practice come to be widely mutually acknowledged, with standards that are recognized and not challenged? According to Goldberg:

> This is a hard question to answer, and in any particular case the boundaries may be ill-defined. Unlike the case involving professions and institutions, where both the practices and their standards may be made explicit and communicated, and where enforcement mechanisms are often in place, the sorts of practice that emerge e.g. in the course of a marriage (or a friendship, or a book group, or a gardening club, etc.) are often inexplicit and never communicated, and it can be unclear whether the practice is widely recognized enough, and its standards sufficiently acknowledged, to constitute a "legitimate" practice in my sense.
>
> (2018, 175)

But it would be a mistake to think that this poses a problem for anything we need be committed to in the present context. In particular, it does not pose a problem for getting a shared grip on when particular cases involve entitlements to normatively expect, and when they do not. This is because, as Goldberg himself rightly points out: "the legitimacy of any epistemic assessment involving standards sanctioned by the practice will be unclear to precisely the same degree that there are uncertainties regarding the legitimacy of the practice itself" (2018, 175).

All of this highlights an important difference between Brown's Kant example and our actual epistemic practices. However, it may leave untouched the core point of Brown's objection. As I understand it, the core point of her objection is that the possibility of our practice of epistemic interdependence seems at most to be underpinned by *predictive* and not *normative* expectations that we have concerning one another's intellectual conduct. That is to say, only predictive epistemic expectations meet the enabling condition on practice generated entitlements.

STANDING   153

Return to the doctor example. On closer inspection, it does seem possible for a patient to participate in the practice of relying on their doctor for medical treatment even if they are not entitled to *normatively* expect her to be reliable. Arguably all that is needed is that they are entitled to predictively expect her to be reliable. So, it seems, at most, predictive expectations meet the enabling condition. If so, then all one is *entitled* to vis-à-vis the practice of relying on their doctor is a predictive expectation about their medical competence (assuming the practice is legitimate).

I think this objection rests on a misunderstanding. Continuing with the doctor example, notice that a crucial element of the practice at hand is a *mutual understanding* between participants that the patient is entitled to the relevant predictive expectations concerning their doctor's medical competence. My doctor is not oblivious to the fact that I do, and am entitled to, predictively expect her to have an appropriate degree of professional medical competence. Her awareness of this fact is arguably an essential ingredient of the very practice we are engaged in. Interestingly, the fact that my doctor knows—or at any rate *ought* to know—that I have these predictive expectations (to which I am entitled), explains why I am also entitled to have a set of *normative* expectations concerning her medical competence. Consider: were my doctor to become aware that the predictive expectations (to which I am entitled) concerning her medical competence happen to be inaccurate—that is to say, were she to become aware that she *lacks* the relevant medical competence—and were she to continue treating me anyway, my doctor would be in gross violation of central norms of the medical profession. So, to the extent that she engages in the practice, my doctor had better ensure that the predictive expectations I am entitled to, concerning her medical competence, are accurate. But this is just another way of saying that I am also entitled to *normatively* expect my doctor to have the relevant medical competences.

While I am sure it is more controversial, I want to suggest that the same structural point can be made about our general practice of epistemic interdependence. The basic idea is as follows. Other members of the epistemic community should know that I have a set of predictive expectations concerning the general running of their intellectual lives (*in the restricted way noted above*).[20] If some member of the epistemic community knows that a subset of these expectations (to which I am entitled) are inaccurate—that is to say, if they know they lack the relevant epistemic competence—but carry on anyway (say, by continuing to make

---

[20] What is the force of this "should"? Is it epistemic, or somehow practice generated? I am not entirely sure, and I suspect it is both. But because I am remaining neutral on the questions about what grounds epistemic normativity—for example, I am not committing myself, as Goldberg does, to a view according to which epistemic normativity itself gets a grip on us in virtue of social expectations—I don't think this is worrying for me. If I was committed to the idea that epistemic normativity gets a grip on us in virtue of social expectations, then there might be something problematic about telling a story about why we are entitled to those expectations that included ineliminable reference to an epistemic "should" here.

154 EPISTEMIC BLAME

assertions on a certain subject matter), they would be flouting central norms of the practice of epistemic interdependence. So, to the extent that they engage in the practice, they ought to ensure that the relevant predictive expectations I am entitled to are accurate. But this is just another way of saying that I am also entitled to *normatively* expect them to have the relevant epistemic competence.

Notice that this idea explains why Brown's Kant example misses its target. Mutual recognition of one another's expectations just is part of what it means for something to be a genuine social practice. The fact that the Kant example lacks such mutual recognition entails that it is not an example of a social practice, and so not something Goldberg is committed to saying generates entitlements to normatively expect.

There is certainly more to say on this issue. But it is enough for present purposes to make the following conditional claim. If the foregoing story is plausible, or on the right track, then the relationship-based account of epistemic blame is poised to provide a general, detailed, and nuanced framework for making sense of the business condition in the epistemic domain. The normative expectations at issue in Goldberg's work just are examples of sorts of expectations that are—according to the relationship-based account of epistemic blame—partially constitutive of our epistemic relationships with one another. I will fill out this nuanced framework in more detail in the next section. First, I want to address a couple of other worries about the connection between the relationship-based framework and my approach to the business condition. Doing so will help further motivate the *need* for a nuanced framework for making sense of the business condition in the epistemic domain.

One might worry that the explanation I have provided of how the business condition can be met in the epistemic domain is somehow vacuous or trivial. That is to say, one might object that I have explained how the business condition can be met in terms of the idea of epistemic relationship impairment, but then maintain that my notion of an epistemic relationship simply amounts to "the thing that makes our epistemic failings one another's business." However, this would be a mistake. For a start, this is not what my notion of an epistemic relationship amounts to. Rather, I have given independent support for the claim that, whether we are aware of it or not, most of us have expectations, intentions, and attitudes toward one another, simply in virtue of being parties to a mutually recognized practice of informational exchange and co-ordination—intentions, expectations, and attitudes that are thus oriented toward our epistemic agency in distinctive ways. Given my understanding of relationships as sets of intentions, expectations, and attitudes, these intentions, expectations, and attitudes partially comprise what I have called the GER. More than that, drawing on Goldberg, I have just offered an account of why the epistemic expectations that partially comprise the normative ideal of the GER are ones we are entitled to have. So, there is a good deal of substantive theory underpinning my notion of an epistemic relationship—theory that can be articulated independently of any claims about the business condition.

There is, however, a second sense in which one might worry that the account I have offered is somehow vacuous or trivial. In particular, one might worry that an implication of my account is that *everyone's* epistemic conduct is one's business, and if everyone's epistemic conduct is one's business then this may seem to make the whole idea of a business condition on epistemic blame vacuous or incoherent. What's the point of condition on standing to blame that's always met?

In order to deal with this worry, I will emphasize two points. First, recall the degree-regulating conception of the business condition that I am working with. In section 6.1, I defended the business condition in a more general context by arguing that it is most plausibly understood as a constraint on the *degree* or *form* of blame it is fitting to direct toward someone, rather than a simple on-off switch determining a "yes" or "no" answer to the question of whether it is fitting to blame someone. The point here is that such a condition still has a "point," even if it is true that everyone (or at least a very large number of people) meets it. And this is because people can meet the degree-regulating form of the business condition in different ways. Indeed, on a second but closely related note, in my view the GER is plausibly a kind of baseline for epistemic blame, to which a more realistic discussion must add details that arise when accounting for the nuances of the other relations in which actual people stand with one another. For example, as I have noted a number of times already, in addition to the GER, people of course also stand in professional and institutional relationships, as well as a wide variety of personal relationships.[21] Each of these relationships is structured by practices which generate more specific kinds of epistemic expectations (Goldberg 2018, 160–5).

According to my account, modifications to intentions and expectations that partly comprise more specific kinds of relationships, but which are nevertheless oriented toward our epistemic agency, provide structure for thinking about how epistemic blame interacts with other normative domains. In the next section, I develop a detailed account of how this further structuring of epistemic blame arises.

6.5 Epistemic Expectations in Other Relationships

In order to prevent the relationship-based account from predicting that all epistemic failings are everyone's business in the same way, I have said that we need to consider further layers, or ways the GER can be impacted, depending on the epistemic expectations involved in other, more specific kinds of relationships we stand in with various individuals. I have suggested treating the GER as a kind

---

[21] I also used the example of a kind of personal relationship one can have with oneself in one's pursuit at becoming better at chess (see Chapter 5, section 5.3.2).

156   EPISTEMIC BLAME

of baseline upon which additional expectations, intentions, and attitudes can become legitimate, as a result of further practices that individuals may be involved in. We thus need to flesh out the properties that the epistemic expectations of these more specific relationships can have, in order to better understand how they interact with the GER.

First, a clarification. Henceforth, when I say that an intention or expectation "impacts" or "interacts with the GER," more carefully put I mean that it influences or changes how the GER shapes token blame responses that one party to the more specific relationship might direct toward an epistemic failing of another party to that relationship. For example, when A and B stand in no personal, professional, or other kind of practical relationship, then perhaps the GER alone shapes any token blame response A might direct toward B for an epistemic failing. A might modify their standing intention to epistemically trust the word of B in domain D, for example (as a reflection of a judgment of GER impairment). But when A *also* stands in some further relationship with B—let's say B is A's dentist—the expectations and intentions constitutive of their "dentistry relationship" impacts the GER. That is, it influences or changes how the GER shapes token blame responses A might direct toward B for an epistemic failing. For example, when it is revealed that B does not know the proper safety procedures for removing a cavity (while B is removing A's cavity), not only will A adjust their intention to epistemically trust the word of B on those safety procedures, they might also immediately adjust their intention to trust B's word in a wide range of other domains—perhaps because the significance of their disregard for epistemic goods in this context implies a wide-ranging form of epistemic viciousness.[22] But also, and more obviously, A will simply manifest other kinds of blame-response altogether, plausibly including the reactive attitudes narrowly construed. In sum, as indicated in Chapter 4, section 4.3.1, the dentistry relationship between A and B not only influences the *strength* of A's epistemic blame, but also the role epistemic blame, per se, plays alongside other forms of blame, when A blames B for an epistemic failing. These are the ideas I will be spelling out in detail in what follows.

My approach will be to start with *professional* relationships, moving on to relationships between *experts* and *laypersons* more generally, and then on to *institutional* and *interpersonal* relationships. This is not intended as an exhaustive account of all possible relationships involving epistemic expectations which may impact the GER. But I think it's a good start, and a helpful way to establish some central claims. As should become clear, the ordering I propose is helpful because each of these types of relationship has an increasing number of features that *differentiate* the epistemic expectations they involve from the baseline set constituting the GER. I will ultimately be arguing that once we get to a certain point in

---

[22] This is the sense in which, in addition to standing in the GER, A also has their own unique sort of "epistemic relationship" with their dentist.

our consideration of these differences, the relationship in question may no longer appropriately be regarded as capable of impacting any kind of *epistemic* relationship, directly, even though it may involve intentions and expectations that in some sense concern epistemic matters, as all relationships can.

6.5.1 Professional Relationships

By "professional relationships" I mean the kind between doctors and their patients, lawyers and their clients, accountants, building contractors, civil engineers and their clients, and so on. In some ways, this is obviously a fairly diverse list, but what unifies it is the (often legally binding) *contractual* nature of these relationships, along with the fact that, in most instances, one party to the relationship—the professional—will have a certain expertise that the other party lacks, and which is a central *reason* for the latter's participation in the relationship.

In my view, the epistemic expectations characteristic of professional relationships have the following important properties:

Asymmetry: The epistemic expectations between parties to the relationship are *asymmetrical.*

Domain constraint: The epistemic expectations concern a relatively *narrow domain of propositions.*

Normative overlap: The epistemic expectations appear to *overlap* with other normative domains (in complex ways).

There may of course be other properties worth discussing. But these three seem most salient when considering the way professional relationships can impact the baseline of the GER. Let me explain what I have in mind.

First, one thing that is definitive of, for example, your relationship with your doctor, is that the epistemic expectations between you and your doctor are asymmetrical: your doctor is not entitled to expect the same things that you are of them, whether epistemically speaking, or otherwise.[23] This is all I mean when I say that the epistemic expectations involved in professional relationships typically have the property of **asymmetry**. Second, the epistemic expectations involved in professional relationships tend to be oriented around a relatively narrow range of propositions, or topics of concern. Again, sticking with doctors, the epistemic expectations involved in a doctor-patient relationship, as such, are oriented around how to promote a patient's health. This is all I mean when I say that the

---

[23] Interestingly, perhaps one of the most important loci of asymmetry between layperson and expert is precisely the epistemic dimension of the relationship.

158   EPISTEMIC BLAME

epistemic expectations involved in professional relationships have the property of **domain constraint**. Third, the epistemic expectations involved in professional relationships may often be epistemic "in content only," while the normative domain they are properly a part of may either in some sense be mixed between epistemic and practical, or be entirely non-epistemic. To see this, consider the following.

When you are entitled to expect that your doctor knows the treatment protocols for familiar disease X, it's true that this is an "epistemic expectation" in some sense—as Goldberg himself has argued extensively. But it's also true that were the doctor to fail to know this, under certain circumstances, it seems obvious that you would be entitled to blame them in a way that is more than just epistemic. Fitting this into our framework for thinking about the connection between blame, relationships, and normative expectations, my point is simply this: when someone who is party to a professional relationship modifies their intentions and attitudes in response to a judgment that the relevant expectations have not been met, the blame response constituted by these modifications will likely be something other than epistemic in nature. This is what I mean when I say that the "epistemic expectations" involved in certain professional relationships exhibit **normative overlap**.

There are two things to discuss in light of all this. First, given this understanding of their properties, how do the epistemic expectations of professional relationships interact with the GER? In what ways, exactly, are the epistemic expectations involved in these relationships capable of impacting the normative contours of the GER? The second thing to discuss is the following. What do these considerations have to do with the business condition on standing to blame? How is our understanding of the business condition in the epistemic domain enriched by thinking about the epistemic expectations involved in these more specific kinds of relationships?

Answering my first question requires considering how the properties of **asymmetry**, **domain constraint**, and **normative overlap** affect the capacity of the epistemic expectations involved in professional relationships to impact the GER in any meaningful way. Let's consider these in turn, starting with **asymmetry**.

We might wonder whether **asymmetry** prevents the epistemic expectations involved in professional relationships from impacting the normative contours of the GER altogether. One reason might be that **asymmetry** somehow rules them out as expectations that are in any real sense germane to *relationships*, per se. Perhaps the expectations that are germane to relationships, as a matter of their nature, cannot be asymmetrical or lopsided, in the sense that one party to the relationship cannot have radically different expectations than another—perhaps because of something to do with *reciprocity* and the *joint* nature of anything deserving the title of a "relationship." If the kinds of expectations we have toward, say, our lawyers or doctors, are not germane to any kind of genuine *relationship* after all, then perhaps we should regard them as incapable of impacting the GER. But it is easy to see that asymmetrical expectations are a part of genuine relationships. There are many examples of things we immediately recognize as relationships which involve expectations that are asymmetrical or lopsided in precisely this way. Think for example of the relationship between a father and son, or a teacher and their students. While a young child is arguably entitled to expect certain forms of care and concern from their father at a young age, the same is not true regarding the expectations the father is entitled to have of his child. I see no reason why the asymmetry of the epistemic expectations involved in professional relationships undermines their capacity to impact the normative contours of the GER.

Let's move on to **domain constraint**. On the face of it, the fact that the epistemic expectations involved in a given professional relationship are oriented around a highly circumscribed locus of concern shouldn't matter when it comes to assessing their capacity to impact the GER. At most, the property of **domain constraint** simply seems to imply that the *range* of propositions over which a given professional relationship can have an impact on the GER will be correspondingly circumscribed. Still, at least two points are worth making here. First, even though the epistemic expectations germane to a given professional relationship will be narrowly circumscribed (in a doctor-patient relationship, for example, they may concern only medical matters of a certain sort), a person's beliefs about whether these expectations have been met will nevertheless stand in important inferential relations with other beliefs, which in turn may have relevance for the GER. Returning to my point in the dentist example from earlier, if you judge that your dentist should have known some proposition p, in the sense that by failing to know p they put you at undue risk of harm, chances are good your awareness that they failed to meet an important epistemic expectation in the domain of dentistry will lead you to be cautious about epistemically trusting them on other matters too. The basic thought is this. Because your dentist is a *dentist*, when they epistemically fail in a certain way, this may lead you to epistemically trust them less, not just about dentistry, but on a range of other things too. Again, perhaps this is because the significance of their epistemic failing in this context implies a wide-ranging form of epistemic viciousness. The specifics of the case will determine the extent to which such an inference is justified, but the key point here is simply that, despite being narrowly circumscribed, the epistemic expectations germane to a given professional relationship may be capable of having an impact on the GER that extends well beyond the domain of propositions they most immediately concern.

The second point worth making is that the normative expectations involved in a given professional relationship may extend beyond the propositional altogether, in ways that may nevertheless seem epistemic. For example, professional relationships often involve expectations that the expert in the relationship will have a

160 EPISTEMIC BLAME

certain degree of *know-how*, not just propositional knowledge. We expect a surgeon to have a certain degree of know-how (*lots* of know-how) when it comes to operating their instruments without causing excessive discomfort; we expect a lawyer to have a certain degree of know-how when it comes to constructing their case persuasively, and so on. A case might be made to count these normative expectations as a kind of epistemic expectation. If so, then perhaps an important additional question is whether or to what extent those epistemic expectations are capable of impacting the GER. To what extent do they have the capacity to shape the nature of a person's *epistemic* blame response?

This is an interesting question because, on the face of it, we might think that a surgeon's ineptitude at handling her scalpel should have no bearing on the nature of one's epistemic relationship with them, and so no capacity to impact the nature of a would-be instance of epistemic blame, even if it amounts to falling short of an "epistemic expectation" that is germane to your professional relationship with them. However, while perhaps raising interesting questions worth discussing elsewhere, I think for present purposes we can regard this as largely a terminological issue, not a substantive one. It seems fair enough to restrict our understanding of "epistemic expectation" to expectations of a propositional nature (concerning propositional knowledge, justified belief, rational belief, and the like), even if there is a case to be made that our definition should be more expansive. I will leave this matter for another time.

That said, it does lead naturally to the third property of epistemic expectations involved in professional relationships that I would like to consider, namely **normative overlap**. Restricting ourselves even just to normative expectations of a propositional nature, if it turns out that certain expectations partially comprising professional relationships are not strictly speaking *epistemic*, even though they might *seem* epistemic in some sense, then we may have reason to doubt whether it is helpful or accurate to think of them as having the capacity to impact the GER in a meaningful way. For example, again, if it turns out that your expectation that your doctor knows the treatment protocols for familiar disease X is really, perhaps despite initial appearances, a *moral* expectation (perhaps it appears epistemic because it happens to be *about* the state of their knowledge) then we might wonder: how can the doctor's failure to meet this expectation have an impact on your *epistemic* relationship with them? Correspondingly, how can any instance of epistemic blame you might direct toward your doctor be colored by, or partially constituted by, an adjustment to whatever intentions and attitudes you form as a result of judging that your doctor fails to meet this expectation? Surely such intentions and attitudes would at best be relevant to our understanding of what *morally* blaming the doctor (partly) consists in—not what epistemically blaming them consists in? We might wonder whether *any* of the normative expectations germane to a given professional relationship are "strictly speaking" epistemic expectations, at least in a sense that is relevant for our understanding of epistemic blame.

My response to this important question is twofold. First, even *if* we want to regard the expectations at issue here as strictly speaking moral, the fact that they concern the doctor's state of knowledge means that, when the doctor fails to meet them, this can tell you something important about their intellectual life. The example above seems like one way of learning that your doctor does not have her intellectual house in order. Reflecting this fact, it may be entirely appropriate for you to adjust certain intentions and attitudes you have which are oriented specifically toward her epistemic agency. And so, this failure of expectation may have an impact on the GER in this way. This point is closely related to the one just made about **domain constraint**.

But, second, **normative overlap** requires us to emphasize again that there are at least *two* dimensions to what I mean when I talk about epistemic blame interacting with other normative domains (Chapter 4, section 4.3.1). Relationships can impact the GER by modulating *strength* of epistemic blame. But relationships can also impact the GER by modulating how much of a role modifications to the intentions and expectations constitutive of the GER themselves ought to play in a response to an epistemic failing. Sometimes, when my doctor epistemically fails, there is arguably less of a role for epistemic blame, and more of a role for moral blame—in comparison with, say, when my pub quiz teammate epistemically fails, or some random stranger epistemically fails in a low-stakes situation. Not only do I direct a stronger epistemic blame response toward my doctor (to the extent that I focus on the epistemic dimension of the situation, specifically), I direct different kinds of blaming attitudes toward them altogether, such as the moral blaming attitudes of indignation or resentment. This is just another way in which professional and other kinds of relationships can impact the GER.

What we are finally seeing in detail is how, rather than running roughshod over the platitude that epistemic blame interacts with other normative domains, the relationship-based account naturally accommodates this platitude and even gives it considerable structure. This structure arises out of a simple thought: epistemic blame interacts with other normative domains to the extent that the GER can be impacted by our other relationships. As I noted in the Introduction, this has broader significance in that it illuminates the bigger-picture idea that the epistemic domain is somehow intertwined with other normative domains. The relationship-based account of epistemic blame illuminates an important site of the interaction between the epistemic and practical domains. That said, I've also noted that there are many other sites of interaction between these domains, and corresponding literatures discussing them. In many cases—such as the pragmatic or moral encroachment debates—the very *point* of those debates concerns whether, or to what extent, the relevant kind of interaction in fact takes place (e.g. do stakes, or the risk of moral harm, really affect the evidential threshold for justification or knowledge?). What is interesting about the relationship-based account of epistemic blame in this context, then, is that it sheds light on

162 EPISTEMIC BLAME

connections between the epistemic and other domains independently of debates about things like pragmatic or moral encroachment.

It is worth pausing to emphasize the significance of this result. A common complaint about the very idea of epistemic blame is that it is unclear whether, or to what extent, it is distinct from other kinds of blame. Part of the issue is a variation on the puzzle of epistemic blame: how could there be genuine *blame* responses that are uniquely at home in the *epistemic* domain? I spent the first half of this book answering that question. But I think another part of the issue is simply a recognition of the fact that, if there is an epistemic kind of blame, it clearly interacts in complex ways with other dimensions of our blaming practices— perhaps in such complex ways that it seems hopeless how we might disentangle the epistemic from other elements at play. And if it is hopeless, then perhaps we should avoid putting too much weight on the idea that there is an epistemic kind of blame.

What I am proposing is that the relationship-based framework provides a principled way of doing this disentangling. Again, the thought is: the extent to which our *epistemic* relationships are impacted by other relationships—that is, the extent to which the intentions and expectations partially constitutive of the former, interact with intentions and expectations partially constitutive of the latter—just is the extent to which our epistemic blame responses interact with non-epistemic considerations and responses.

Of course, in a sense this simply shifts the bump in the rug. How can we measure the extent to which one relationship is impacted by another, for example? I do not mean to suggest that there is a precise answer to this question. But I also do not think we need one. The way epistemic blame interacts with non-epistemic considerations and responses often just is an imprecise matter. My proposal nevertheless gives us valuable traction on this issue, in the sense that it frames the mechanisms at play in terms of an entirely familiar phenomenon.

Notice: we have an independent grip on what it means to be in one kind of relationship rather than another. We also have an independent grip on how the dynamics of one kind of relationship—say a friendship—can be impacted by the dynamics of another—say a business partnership. Many of us have experienced the shift in expectations and intentions that results when entering a professional relationship with someone who was previously "just a friend." And we are familiar with the way our responses to impairments to our relations with that person can change as a result, too. My point is that we can think of the interaction between epistemic blame and other non-epistemic considerations and responses along these familiar lines. Sometimes, the nature of our responses toward someone for an epistemic failing will have a different strength or normative character, in virtue of the fact that expectations constitutive of relationships beyond the GER are at play. In those cases—which may be common, if not the norm—our epistemic blaming practices, precisely to that extent, take on these different dimensions.

Before moving on to our examination of other kinds of relationship, it will be helpful to consider the second bigger issue I wanted to address. I asked: how is our understanding of the business condition in the epistemic domain enriched by thinking about the epistemic expectations involved in more specific kinds of relationships? In my view, one fairly clear answer is the following. Because you stand in a professional relationship with your doctor, the epistemic expectations involved in this relationship partially determine which of your doctor's epistemic failings *matter*, and to what extent, in addition to constraining the nature of your reactions to them for making those failings. Thus, when your *doctor* fails to know the treatment protocols for familiar disease X, this may matter in a very different way than when your uncle, who's always showing off about how much he knows about X, fails to know the treatment protocols for X. It matters in a different way because you have a (legitimate) expectation that they know those protocols. Correspondingly, your response toward them for not knowing the protocols will be different than any response you might have toward your uncle for not knowing them—and this is because your response will be partly *constituted* by modifications to the intentions and attitudes that you have which are connected to this normative expectation in the first place. Put in the language of the business condition, because of these additional normative expectations, your doctor's epistemic failings can be your business to a greater degree than, say, the epistemic failings of your uncle, or the epistemic failings you may happen to notice of a stranger on the street.

Generally speaking, the results of the foregoing discussion can be summarized as follows. We gain a better understanding of the business condition in the epistemic domain simply insofar as we learn more about the nature of our entitlements to expect in different kinds of relationships. The more we learn about what, specifically, a person is entitled to expect as a function of a given relationship, the more we learn about what sorts of normative failings will count as their business, and why. Thus, the more we learn about what it takes to have the standing to blame in various contexts. With this in mind, let's examine the epistemic expectations involved in a few other kinds of relationships.

6.5.2 The Expert-Layperson Relationship

We might say that experts and laypersons stand in a kind of relationship. This idea is inspired by Goldberg, when he writes: "Related to this first class of epistemic expectations (those we have of professionals) are the epistemic expectations we have of experts in their field. We rely in very complicated and indirect ways on scientists of various kinds" (2018, 162).

Goldberg's point about reliance is connected to his argument—seen above—about what entitles us to epistemic expectations. According to Goldberg, the fact

164 EPISTEMIC BLAME

that we have a *practice* of relying on experts, albeit in "complicated and indirect ways," is what makes the epistemic expectations we have of those experts legitimate—assuming, of course, that this practice has the properties laid out earlier that would render these expectations a form of "practice generated entitlements." I will not get into the question of whether Goldberg is correct that we have an entitlement to these epistemic expectations, or, if so, what grounds them—let alone what their contents are exactly. Instead, I'll work with a fairly intuitive and rough view of what I think Goldberg has in mind. My aim is simply to sketch the contours of these epistemic expectations, in order to assess the extent to which they are capable of impacting the GER. I think there is enough plausibility to the idea that we are entitled to expectations along the lines I'm about to suggest that it would be useful to have an account of how they are capable of impacting the GER.[24]

A layperson in a given domain is simply someone who is not an expert in that domain. What is an "expert"? Following Alvin Goldman, we can start with the following:

> Someone is an expert in domain D iff they have more true beliefs and/or fewer false beliefs in D than most people do. Also, they typically have skills or dispositions to generate more true answers to questions in D that they haven't previously thought about than most people would be able to generate.
>
> (Goldman 2001, 92)

In addition to having Goldman's properties, "experts" in the sense I want to focus on play an institutionalized role partly in virtue of having these properties. Note that someone might be an expert in Goldman's sense without even realizing it. Such cases may introduce important complications for the idea that expert-layperson relationships can impact the GER. By restricting our focus to experts who play a recognized role in an institutionalized setting, we can set those complications to the side.

The most straightforward examples of experts, in my sense, are scientific researchers in various fields working in universities or other organizations. The sort of thing I want to suggest we are entitled to expect of experts is precisely that they have more true beliefs and/or fewer false beliefs regarding the domain in which they are an expert than most people do, as well as that they will have skills or dispositions to generate more true answers to questions in that domain than

---

[24] While my discussion here focuses on experts and laypersons, it seems clear that experts may stand in distinctive kinds of relationships with other experts too. These relationships may have their own unique dynamics. It is worth noting that, according to the definition of "expert" I use below, an expert in one domain can of course be a layperson in many other domains. So, in this sense, our focus on expert-layperson relationships covers a wide range of possible cases. What might require special treatment elsewhere are relationships between experts *in the same domain*.

most people would be able to generate. Note that this is not yet to say anything about the conditions under which we are entitled to expect someone to *be* an expert. It is only a claim about what we are entitled to expect of someone, given their role as an expert.

These epistemic expectations plausibly have the same properties as those I've outlined for epistemic expectations involved in professional relationships (**asymmetry, domain constraint**, and **normative overlap**). These epistemic expectations are asymmetrical, domain specific, and likely overlap with other normative domains in complex ways. But it is also plausible that they have at least one additional salient property—one that is perhaps related to **asymmetry**—I'll call it **asymmetry of awareness**. Typically, in addition to having a set of expectations toward experts that experts do not have toward laypeople, token laypersons are the only parties to the relationship who would seem to have *any* attitudes whatsoever toward the other party. Typically, an expert that a layperson has legitimate epistemic expectations of will not be aware of that layperson's existence.

I have already examined in detail how the first three properties of these epistemic expectations function vis-à-vis the GER. I won't rehash those points here. What bears scrutiny is this additional dimension of the expert-layperson relationship. Does asymmetry of awareness undermine the capacity of the expectations involved in the expert-layperson relationship to have an impact on the GER? One reason we might think so, is if it turns out that normative expectations with this property simply cannot function as constitutive elements of genuine relationships. Perhaps the normative expectations that are germane to genuine relationships must, as a matter of their nature, be such that the *awareness* each party to the relationship has of them is in some important sense symmetrical, in the sense that one party to the relationship cannot have a radically different awareness of the expectations than the other party. Again, perhaps this somehow falls out of the reciprocal and joint nature of genuine relationships.

We need not get into general questions about whether radical asymmetry of awareness undermines the possibility of a genuine relationship. In my view, the asymmetry of awareness involved in the expert-layperson relationship does not undermine the capacity of the normative expectations involved in this relationship to impact the GER for the following reason. Any given expert may be unaware that a token, or set of token, laypersons currently have certain epistemic expectations of them. But if they are responsible experts, typically they will be aware that *there are* laypersons who exist who have certain epistemic expectations of them. It seems to me that these attitudes—even though they are asymmetrical in the specificity of their contents—underly a kind of reciprocity and joint nature of this relationship, which suggests that we should not exclude the epistemic expectations that partly constitute it from having the capacity to impact the GER.

How is our understanding of the business condition in the epistemic domain enriched by thinking about the epistemic expectations involved in the

166 EPISTEMIC BLAME

expert-layperson relationship? In a way resembling the doctor example from earlier, I will use the example of an expert on climate change to illustrate. Let layperson L stand in the expert-layperson relationship with an expert on climate change. The epistemic expectations involved in this relationship will partially determine which of the climate change expert's epistemic failings *matter* for L, and to what extent, in addition to constraining the nature of L's reactions to the expert for those failings. Thus, if it turns out the climate change expert fails to know about the latest important findings in their field, for example, this may matter in a very different way for L than when L's friend, who has a passing interest in climate science, fails to know the latest findings in that field. It matters in a different way because L has a (legitimate) expectation that the climate scientist will know about those findings. L does not have any such expectation of her friend. Correspondingly, L's response toward the expert for not knowing X will be different than any response L might have toward her friend—and this is because L's response will be partly *constituted* by modifications to the intentions and attitudes she has which are connected to this normative expectation in the first place. Put in the language of the business condition, because of these additional normative expectations—assuming, again, for the sake of argument, that L is *entitled* to have them—the climate change expert's failing is L's business to a greater degree than, say, the epistemic failings (if they can be called as much) of her friend.

It's interesting to consider how the "sting, force, and depth" of this sort of blame response will compare with that of the sort we discussed in professional relationships. I do not know how to answer that question. However, crucially, I don't think answering it matters here. My primary concern at this point is defending the relationship account against the accusation that it predicts that all epistemic failings are everyone's business in the same way. I'm interested in showing not only that that's *not* the case, but also, offering some structural details about *why* it's not.

6.5.3 Institutional and Personal Relationships

Perhaps epistemic blame can be affected not just by professional and layperson/ expert relationships, but also by institutional and personal relationships, via the epistemic expectations involved in them. Here again is Goldberg:

[W]e have epistemic expectations of various people playing other institutional roles. We expect the relevant individuals to know what responsibilities accrue to them in virtue of their occupying the role they do; and when these responsibilities include responsibilities to know, or to inquire, or to be familiar with sources of information, etc., our expectations of them have an epistemic content. Thus we expect religious leaders to be knowledgeable of the basic aspects of their religion's practices, and to be knowledgeable as well of any elementary doctrine associated with the religion. We expect the head of a charitable organization to be familiar with the basic needs that her organization addresses, and to know as well when the organization's practices come under legal scrutiny. (2018, 163)

Goldberg adds to this list academic chairs, police officers, members of a sports team, members of a club. He goes on:

But it should also be clear that our epistemic expectations of others go beyond those generated in professional or institutional contexts. Some of our expectations are generated in connection with the ongoing practices that have emerged in our interpersonal relations with one another: our business partners, colleagues, fellow students, friends, or family members. (164)

By now I think we are familiar with the basic gist of how to spell out the connection that may or may not hold between these additional sorts of epistemic expectations and the GER. So, I won't get into the details here.

But I will address one point raised earlier. Some of the expectations involved in these additional relationships may have properties that undermine their capacity to impact the GER *qua* epistemic relationship—something we might call **normative irrelevance**. Let's focus on personal relationships. Consider John Gibbons' example of partners with an established practice of leaving post-it notes on the fridge to let one another know what ingredients they need on their next shopping trip (Gibbons 2006). Perhaps certain normative epistemic expectations have arisen out of this practice, such as the expectation that a member intending to make a mushroom omelet in the morning ought to know whether they need mushrooms, if mushrooms are currently listed on the post-it note. Does this epistemic expectation have the capacity to partially shape a given blame response within this relationship? Does it have the capacity to impact the GER? I am doubtful of this. To give a sense of why I am doubtful, note that there seems to be an important difference between this example and, say, the dentist example I discussed earlier in this regard. Here's what I have in mind.

In the example just used, it is not clear to me that the partner is really entitled to infer anything about the other partner's running of their intellectual lives more generally by virtue of the fact that they failed to live up to the epistemic expectation regarding the post-it note. The oversight may simply indicate that the partner was being lazy that morning. Laziness in this context is not plausibly linked to epistemic irresponsibility in the way it is (or can be) in the context of being a dentist, and when we are talking about expectations that have to do with central facets of being a *good* dentist. Generally speaking, it may be the case that many of the normative expectations involved in personal relationships (even when they

168   EPISTEMIC BLAME

seem to be, on the face of it, "epistemic" in nature) are not really capable of impacting the GER directly. So, they may be of less or no relevance when it comes to giving structure to our understanding of how epistemic blame interacts with other normative domains.

A central aim of the present section has been to make sense of just one condition on standing to blame—one that seemed to raise an especially interesting question in the epistemic domain. To close this chapter, I turn now to briefly consider a few other standing conditions that have been discussed in the moral philosophy literature, and examine the issue of whether their epistemic analogues pose any further interesting questions or problems.

6.6 Other Conditions on Standing to Epistemically Blame

As I noted in section 6.1, some moral philosophers maintain that a "non-hypocrisy condition" requires that blamers not manifest the same flaw that they attempt to criticize in another (Fritz and Miller 2018, 119). I also noted that, perhaps relatedly, a "non-complicity" condition requires that the would-be blamer not be complicit in the wrongdoing involved in the target of their blame (Bell 2013).

On the face of it, I find it easier to make sense of the idea of "epistemic hypocrisy" than I do "epistemic complicity." This is likely because the term "complicity" sounds like it implies *action* in a way that does not immediately fit with our typical understanding of epistemic failings. Meanwhile, "hypocrisy" doesn't necessarily have an action-based ring to it. A very ordinary use of "hypocrisy" attaches to *belief*, just as much as action. Someone can be a hypocrite for holding sexist beliefs while accusing others of sexism, for example. I don't mean to present this as an example of "epistemic hypocrisy," however. My point is just that we likely shouldn't anticipate a difficult time filling out the notion of epistemic hypocrisy, or understanding how it's possible.

It seems to me fairly straightforward that the non-hypocrisy condition in the epistemic domain constrains epistemic blamers in the following way. Those who have performed epistemically badly in the same or similar way as a target of blame, may lack the standing to blame their target, even if the target is epistemically blameworthy.[25] Just as with the business condition, if this condition has any plausibility, it should be understood as constraining the strength, degree, or kind of blame as opposed to functioning like an on-off switch.

---

[25] The conditions on whether someone has failed in a way "similar" to the target of blame might include a role for how *recently* the failing occurred. I'll set this issue to one side in order to stay focused on the bigger picture.

Is there a non-hypocrisy condition on standing to epistemically blame? Rather than directly answer this question, I'll take a step back and make the following point. Ultimately, I am more interested in being able to make sense of the very idea of standing conditions in the epistemic domain, with a view to examining whatever implications this may have for our understanding of epistemic blame. My aim is to be relatively neutral on the question of whether there *are* such conditions in the first place, given that many (though not all) theorists in moral philosophy take them seriously. The non-hypocrisy condition seems to be more predominantly endorsed than the business condition, so I won't weigh in on this matter any further, except to say: any plausibility the non-hypocrisy condition has in the moral domain, there seems to be no in-principle reason why it (suitably spelled out) shouldn't carry over to the epistemic domain.[26]

What about the non-complicity condition? What would it mean to be complicit in an epistemic failing? On one hand, the apparent oddity of this question is yet another reflection of the *private* light in which many of us tend to see our epistemic lives. Perhaps it's impossible to be complicit in someone else's epistemic failing because such a failing is inherently their *own*, in some sense. This thought is obviously closely related to the skepticism we might have about the business condition in the epistemic domain, just discussed at length.

Of course, one thing to note immediately is that the business condition is what we might call a *positive* condition on standing to blame. It specifies something that must *be* the case in order for blame to be fitting or appropriate. Meanwhile, the non-complicity condition, as the name suggests, is what we might call a *negative* condition on standing to blame.[27] It specifies something that must *not* be the case in order for blame to be fitting or appropriate. As such, I don't think it raises the same sort of existential concerns for the idea of epistemic blame that the business condition seemed to, which is one reason I prioritized so heavily discussion of the latter. Let me explain.

A positive condition states that blamers must meet condition C in order to have the standing to blame. If *no one* meets condition C, then no one has the standing to blame. So, no one can appropriately epistemically blame anyone else. This would be a puzzling if not outright worrying result for the idea of epistemic blame. Meanwhile, a negative condition states that blamers must *not* meet condition C in order to have the standing to blame. If *no one* meets condition C, then, for all we know, no one's standing to blame is impeded by this condition. So, for all we

---

[26] Perhaps one worry is the following. Given well-known findings about the deep and pervasive tendency we *all* have to think in biased ways (and where the operation of these biases is often opaque to self-reflection), we might worry whether anyone really meets a non-hypocrisy condition on standing to epistemically blame. I'm not inclined to think this is a very serious worry. I think it's true that we're all imperfect believers and inquirers. But I don't think we're all equally as bad, all the time.

[27] The point to follow could also be made for the non-hypocrisy condition.

170 EPISTEMIC BLAME

know, people really can appropriately epistemically blame one another. On the face of it, this doesn't seem to present us with any puzzling or outright worrying thoughts about epistemic blame.

To be sure, one might worry that if it's literally impossible to be complicit in another person's epistemic failing, then it does sound bizarre—bordering on nonsensical—to talk about a "non-complicity condition" on standing to epistemically blame. Rather than engaging with this sort of worry directly, I'll point out that it very likely *is* possible to be complicit in another person's epistemic failing. For example, it's not difficult to imagine a teacher being "epistemically complicit" in a student's tendency to affirm the consequent, for example, or to think that climate change isn't real. Perhaps the student's epistemic failings are themselves a result of the teacher's bad teaching. If so, then it seems the teacher may lack the standing to epistemically blame the student. One issue with this example is that, if the teacher really is so complicit in the student's epistemic failings here, the student may not be epistemically blameworthy in the first place. Perhaps the fact that they had such a bad teacher gives them a good excuse for their epistemic failing.[28]

There are likely cases in between a kind of deep complicity that serves as an excusing condition for the other epistemic agent, and a lack of complicity altogether, such that a person can lack the standing to epistemically blame another for reasons of complicity.[29] Elsewhere, I examine three additional ways we can be complicit in the epistemic domain: by manipulating an agent to epistemically fail, by engaging in bad joint inquiry, and through group unjustified belief.[30] Intuitive examples of the first type might be things like indoctrination or brainwashing. Intuitive examples of the second and third type might be certain forms of political activism, extremist organizations, or a group pursuing a corporate agenda (e.g. an oil company's selective reliance on "climate scientists"). In each case, interesting challenges arise in identifying something that is simultaneously a form of *complicity*, and which specifically concerns the *epistemic* domain. But I argue that these challenges can be met.

Again, I'm mostly inclined to think that, owing to its status as a *negative* condition on standing to blame, the non-complicity condition simply does not present as urgent a set of issues for us to deal with in the context of a discussion about epistemic blame. The foregoing is simply a brief sketch of the sorts of things we might say if we wanted to pursue these matters further.

---

[28] Similar questions may of course arise about complicity in the moral domain.

[29] Lani Watson suggested to me that the consumption of news from unreliable sources may be a case in point. Perhaps a news source like the *Daily Mail* is complicit in the formation of its readers' false beliefs, but the readers are not themselves blameless for forming false beliefs on the basis of choosing to read the *Daily Mail.*

[30] Boult (forthcoming).

6.7 Conclusion

This concludes my discussion of standing to epistemically blame. We have now considered a variety of standing conditions in the epistemic context, but my primary focus has been the business condition. It is not immediately obvious how to make sense of epistemic blame in light of considerations about the business condition on standing to blame. The relationship-based account provides tools for making this clear. Moreover, careful attention to this issue allows us to connect the relationship-based account to recent work on practice generated entitlements to expect. This in turn paved the way for a more structured analysis of the variable nature of epistemic blame, including providing a principled account of the extent to which blame for epistemic failings can sometimes—perhaps often—interact with a variety of normative perspectives.

7

The Value of Epistemic Blame

In the first part of this book, I argued that there is conceptual space for epistemic blame. I also defended an approach to filling that space. The relationship-based account can explain what makes epistemic blame more significant than mere negative epistemic evaluation, without invoking attitudes, behaviors, or practices that seem out of place in the epistemic domain. The account also enables fruitful exploration of two clusters of issues in the ethics of epistemic blame. In this final chapter, I turn my attention to a third question in the ethics of epistemic blame. Should we epistemically blame one another? What is the value of this practice? And might there be some other way of responding to each other's epistemic failings that is somehow better or more worthwhile?

I approach these questions, first, by focusing on a case study that is useful for examining the value of epistemic blame. My case study is the realm of democratic participation. I argue that epistemic blame—as understood on the relationship-based model—has value insofar as it constitutes a distinctive way of holding others, especially leaders, to account in the democratic sphere. I argue that there is independent plausibility to the idea that democratic citizens have a (defeasible) *responsibility* to hold their leaders to account in certain ways. A good way of making sense of this responsibility is in terms of epistemic blame as epistemic relationship modification. This case study paves the way for more general observations about the value of epistemic blame. The chapter turns to a detailed examination of whether certain kinds of *positively valanced* epistemic relationship modification might be more fitting or productive (or both), as ways of responding to culpable epistemic failings. I argue on the basis of considerations about autonomy, efficacy, and social justice that they are not.

7.1 Preliminaries

What do I mean by the "value" of epistemic blame? There are at least two dimensions along which we can evaluate a response: (i) in terms of its instrumental value; and (ii) in terms of its aptness or fittingness. It may be fitting for me to resent you for forgetting my birthday, and to express this resentment next time I see you. But whether or not doing so will ultimately have a beneficial outcome for our friendship is a different question.

Epistemic Blame: The Nature and Norms of Epistemic Relationships. Cameron Boult, Oxford University Press.
© Cameron Boult 2024. DOI: 10.1093/oso/9780192890580.003.0008

When I speak simply of a response having "value" or being "better" (more valuable) than some other response, what I have in mind is a kind of all-things-considered use of the term combining the two dimensions, and perhaps more. In any given case, it seems we can weigh considerations of fittingness along with considerations about benefits to arrive at a "deliberative" judgment about what we should do.[1] Of course, weighing these considerations is a complex matter, and difficult questions will arise about how to do it. We might even think that these dimensions are incommensurable (Srinivasan 2018). Since I think we can sensibly talk broadly of the value of a response in a way that takes both considerations into account at once, I am not convinced that they are incommensurable. However, rather than committing myself to this view, I will for the most part focus on just one or the other of these dimensions at a given time, using the terms "beneficial" and "productive" to pick out the dimension of instrumental value, and "apt," or "fitting" to pick out the dimension of fittingness.

The value of epistemic blame is a large and potentially unwieldy topic. It is worth pausing to consider the methodological options we have in approaching it. One strategy might be to start from the ground up and develop a fully general and foundational theory of the value of epistemic blame. Perhaps such a theory would first establish certain claims about human values more broadly, and proceed to argue that epistemic blame plays some fundamental role in promoting those values, thereby enriching our capacity to live full human lives. Alternatively—or perhaps as a step toward a more general theory—we could look at the issue from a narrower angle, for example by examining specific contexts in which epistemic blame seems prima facie valuable, and proceed to work out the details. We might also examine the merits of certain concrete alternatives to epistemic blame. By putting a variety of such considerations together, a broader inductive case for epistemic blame may begin to emerge. I have chosen to pursue the latter strategy in this chapter. My primary reason for doing so is that developing a fully general and foundational theory of the value of epistemic blame is beyond the scope of this chapter. Indeed, doing so would likely be a book-length project in its own right. But also, by looking at the value of epistemic blame in specific contexts, and by focusing on concrete alternatives, our approach will reveal fruitful connections between the ethics of epistemic blame and a variety of other debates—including the value of democracy, the harm of paternalism, and questions about social justice. This is useful given my broader aspirations in this book of making visible a wide range of underexplored issues in the ethics of epistemic blame, and also to demonstrate the power and fruitfulness of the relationship-based account.

In the next section, I argue for the value of epistemic blame—understood as a kind of negatively valanced epistemic relationship modification—on the basis of

---

[1] See Schroeder (2011), Wedgwood (2007), and Williams (1973) for use of the "deliberative ought."

174 EPISTEMIC BLAME

claims about its fittingness and benefits in the sphere of *democratic participation*. Before getting started, I want to acknowledge that there are of course many systems of political governance that we might use as lenses for examining the value of epistemic blame. For example, we could look at epistocracy, lottocracy, various hybrid models, and so on. My focus is on representative democracy, mainly because it is the political system I am most familiar with. But representative democracy is also regarded by many as the best—or least bad—form of political governance we have so far been able to come up with. Of course, a lot of heated debate concerns not merely how to improve democratic systems, but also whether they should be replaced altogether. To my mind, some of the most powerful recent criticisms of democracy argue for various forms of epistocracy as an alternative (Brennan 2016, 2020). If we can demonstrate the value of epistemic blame for representative democracy, I suspect it will be even easier to do so for epistocracy (a number of the arguments I make in what follows should straightforwardly transpose into an epistocratic framework). But I will not argue for this claim here. I leave the project of examining the value of epistemic blame within other political frameworks for another time.

7.2 Two Kinds of Political Epistemic Responsibilities

I turn now to an argument for the value of epistemic blame, one focused on claims about its fittingness and benefits in the sphere of democratic participation. I start from the idea that citizens have a defeasible responsibility to hold leaders to account for their culpable epistemic failings. I then argue that epistemic blame, understood as a kind of epistemic relationship modification, is a uniquely good way of fulfilling that responsibility. Since fulfilling this responsibility is valuable, epistemic blame is valuable.

Many find it natural to maintain that democratic participation comes with certain responsibilities. There is such a thing as being a responsible democratic citizen. Many also find it natural to suggest that there is an epistemic dimension to these responsibilities. We might even hold that democratic participation generates "epistemic responsibilities," such as being informed about the issues of the day, understanding some basics about the political process, or conducting one's politically relevant belief-forming processes and acts of inquiry in ways that meet certain epistemic standards.[2] I will call these "political epistemic responsibilities" (PERs).

---

[2] What is a "politically relevant belief-forming process"? A "political belief" is any belief that is of direct relevance to decision making on political issues (such as whether to increase the national deficit, foreign aid, or to have public health care). A politically relevant belief-forming process is a belief-forming process aimed at forming a political belief (consciously or otherwise). The boundaries of what counts as a political belief are vague and broad. But there are nevertheless clear-cut examples, such as those just listed.

THE VALUE OF EPISTEMIC BLAME   175

Consider a distinction between two different kinds of PERs:

Personal PER: a defeasible responsibility to meet certain epistemic criteria in contributing to the democratic decision-making process.

Interpersonal PER: a defeasible responsibility to hold others to account for culpably failing to meet certain epistemic criteria in contributing to the democratic decision-making process.

Questions concerning Personal PERs include: what is the nature of the responsibility at play?[3] What exactly are the epistemic criteria? Do people have a defeasible responsibility to be "well-informed" about certain issues? What counts as "well-informed"? And how do we *tell* whether someone meets this criterion or not?[4]

I want to set all these questions aside and focus on Interpersonal PERs. I am interested in how Interpersonal PERs interact with the nature and value of epistemic blame.

7.3 Interpersonal Political Epistemic Responsibilities

Two questions we can ask about Interpersonal PERs are what I will call the "target question" and the "condition question." The target question is: who exactly do ordinary citizens in a representative democracy have a responsibility to hold to account for culpable failures to meet certain epistemic criteria in contributing to the democratic decision-making process? Potential options include:

- Other citizens
- Media producers (organizations; or individual actors in professional roles, such as an individual journalist, or news reporter)
- Special interest groups (organizations; or individual actors in professional roles)

---

[3] See Boult 2021d for discussion of how different conceptions of the value of democracy connect with different views about the nature of the epistemic responsibilities of citizens. To take one example, I argue that pure-proceduralist conceptions of the value of democracy—ones that seek to ground the value of democracy in terms of standards internal to a procedure, such as fairness—do not seem to imply that democratic participation, of its own accord, generates substantive epistemic responsibilities for citizens. Meanwhile, epistemic conceptions of democracy—ones that seek to ground the value of democracy in terms of its supposed tendency to produce epistemic goods (such as *correct* decisions)—do seem to imply that democratic participation generates epistemic responsibilities for citizens, minimally a responsibility to meet whatever epistemic criteria is required of individuals in order for the system as a whole to be likely to produce epistemic goods.

[4] A number of political theorists tend to rely on survey data about political ignorance in discussing how informed voters are. See Arthur Lupia (2016) for excellent critical discussion. One of Lupia's central claims is that a good deal of work needs to be done to articulate a clear logic getting us from claims about survey data, to claims about what he calls "voter competence" (see esp. chapters 15 and 16).

176 EPISTEMIC BLAME

- Political representatives (parties; or individual actors in official roles: MPs, the President, Prime Minister, etc.)
- Bureaucrats
...and so on.

I will not get into much detail about who can be an appropriate target of Interpersonal PERs. I am sure a case could be made for any one of these targets, though challenges will vary across them. Instead, I will assume for the sake of argument that *political representatives*, where this can include both individuals (such as an MP, or the Prime Minister) and groups (such as parties), can be appropriate targets of Interpersonal PERs. In my view, if anyone is an appropriate target of Interpersonal PERs, political representatives are. Henceforth I will simply refer to political representatives, where this includes both individuals and groups, as "leaders."

My suggestion is that citizens have a defeasible responsibility to hold their leaders to account when they culpably fail to meet certain epistemic criteria in contributing to the democratic decision-making process. For example, if it is revealed that leader X made an egregious epistemic error by relying on misleading intelligence when signing off on a missile strike that accidentally killed dozens of civilians, it seems citizens have a defeasible responsibility to hold leader X to account, not just for the deaths of the civilians, but also for the careless intellectual conduct committed in performing their official role as leader.[5]

The condition question is about how to further specify the sense in which citizens have a responsibility to hold their leaders to account. What does it take for a citizen to *count* as holding X to account in the manner required by an Interpersonal PER? This is obviously a big question. Perhaps citizens can hold leaders to account in different ways. For example, one way to hold leader X to account might be by *not voting for them* at the next election. Another might be by attending rallies and protests dedicated to calling leader X out for their failings. Yet another might simply be by deciding not to pay attention to leader X's antics any longer—say, by avoiding social media posts of the leader, or changing the channel when they come on the news.

I am not convinced that these initial suggestions adequately capture the full range of our Interpersonal PERs in this context. For one thing, keeping in mind

---

[5] Citizens must of course be *aware* of the epistemic failing at issue, or rather, it must be the case that they in some sense ought to be aware of the failing at issue. I will simply talk about citizens *knowing* (or citizens who ought to know) that a relevant leader has epistemically failed. An additional complex issue surrounds how ordinary citizens are supposed to be able to tell whether a leader has epistemically failed, or is just being insincere. Given the complexity of political motivations, and the ability of leaders to deploy sophisticated tools to manipulate public perception, it is often difficult to tell whether a leader has culpably epistemically failed, or whether they have deliberately made a decision to appear as though they've culpably epistemically failed in the service of some other aim. One way to deal with this issue might simply be to require only that a citizen has *reasonable* belief that a leader has culpably epistemically failed. This may allow us to more or less side-step the issue altogether.

the defeasible nature of Interpersonal PERs, I find it plausible that citizens have a responsibility to do *more* than merely stop paying attention to the antics of their leaders. But also, and conversely, it strikes me as a step *too far* to suggest that any given citizen has a responsibility to modify their voting behavior, or attend rallies or protests, because of an epistemic failure of some leader. Of course, these sorts of actions may be entirely fitting or appropriate. But that is not yet to establish that citizens have a responsibility to undertake them as ways of holding their leaders to account for culpable epistemic failings. Citizens may well have responsibilities to do things that will be likely to *affect* their voting behavior, or their motivation to attend protests. But my point is that obligating them to undertake such actions directly, in response to the culpable epistemic failings of their leaders, seems in some sense too strong.

Perhaps epistemic blame is useful here. As a response that is at once a way of holding to normative expectations (SIGNIFICANCE), and capable of being rendered legitimate by culpable epistemic failings (FITTINGNESS)—epistemic blame seems uniquely suited to playing a role in Interpersonal PERs.[6] It seems uniquely suited in that it is simultaneously an engaged enough sort of response to be a way of holding accountable, without being *too* engaged—for example, in the way that obligating citizens to direct their voting choices in one direction or another, or attend protests, may in some sense go too far.[7] If citizens have a responsibility to hold leaders to account for their culpable epistemic failings, and if epistemic blame is uniquely positioned to play this role, we might even say that citizens have a defeasible responsibility to epistemically blame their leaders when their leaders culpably fail to meet certain epistemic criteria in playing their official roles. Call this the "epistemic blame claim."[8]

The idea that we sometimes have a responsibility to *blame* people might seem odd. It intersects in crucial ways with the discussion I take up in the second part of this chapter. There I will examine whether—or in what way—we ought to epistemically blame anyone at all. However, I think many can agree that there is something compelling in the vicinity. For instance, blame sometimes seems to be what is called for in light of considerations about one's self-respect in certain circumstances. You've just discovered that your long-term partner has been cheating on you with one of your work colleagues for months. They had no intention of letting you know; you simply found out because they left their phone in the car and the screen-locked part of a bunch of messages that arrived

---

[6] For detailed discussion of SIGNIFICANCE and FITTINGNESS, see Chapter 1, section 1.6.

[7] I will discuss in section 7.4.3 how epistemic blame may be a sort of response that can affect, or be motivationally connected to, citizen voting behavior.

[8] Even if citizens have a responsibility to hold their leaders to account, and even if blaming is *one* way to do this, they may nevertheless have still *other* ways of holding their leaders to account—ones beyond those I considered above—and so can meet their Interpersonal PERs without epistemic blame. This is a fair point. But my methodology should not be seen as hostage to it. I take the considerations so far simply to give some intuitive plausibility to the epistemic blame claim, enough plausibility to function as a useful angle from which to examine the nature and value of blame.

178   EPISTEMIC BLAME

throughout the day made it obvious. Other things being equal, it seems like blame is called for here. Under certain circumstances, anything less may amount to a kind of disrespect of your own self-worth in an unjust way. Perhaps this is because by blaming them you show that certain facts about the "normative landscape" (Sliwa 2019) need addressing, or that a certain balance in what you are owed as a party to the relationship (or even fellow human being) has been upset and needs reparation. Were you *not* to blame your partner, perhaps you'd be leaving these matters unaddressed (or inadequately addressed), and that seems like a form of disrespect of oneself.[9]

In the case of democratic participation, perhaps what generates the defeasible responsibility to epistemically blame our leaders when we know (or ought to know) they have culpably epistemically failed in playing their official roles, is that we *owe* it to ourselves and our fellow citizens to hold those leaders to account in certain ways—and anything less than epistemically blaming them, under certain circumstances, can amount to diminishing the worth of the democratic process, or the group of citizens as a whole, in an unjust way. When it is revealed that leader X made an egregious epistemic error by relying on misleading intelligence when signing off on a missile strike that accidentally killed dozens of civilians, anything less than epistemically blaming X for these epistemic failings can easily seem to amount to a kind of tacit diminishing of the worth of the citizenry of which one is a part. After all, the citizenry elected X to represent them. Representing a group of citizens comes with certain responsibilities, including epistemic ones. X's failure to live up to that responsibility calls for certain reactions on behalf of the citizenry.

A central issue in determining whether the epistemic blame claim is itself either too demanding, or too weak, is settling on what sort of thing epistemic blame *is*— or in other words, settling on how we want to approach SIGNIFICANCE and FITTINGNESS. While I think the epistemic blame claim is intuitive and plausible, we still run the risk of demanding too much of citizens, depending on how we cash out, in more detail, the nature of epistemic blame. I turn now to explore and hopefully resolve what I see as a potential tension between the epistemic blame claim and some ways of thinking about the nature of epistemic blame we've encountered in this book.

7.4 Comparing Accounts of the Epistemic Blame Claim

We have examined three broad approaches to the nature of epistemic blame in this book. In this section, I argue that my preferred account is especially well-positioned to avoid generating a tension with the epistemic blame claim. I will also

---

[9] For defenses of the value of blame along these lines, see Sher 2006, Scanlon 2008, and Franklin 2013. For defenses of *angry* blame, see Reis-Dennis 2019 and Cherry 2021.

THE VALUE OF EPISTEMIC BLAME   179

argue that the other approaches we have considered appear to do just the opposite. If this is right, it may even amount to a further source of support for my relationship-based approach to epistemic blame. But my primary concern is to further develop my argument for the value of epistemic blame, understood as a kind of epistemic relationship modification.

7.4.1 Responsibility to Resent

Recall that, according to the emotion-based view, epistemic blame is the manifestation of reactive attitudes such as indignation and resentment, directed toward a target as a result of the judgment that the target has (culpably) violated some epistemic norm. This is one way we might try and accommodate SIGNIFICANCE and FITTINGNESS. Of course, we looked at three different approaches to this general idea: the bold approach, the moderate approach, and the sui generis approach. I will address nuances that arise in the present context as they come up.

There seems to be a tension between this general understanding of the nature of epistemic blame and the epistemic blame claim. Recall, the epistemic blame claim says:

> citizens have a defeasible responsibility to epistemically blame their leaders when their leaders culpably fail to meet certain epistemic criteria in playing their official roles.

Taking the emotion-based view on board, this becomes the claim that:

> citizens have a defeasible responsibility to direct certain negative emotional responses (+ some judgment condition) towards their leaders when their leaders culpably fail to meet certain epistemic criteria in playing their official roles.

On the bold account, the sorts of negative emotional responses at issue are the reactive attitudes narrowly construed. Is the resulting epistemic blame claim plausible? Not in my view. In particular, it seems too demanding to require of ordinary citizens (in the sense of assigning them a responsibility) that they manifest reactive attitudes narrowly construed toward their political leaders for epistemically failing. And the issue is not equivalent to the familiar problem that reactive attitudes narrowly construed are not fitting responses to epistemic failings. Suppose you are unconvinced by the arguments against the bold view laid out in Chapter 2. The present considerations may even amount to an independent way of challenging the bold view, in the sense that we can raise it while staying neutral on the question of whether reactive attitudes narrowly construed are fitting responses to epistemic failings.

180 EPISTEMIC BLAME

There are perhaps many reasons to be suspicious of the epistemic blame claim as understood on the bold account. First, we might think there is something prima facia odd about assigning someone a responsibility to be indignant or feel resentment about X—regardless of whether X is an epistemic failing or something else. Imagine you are a healthy, materially well-off parent who has just had their first child. It is entirely natural to suggest that—other things being equal—you have a responsibility to undertake certain actions, such as caring for that child. Perhaps it's also natural to think you have a responsibility to be in certain mental states, such as being aware of the child's state of well-being, and being concerned about the child's safety. It sounds less natural, however, to suggest that you have a responsibility to manifest a sense of joy about becoming a parent, or to be in any other emotional state for that matter. Of course, such attitudes might be entirely fitting or appropriate. But this is not the same as saying that you have a responsibility to manifest them. To put it one way, it seems your responsibilities as a parent don't penetrate quite that far, or in quite this way, into your own private mental life.

My main concern, however, is that it seems fair to allow that some of us simply prefer to be more "cool-headed" about our approach to democratic participation. Consider: voter X does not necessarily fall short of doing their duty as a democratic citizen by not manifesting certain negative emotional responses toward their political leaders when they culpably epistemically fall short. Perhaps voter X simply prefers not to get emotional when it comes to their public responsibilities. Voter X's responsibilities as a democratic citizen don't penetrate this far into their own private mental life.

What about the moderate or sui generis approaches to the emotion-based view? One way of cashing out the moderate approach is to focus on things like flickers of irritation, vague annoyance, and disappointment. In Chapter 2, I argued that these reactions simply don't amount to ways of holding others to normative expectations in the way requisite of blame.[10] So, it seems that this way of filling out an emotion-based view is a non-starter. The other way of taking the moderate approach is to focus on emotion-stances rather than emotion episodes. I think it's clear, however, that if the problem we have identified holds for emotion-episodes, it holds for emotion-stances as well. It seems equally problematic to maintain that citizens have a responsibility to be disposed to undergo certain emotion episodes in the relevant circumstances, etc.

---

[10] What about the distinction between "mere disappointment" and "reactive disappointment" (Chapter 2, section 2.3.2)? A familiar point is again applicable here: *reactive* disappointment may very well be a way of holding others to normative expectations (or something close, such as what Telech and Katz 2022 call "normative hope"). But as a kind of interpersonally robust negative emotional response, it seems too much to say that citizens have a *responsibility* to direct it towards their leaders for culpable epistemic failings. Meanwhile, I have argued that *mere* disappointment is simply not a way of holding people to normative expectations.

THE VALUE OF EPISTEMIC BLAME   181

What about the sui generis approach to the emotion-based view? The general issue facing the sui generis approach surfaces quite clearly in this specific case. It seems likely that any plausible formulation of a sui generis "emotional response" for the epistemic domain—such as an adjustment of epistemic trust—simply threatens to collapse into something very much like my preferred account. As I will argue shortly, it does seem plausible that, under certain circumstances, citizens have a responsibility to adjust their epistemic trust in their leaders for epistemically failing. But rather than supporting an emotion-based approach to epistemic blame, this fits neatly with a relationship-based approach to epistemic blame.

7.4.2 Responsibility to Desire

Recall that on the desire-based view, epistemic blame consists in a characteristic set of dispositions—ones that we may ordinarily associate with epistemic blame, such as dispositions to reproach, feel upset, and verbally request reasons—unified in their causal connection to a belief-desire pair. According to Brown, the belief in question is that an agent has "believed badly" (a technical term roughly referring to a culpable violation of an epistemic norm), and the desire is that they not have believed badly. On this account, epistemic blame is what happens when a person's desire that someone not have culpably violated an epistemic norm is frustrated.

There may be a tension with the epistemic blame claim here as well. Taking the desire-based view on board, the epistemic blame claim becomes:

> citizens have a defeasible responsibility to (believe and) desire that an epistemic norm not have been violated (+ disposition to behave in ways characteristic of epistemic blame) when their leaders culpably fail to meet certain epistemic criteria in playing their official roles.

As with the emotion-based account, this claim strikes me as implausible. It seems to me too demanding to require of ordinary citizens that they have certain desires about epistemic norms not being violated. There may be many reasons for this. Here are a couple that come immediately to mind.

First, broadly speaking, as with the line of thought regarding emotions, the idea that people can have a responsibility—especially a political (i.e. public) responsibility—to desire certain things can seem a bit odd. Second, and relatedly but more specifically, we should be able to assess whether a given citizen has performed their epistemic-political duties without getting into the messy and seemingly quite private business of determining what they desire. It seems to me that whether a citizen wants to be doing what's required of them in holding a leader epistemically accountable is much less important—if important at all—in

182 EPISTEMIC BLAME

comparison with the question of whether they in fact make certain adjustments in their relations with that leader. Again, some desires may be entirely appropriate or fitting. But that does not establish that citizens have a responsibility to manifest them. Of course, what I mean when I speak of citizens "adjusting their relations" with a given leader is only suggestive at this point. But by turning to the relationship-based account of epistemic blame, I can give this some shape.

7.4.3 Responsibility to Adjust Epistemic Trust

As we are by now familiar, the relationship-based account says that epistemic blame is comprised of a judgment that someone is epistemically blameworthy, and a modification to one's epistemic intentions, expectations, and attitudes toward that person in a negatively valanced type of way made fitting by that judgment. How does this jibe with the epistemic blame claim? Taking the account on board, the epistemic blame claim becomes:

> citizens have a defeasible responsibility to modify their epistemic relationship (including the role for judgment) with their leaders when their leaders culpably fail to meet certain epistemic criteria in playing their official roles.

If we assume that reductions of epistemic trust are paradigm forms of epistemic relationship-modification, the epistemic blame claim need only imply that citizens have a responsibility to reduce their epistemic trust in their leaders under certain circumstances (as a reflection of a judgment of epistemic blameworthiness).

Rather than generating a tension, this strikes me as entirely plausible. The issues that arise when taking the emotion-based and desire-based accounts on board do not arise here. Unlike negative emotions and desires, it does not seem overly demanding to assign citizens a defeasible responsibility to make these adjustments to their interpersonal relations with their leaders when those leaders culpably epistemically fail under certain circumstances.

In my view, not all properties of the relations that obtain between citizens and their leaders "really matter" for the health of a representative democracy. Getting into questions about emotions and desires can easily seem too messy, to go too far, or be entirely irrelevant to what really matters. Someone might object here that, at least in some cases, emotions are exactly what really matters when it comes to certain forms of democratic participation. For example, Myisha Cherry's (2021) defense of "the case for rage" may be a case in point. Cherry argues that certain forms of anger—what she calls "Lordean rage"—are not merely *acceptable* responses to racial injustice, they are necessary for effecting change. Lordean rage is distinctive in that it *motivates productive action, builds resistance,* and is *informed by an inclusive and liberating perspective.* The connection between

Lordean rage and Interpersonal PERs—that is, citizens' responsibilities in holding others to account for their *epistemic* failings—strikes me as worthy of further investigation. In any case, the business of how citizens are prepared to *epistemically trust* and rely on the word of their leaders has real, immediate consequences. Here is an argument for this claim.

Consider a group of voters who is smart enough to realize that leader X is not very epistemically responsible, at least some of the time. These voters are sub-personally motivated to look the other way, and to keep epistemically trusting leader X. Leader X asserts things that sound (to members of the group) like they are in this group's best interests. So, they keep voting for leader X. Assume that, were the members of this group to negatively adjust their epistemic trust in leader X, they would be more likely to come to realize they are not actually doing anything that is in their best interest, and become at least less inclined to vote for X. If that is true, it seems like a better outcome.

This is obviously a simplified view of the dynamics of voting in a representative democracy, as well as how voter perception of leaders' intellectual conduct may interact with questions about who they will end up voting for. But the basic idea is straightforward and plausible: when members of a representative democracy have healthy *epistemic* relationships, this is quite plausibly a good thing for that democracy.

The previously considered accounts of epistemic blame have components that also seem like ways of adjusting interpersonal relations, and generally to be potentially useful in the democratic context. But I have argued that they also come with conditions that seem either irrelevant, or too demanding. So, a potential virtue of the relationship-based account is that, by focusing more directly on a broader notion of relationship modification in the epistemic domain, we can get at something important, without raising issues that the other accounts have raised. The context of democratic participation reveals a way in which my preferred account of epistemic blame focuses on what matters.

This may amount to another form of support for the relationship-based account of epistemic blame. But my primary concern is to argue that examining the connection between the epistemic blame claim and views about the nature of epistemic blame reveals insights into the value of epistemic blame. At least when understood in the correct way, epistemic blame is beneficial because it helps facilitate responsible democratic participation, by being a distinctively fitting way of holding leaders to account for their culpable epistemic failings. One way of explaining why the epistemic blame claim seems plausible is that it recommends something that is good for democracy. So, it looks like we have identified at least one way epistemic blame can play a valuable role in our lives.

This is just a broad-brushstroke argument for the value of epistemic blame. There are surely all sorts of tricky issues involved in further specifying claims about what is "good for democracy." But this section gives an idea of how to start filling in the details of a promising line of thought.

184 EPISTEMIC BLAME

7.5 The Value of Negatively Valanced Epistemic Relationship-Modification

We have seen that one argument for the value of epistemic blame appeals to considerations about democratic participation. According to the argument, epistemic blame is valuable because it is a fitting way of holding leaders in representative democracies to account for their epistemic failings, and this in turn contributes to the healthy functioning of the democratic process.

Still, we might wonder whether there are other ways of holding our leaders to account for their epistemically blameworthy failings which might be more fitting, or more beneficial, or both. More generally, perhaps there are better ways of responding to one another for epistemically blameworthy conduct than by adjusting our epistemic relationships in ways characteristic of epistemic blame.

Note that I have not committed to many specifics on what forms of epistemic relationship modification can count as epistemic blame. I have taken a pluralist stance on vehicles of epistemic blame, so that we can allow a range of options without distracting from my initial bigger picture aims. I have, however, claimed that a paradigm form of epistemic relationship modification (in epistemic blame) is the suspension of a default presumption of epistemic trust. I have also more broadly focused on responses that amount to what we might call a "cooling" of the epistemic relationship—in other words, *negatively valanced* forms of epistemic relationship modification. In Chapter 3, section 3.2, I characterized the idea of a "negatively valanced" response as a response that manifests a negative evaluation. In the present context, it will be helpful to sharpen this a bit further along the following lines. Call a response "negatively valanced" just in case it expresses a judgment that something is bad (whether epistemically, morally, aesthetically, and so on), or has the potential to be bad, where "having potential" is determined by some contextually specified threshold. I leave the "something" in this formulation deliberately open-ended, so we can cover responses to actions, attitudes, viewpoints, capacities, people, and their character traits.

Perhaps the most salient contrast to consider at this point is whether responses that amount to a kind of "warming"—or, more *positively valanced* forms of epistemic relationship modification—would be better ways of modifying our epistemic relationships in response to epistemically blameworthy failings (at least under certain circumstances). I will understand a "positively valanced" response as one that expresses a judgment that something is *good* (whether epistemically, morally, aesthetically, and so on), or has the potential to be good, where "having potential" is determined by some contextually specified threshold. I will offer some examples of what I have in mind shortly.

To get a handle on this issue, consider a case:[11]

---

[11] Thanks to Tim Kwiatek for this example, and for encouraging me to examine this issue. Thanks also to Eugene Chislenko for pressing me to consider this issue in more depth.

YouTube: Dave's old friend, Carl, has been spending too much time alone. One day they get to chatting on the phone and he tells Dave about how anxious he's become. Dave asks why, and Carl says he is concerned about the "spread of evil." Puzzled by this uncharacteristic remark, Dave asks for clarification. Carl explains that he sees evidence of devil worshippers kidnapping children as orchestrated by the wealthiest people in the country. Last year, Carl saw some strange QAnon protests on the street. This led him down a YouTube rabbit hole. Now he's calling Dave to spread the word.

Dave judges that Carl's method of inquiry and belief formation about the spread of evil is epistemically blameworthy. But he is also concerned about the well-being of his old friend. We might take this to suggest that, sometimes, the right way to modify a relationship in light of someone's epistemic blameworthiness is to make the relationship closer, not more distant. Set aside the question of whether such a thing should be called "epistemic blame" or something else, and consider the proposal in its own right. The proposal is that sometimes our epistemic relationships ought to be "warmed" in response to judgments of epistemic relationship-impairment. To put it one way, the general thought is that sometimes the sort of response in Angela Smith's (2013, 38) loving mother case is what's called for (Chapter 3, section 3.2). In Smith's case, the mother intends to love her son more upon judging that he is morally blameworthy. In the epistemic version of these cases, the idea is that, rather than suspending a presumption of epistemic trust, and engaging in other negatively valanced forms of epistemic relationship modification, sometimes we ought to intend to better understand the source of the epistemic failing, or to steer the person toward better appreciating the epistemic reasons available, or perhaps intend to behave in certain ways that will set an example. I will use these as paradigmatic examples of epistemic relationship warming. I classify them as instances of "warming" as opposed to "cooling," just to the extent that they are positively, rather than negatively valanced. That is to say, they can be expressions of a judgment that something is (epistemically) good, or has the potential to be (epistemically) good, where "having potential" is determined by some contextually specified threshold.

We can of course make other judgments in epistemic relationship warming—notably, that the person has epistemically failed, for instance. But the point is that warming is not first and foremost an expression of *that* judgment. In seeking to empathetically understand someone, we seem to express the judgment that their viewpoint has value, that it is something worth seeking to understand. This is arguably part of the very nature of empathy.[12] In steering someone toward better appreciating the epistemic reasons available, we seem to express the judgment that they have rational capacities that are worth engaging. It is perhaps difficult to see

---

[12] That is to say, a person does not seem to count as genuinely *empathetic* if they do not regard the viewpoint they seek to understand as worthy of understanding and thereby having some kind of value.

186 EPISTEMIC BLAME

why one would bother trying, if one did not have some confidence in, and appreciation of, a person's rational capacities. And I think a similar point can be made about setting an example. By overtly setting an example, one expresses the judgment that whatever epistemic virtue they seek to embody is a valuable thing. This is presumably part of the very reason one would overtly attempt to embody a virtue. So, I think these are all ways of expressing a judgment that something is good, or at least has the potential to be good within some contextually specified threshold.

One reason to take the "relationship-warming proposal" seriously is that sometimes we might be concerned that distancing ourselves from people in response to epistemically blameworthy failings constitutes an objectionable form of giving up on them. Perhaps this can have harmful effects for whomever has to deal with them next, for example. What may seem objectionable here is that epistemic blame amounts to washing our hands of the person we blame, all the while doing nothing to correct their epistemic failings or preserve what could otherwise be a well-functioning epistemic relationship.[13]

I agree that YouTube is a case where a kind of relationship warming may be more appropriate (and perhaps even more instrumentally valuable) than a kind of cooling. But we must keep the implications of this observation clearly in view. First, just because one sort of case calls for a kind of warming of course does not entail that all—or even very many—types of case call for warming. I will examine the prospects of a broader application of the warming approach shortly. Before doing that, however, I would like to suggest that even in YouTube it is not entirely clear that a warming of the *epistemic* relationship is what's called for in the first place.

For example, perhaps a warming of Dave's *friendship* with Carl is what's called for. It may seem like Dave should intend to check up on Carl a bit more frequently, and to ensure that Carl knows he is there if he needs emotional support. Perhaps this can be consistently done while modifying his epistemic relationship with Carl in a negatively valanced way. It does seem possible to do these things simultaneously. If you are like me, you have at least a few friends whom you regard as somewhat epistemically untrustworthy. What is to stop us from continuing these friendships—and perhaps even "warming" them up on occasion—while further reducing our epistemic trust in these friends?

Continuing with YouTube, in my view, failing to suspend his presumption of epistemic trust toward Carl (on certain matters)—for example, by leaving his levels of epistemic trust where they are, so to speak, and intending to try harder to understand where Carl is coming from, seeing to it that he better appreciates the

---

[13] These ideas are all due to Tim Kwiatek.

epistemic reasons he has, or deliberately setting an example (even when Dave knows that Carl is epistemically culpable)—may actually amount to a way of disrespecting his friend qua epistemic agent. It may be a way of manifesting a kind of deficiency of epistemic normative expectation of Carl, perhaps in a way similar to some of the examples of epistemic harm considered in Chapter 5.[14] The forms of epistemic relationship warming we are considering here run the risk of being paternalistic—in some sense—or otherwise threaten to undermine Carl's autonomy. This point is even more plausible when it comes to cases that do not involve old friends. So, I turn now to consider the prospects of generalizing the relationship-warming proposal.

First, what exactly does it take for an action or attitude to be "paternalistic"? According to George Tsai, "Loosely characterized, the term paternalism refers to behavior aimed at promoting another person's good that treats her like a child, or someone who cannot be trusted to look after her own good" (Tsai 2014, 1). According to Elizabeth Jackson, "Paternalism is the practice of limiting the free choices of agents, without their consent, for the sake of promoting their best interests" (Jackson 2022).[15]

In a recent overview of the literature on paternalism, Jessica Begon (2016) points out that discussions of paternalism are often framed as though anti-paternalism is the "standard view," and that there may be interesting philosophical reasons to be (more) paternalistic under circumstances than the standard view allows. Begon challenges this way of framing the discussion. She notes that there are cases in which certain paternalistic actions intuitively seem called for (think about laws mandating the use of seatbelts, or prohibition of slavery contracts). Moreover, often those challenging paternalism are only committed to the claim that there is something prima facie bad about paternalism. I will not get into this dispute here. I will assume for sake of argument that there is something prima facie bad about paternalism, and that this has something to do with the risk of undermining an agent's autonomy. A more precise articulation and defense of the harm of paternalism would take us too far afield for present purposes.

It is also worth pointing out that a recent literature has begun to focus on the concept of "epistemic paternalism." Jackson considers multiple ways of defining epistemic paternalism. The basic idea is that epistemic paternalism involves interfering with an agent's evidence or belief-forming practices without their consent, and with an epistemic motivation (Jackson 2022). Given that our main

---

[14] Recall how excessive and deficient normative epistemic expectations can be involved in epistemic harms, such as epistemic exploitation, gaslighting, and varieties of testimonial injustice (Chapter 5, sections 5.5 and 5.6).

[15] Jackson points to Mill (1869), Dworkin (2010), and Grill and Hanna (2018) for canonical formulations of "paternalism."

188   EPISTEMIC BLAME

focus is the epistemic domain, one might wonder whether my worry about the epistemic relationship-warming proposal is more appropriately framed in terms of a worry about epistemic paternalism, as opposed to paternalism simpliciter. However, I am not convinced that there is really an important distinction to draw between epistemic paternalism and paternalism simpliciter. More importantly (and relatedly), I don't think it will matter for present purposes whether my worry is framed in one way or the other along the lines of this distinction. So, henceforth I will simply use "paternalism."[16]

Working with our rough idea of paternalism, is it plausible that epistemic relationship warming of the form I have in mind is paternalistic? Can things like getting someone to see the reasons they have, setting an example, or trying to better understand someone's perspective count as paternalistic?[17] This idea might seem like a non-starter, mainly because of the condition stating that paternalistic acts must be done without the victim's consent. The most plausible forms of epistemic relationship warming will be forms of what we might usefully call "rational persuasion," or at least intimately bound up with it. That is to say, rather than being forms of engagement that seek to alter someone's situation without them knowing about it, or doing so somehow against their will—i.e. independently of their consent—epistemic relationship warming is done in full view of the target, and aims to engage their rational capacities more or less directly. We might worry that this fact alone renders it mistaken or misleading to consider them paternalistic. It is fairly common to contrast paternalism with rational persuasion.

But we shouldn't be too quick. I am sympathetic with recent work by George Tsai (2014), who argues that certain forms of rational persuasion can also be paternalistic. Tsai emphasizes that paternalism has a motivational component, as well as a tendency to "occlude an opportunity for someone to canvass or weigh reasons for herself" (84). He argues that we can locate objectionable features of paternalism in these motivational and opportunity-occluding components (not just the non-consent component). If that is right, and if some cases of rational persuasion have the same motivational and opportunity occluding components as other more canonical paternalistic acts, then perhaps those instances of rational persuasion are similarly objectionable.

In a bit more detail, Tsai argues that a paternalistic act's motivation comprises two main ingredients:

---

[16] See Jackson (2022) for helpful discussion of whether epistemic paternalism is really distinct from other forms of paternalism.

[17] To be sure, this is a diverse collection of responses, despite all counting as forms of epistemic relationship warming. It may seem like we must address each of them in turn. However, again, the relevant unifying feature is that they are all positively valanced, in my sense of this term. Moreover, my view is that if we take on board an additional point about *motivation*, which I will introduce in this section, it should be fairly clear that it is unnecessary to address them separately.

(i) distrust in the target's agential capacities, where distrust involves the thought that the target's relevant capacities are deficient or inferior (in some domain or deliberative situation); and

(ii) beneficent concern for the target or her welfare, specifically concern that the target will suffer negative consequences to her welfare as a result of exercising her agential capacities (in some domain or deliberative situation) (2014, 87).

He also points out that paternalistic acts typically "intervene in (intrude on, interfere with, take over) the target's sphere of agency, limiting the target's legitimate exercise of her agency" (88). Tsai's thought is that sometimes cases of rational persuasion can involve precisely these ingredients, and that, all of this taken together is *sufficient* for making an act objectionable in the way paternalism seems objectionable.

Who's to say whether the kinds of attitudes and behaviors I've identified as positively valanced responses to culpable epistemic failings count as paternalistic, even taking Tsai's points on board? After all, what matters, according to Tsai, is how they are motivated, and whether they are opportunity occluding in the relevant way. I cannot hope to establish here whether there is something about epistemic relationship warming that makes it inherently likely to have these features. However, it is an interesting observation in its own right that epistemic relationship warming *can* be paternalistic, despite the fact that it seems to align so closely with rational persuasion. So, I will simply strike a cautionary note: if a token instance of epistemic relationship warming is driven by this combination of motivational ingredients, and has the relevant opportunity-occluding effect, then it may very well be objectionable for reasons similar to the way paternalistic acts are objectionable (i.e. because it threatens to disrespect a person's autonomy). This is an interesting result at least in so far is it may have seemed at first that positively valanced responses are not even in the market for this sort of objectionable feature.

Of course, epistemic blame can have the effect of occluding opportunities for others to think for themselves, too—for example, by "shutting someone down." But one thing to note here is the following. Typical instances of epistemic blame do not seem to occlude opportunities for others to exercise their epistemic agency out of a *beneficent concern* for their well-being. The question of whether to epistemically blame someone, in itself, seems quite disconnected from the question whether you have beneficent concern for them. Perhaps this is an upshot of the *negative* valance of epistemic blame. Of course, sometimes we blame people *because* we care about them, in a sense. But my point is that blame, as such, does not seem constitutively connected to beneficent concern in the way relationship warming does. In any case, I think this is at least partly why epistemic blame does not seem prone to raise worries about paternalism.

7.6 More Arguments Against Epistemic Relationship Warming

My argument so far has challenged the relationship-warming proposal on grounds that it threatens to promote paternalism and undermine autonomy. In this section I present two further arguments.

7.6.1 Inefficacy

One concern directly focuses on the efficacy of attempts at epistemic relationship warming. There may be a kind of principled issue with the epistemic relationship-warming proposal in this regard. Roughly put, we may have reason to worry that the best-case scenarios in which relationship warming might seem called for will also be the sorts of scenarios where it is especially unlikely to bring about desired effects. Let's examine this worry in more detail.

Consider YOUTUBE again. In this case, Dave is pretty seriously concerned about Carl because he has been taken in by conspiracy theories. Of course, details about an individual's psychology and other contextual features of actual cases will be paramount in determining what may or may not be efficacious in responding to someone convinced by a conspiracy theory. But empirical research on conspiracy theories suggests that those who believe them tend to be particularly resistant to counter-evidence.[18] If so, attempts at relationship warming in such cases, perhaps in the form of providing counter-evidence, or getting the target to appreciate the epistemic reasons they have, will be—to put it mildly—likely to fall short.

And here's the rub. In YOUTUBE, it is precisely the fact that Carl is in such dire straits—epistemically speaking, but also otherwise—that motivates the thought that relationship warming, as opposed to cooling, is what's called for. It is what motivates the thought that there is something objectionable about "giving up on them," in the way that relationship cooling supposedly implies. But if the very features that (at least partly) constitute what is concerning about Carl's situation are also the features that make them especially resistant to typical forms of epistemic relationship warming, this may be a sort of principled problem for the relationship-warming proposal.

There is of course an important question further back about what sorts of things can make epistemic relationship warming seem called for. Presumably it is not just a matter of how bad my friend's epistemic position is, let alone whether they are in the grip of a conspiracy theory. Thus, there may be cases in which

---

[18] See Peels et al. (2023) for helpful overview and discussion.

THE VALUE OF EPISTEMIC BLAME   191

epistemic relationship warming seems called for, and is also likely to be efficacious. Here is a different sort of case:

> PRECARIOUS POSITION: Tim's brother James moved abroad two years ago to
> start a new job. Tim and James have always been close, even though it's harder to
> keep in touch now that James lives abroad. Last time they met, Tim noticed
> James commenting a few times on the ill-informed, biased beliefs about climate
> change amongst his co-workers. He commented on it mostly in a light-hearted
> way, as if wanting to downplay the significance of his co-worker's attitudes. But
> Tim also noticed James making dubious remarks here and there, and even
> defending certain unsupported ideas about climate change over dinner ("just
> playing devil's advocate"). Tim thinks that James should know better than to let
> his coworkers influence him in this way. In fact, it seems clear to Tim that—since
> starting his new job—James has come to adopt some epistemically culpable
> beliefs about climate change, or at least adjusted his credences in an epistemically
> culpable way. When deliberating about how to respond, Tim realizes that if he
> flat out *blames* James—for example, by rebuking him, demanding reasons, and
> reducing his degree of epistemic trust—it's likely that James will simply double
> down, or back away from the conversation, and continue to maintain his
> credences as they stand. Meanwhile, if Tim approaches the situation in a more
> positively valanced way, for example by seeking to understand where James is
> coming from, constructively offering alternative points of view, and charitably
> asking James what the reasons for his colleagues' views are, it is likely that James
> will be more willing to adjust his credences in an epistemically advantageous
> direction.

One way of framing the dynamics of the case is to say that James is in an
"epistemically precarious position"—a position such that whether he is likely to
acquire or lose epistemic goods is highly contingent on how other epistemic
agents *respond* to him for his faulty epistemic conduct. In the case, if Tim
responds with epistemic blame, it is likely that James will end up going further
in the direction of his epistemically problematic credences, and lose out on
epistemic goods. If Tim responds with more positively valanced attitudes and
behaviors—i.e. epistemic relationship warming—James' credences will likely be
influenced in an epistemically advantageous way, leading to the acquisition of
epistemic goods. The idea, then, is that this may be a case in which epistemic
relationship warming would be more efficacious, and is therefore the more
appropriate response to a judgment of epistemic blameworthiness.

One thing to consider right away, as we did with YOUTUBE, is whether our
intuitions really track the idea that it is the epistemic relationship between Tim
and James that ought to be warmed and not cooled, as opposed to their relationship as close siblings. Perhaps if a kind of relationship warming is called for, it is

192 EPISTEMIC BLAME

simply that Tim ought to intend to call James a bit more often, or otherwise maintain a positive presence as a brother.[19] Moreover, one might be a hard-nosed epistemic blamer and think: if James is epistemically culpable, then come what may Tim ought to epistemically blame him. He ought to stand up for the epistemic norms that govern our epistemic communities, even if it means losing out on some epistemic goods. This strikes me as an entirely defensible stance. But even *granting* that PRECARIOUS POSITION is a scenario in which epistemic relationship warming would be an appropriate response to a judgment of epistemically blameworthy conduct, we should be cautious about the implications. For instance, one thing to keep in mind is how circumscribed this type of case is, relative to the range of possible scenarios in which we might epistemically blame one another. Tim and James are close brothers who share a mutual admiration and respect. At the very least, then, the case is importantly different from ones involving strangers, for example. It is also different from YOUTUBE, perhaps not necessarily in terms of closeness of relationship, but rather in terms of the nature of the agent's epistemic position. In YOUTUBE, Carl has been taken in by QAnon conspiracy theories. As noted earlier, conspiracy theory beliefs can be particularly resistant to counter-evidence. Meanwhile, we need not have any special reason to think that James's beliefs are especially resistant to evidence (though of course they might be).

There may be other types of cases in which epistemic relationship warming seems called for as a response to a judgment of epistemic blameworthiness. I am sure there is plenty of room for opponents on either side of this issue to focus on features of cases, casting doubt on—or lending support to—claims that actions and attitudes approximating various forms of relationship modification would be called for. Rather than get into further discussion, it strikes me as permissible here to simply invite critics to fill in the details.

7.6.2 Social Justice

Let's return to the context of democratic society more broadly. In this context, in addition to everything we have said so far more or less equally applying, another issue becomes visible: namely, the relationship-warming proposal may end up making unfair demands on epistemic agents that will track structural inequalities surrounding the distribution of epistemic and material resources. To see this, notice that successfully pulling off the sort of thing involved in epistemic relationship warming is a highly burdensome, cognitive resource-heavy human

---

[19] Of course, perhaps nothing whatsoever is called for on behalf of Tim. Indeed, this case may have some distracting features. If so, I suggest considering whether there is some other example, involving someone you care about, doing something you find epistemically culpable in a problematic way, such that you are at least somewhat worried about your relationship with the person.

competence. It requires a significant degree of training, access to information, and freedom from competing demands on one's time and energy. This invites a third sort of objection to the epistemic relationship-warming proposal. The proposal applied in a blanket fashion will lead to injustices tracking structural and systemic inequalities in these areas. To take just one example, it is well-established that in industrialized Western democracies—such as the USA—marginalized groups such as Black citizens or other racial minorities, tend not to have the same access to information, education, and freedom from competing demands on one's time and energy as white or other privileged citizens. This means that, when it comes to a situation in which a member of a marginalized group is confronted with someone doing something epistemically blameworthy, the relationship-warming proposal will call upon the member of the marginalized group to take on epistemic labor in an unfair way. The worry is simply that this renders the relationship-warming proposal unjust.[20]

To make matters worse—and I consider this a separate objection to the proposal—notice that members of marginalized groups are prone to be taken less seriously (e.g. perceived as less credible) in their attempts at epistemic relationship warming. We are familiar from Chapter 5 with a wide range of epistemic injustices and other types of epistemic harm that members of marginalized groups are confronted with on a continual basis. The thought is that, in addition to requiring significant levels of training, access to information, material resources, and freedom from competing demands on one's time, successfully pulling off the labor of epistemic relationship warming obviously requires being taken seriously by one's interlocutor—not only in the form of having one's word epistemically trusted to the appropriate degree, but also in the form of having one's point of view adequately understood by one's interlocutor (Fricker 2007; Hänel 2020; Jackson 2019; Medina 2012a; Pohlhaus 2012). This is then yet another way in which the relationship-warming proposal will lead to unfair demands across epistemic agents, injustices tracking structural social and material inequalities.[21]

Of course, this raises the prospect that my preferred relationship-cooling view is prone to injustice too. After all, paradigm forms of epistemic relationship cooling I have focused on involve suspending one's willingness to epistemically trust the word of another on a certain range of propositions. The resources individuals need to be able to cool their epistemic relationships with others in appropriate ways—for example, identifying the appropriate domain of

---

[20] Perhaps there are forms of epistemic relationship warming that do not require significant levels of training, access to information, and freedom from competing demands on one's time and energy. I leave this question to pursue another time, and welcome suggestions.

[21] Feminist and standpoint epistemologists have long argued that, despite epistemic injustice, members of marginalized groups have a unique understanding of oppression which also gives them major epistemic advantages (Anderson 1995; Crasnow 2013; Toole 2021a, 2021b, 2022). I do not take the proposal sketched here to trade on the idea that members of marginalized groups are at an epistemic disadvantage in all respects.

194 EPISTEMIC BLAME

propositions over which to suspend their presumption of epistemic trust—will also be unequally distributed in most societies.[22] So, doesn't the same worry apply? My response here is to acknowledge that a similar worry may apply. There may be systemic injustices that arise in our epistemic practices as I model them. But I don't think this is first and foremost a problem for my view about the ethics of epistemic blame. This is first and foremost a problem at the level of policy and politics broadly construed. The fact that these injustices exist is just one more reason, among many, that we should be doing more to address structural and systemic inequalities that lead to these injustices.

Someone might respond that the same response is available to the relationship-warming proposal. However, my view is that until such time as these structural inequalities are addressed, discussions about the nature and ethics of epistemic blame should take them seriously into account. These things should be factors that bear on the question of what is reasonable to expect of epistemic agents in their lived epistemic environments. The point is just that relationship modification in the form of cooling rather than warming is considerably less demanding on people's cognitive labor, and less fraught with worries about epistemic injustice.

If we are in the business of answering questions about what is good for society, then taking people's lived epistemic environments into consideration (along with the opportunities various groups have to improve them) seems relevant. It seems more reasonable—given what we have considered so far (including considerations about social justice)—to regard negatively valanced relationship modification as a paradigm of appropriate responses to epistemically blameworthy failings.

We can put the point in the form of the following argument:

Argument from Social Justice

(i) Negatively valanced epistemic relationship modification is not as labor intensive, and does not place as stringent demands on agent credibility as positively valanced epistemic relationship modification.

(ii) An ethics of blame enjoining us to adopt the former, rather than the latter, in response to culpable epistemic failings is thus less likely to track social inequalities in unjust ways.

(iii) This is one source of support for a negatively valanced relationship modification-centric ethics of epistemic blame.[23]

---

[22] Consider someone noticing a bit of epistemically blameworthy conduct in a very specific domain, and then suspending their epistemic trust on basically *everything* that person says. That's what I would call an unsuccessful, or inappropriate form of epistemic relationship cooling. My point here is that training, resources, and freedom from other constraints on one's time, are needed to get this balancing act right. Demands in this regard may be unjust in ways that track social and material inequalities.

[23] See Catriona Mackenzie for an argument about moral blame that is structurally similar to my argument from social justice. Targeting proponents of blame's ability to *capacitate* moral agents, Mackenzie argues:

THE VALUE OF EPISTEMIC BLAME   195

Here is one final concern. Some people have serious aversions to confrontation and conflict. Perhaps epistemic blame is more labor intensive than epistemic assistance *for those people*. After all, epistemic blame may seem more likely to lead to confrontation and conflict than more positively valanced epistemic responses. Doesn't the logic of the Argument from Social Justice imply that this is a mark *against* a negatively-valanced ethics of epistemic blame? Perhaps. But notice: there is always going to be a tension between norms and abilities. As normative theorists, we face the question of what sorts of considerations about our abilities we *should* take into account in understanding what the relevant norms governing our conduct and attitudes *are*. It seems to me that, if a norm demands things that a group of people systematically lack the material and epistemic resources to meet, then this demand has the potential to undermine the very status of the norm. The mere fact that a norm conflicts with some people's aversion to confrontation and conflict does not strike me as having the same potential to undermine the status of the norm.

7.7 Conclusion

This chapter began with a positive argument for the value of epistemic blame. The case study of democratic participation provides a useful lens for examining the relationship between the nature and value of epistemic blame. I argued that in addition to generating further support for the relationship-based account, the discussion revealed one important role for epistemic blame, namely a role in facilitating a healthy democratic process. But there are of course important worries about whether negatively valanced epistemic relationship modification really is the best way for epistemic agents to respond to one another for episte-mically blameworthy conduct. An analogous issue about moral blame is one of the central live debates about blame in moral philosophy. This chapter is a first stab at engaging with this dimension of the ethics of epistemic blame. I have challenged positively valanced epistemic relationship modification on grounds of paternal-ism, efficacy, and social justice.

> these theories tend to operate with highly idealized conceptions of our practices. That is, they assume that moral responsibility exchanges are reciprocal exchanges between parties who are symmetrically situated, in terms of social power, status and capacity. This assump-tion overlooks the impact of social oppression and inequalities of status and power on individual agency and our social practices of holding to account (2021, 165).

According to Mackenzie, recent attempts at "civilizing blame" (see McGeer 2013), by placing greater emphasis on the value of holding to account through *dialogical exchange* (as opposed to expressing negative emotion, or anger), are typically conducted without proper consideration of how social power creates asymmetries in the effects that such dialogical exchanges may have. Various forms of social and epistemic injustice can mean that marginalized persons will most likely be anything but capacitated by such dialogical exchanges, while those in positions of power enjoy a further entrenching in their roles in the social power hierarchy. Our understanding of the very nature of blame—or the type of blame we think we *ought* to embrace as a moral community—should itself be sensitive to dynamics of social power.

Conclusion

We started with a puzzle and ended with political epistemology. What happened along the way?

First, I have argued that epistemic relationships are the key to resolving the puzzle of epistemic blame. Epistemic relationship modification has the right sort of significance to count as a kind of *blame*. But it is also a response that is entirely at home in the epistemic domain. Where negative emotions struggle with FITTINGNESS, and desires about bad believing struggle with SIGNIFICANCE, epistemic relationship modification reconciles these dualling sources of pressure, while generating a wide range of additional theoretical benefits.

Second, solving the puzzle of epistemic blame opens up a new set of questions for social epistemologists. I have identified three main questions in the ethics of epistemic blame:

- What is the scope of appropriate epistemic blame?
- Who are the appropriate epistemic blamers?
- Should we epistemically blame (at all)?

I hope the last three chapters have given a sense of how we can engage with these questions, and what sorts of issues we confront in doing so. I also hope they further illustrate the power and fruitfulness of the relationship-based account of epistemic blame. Indeed, I have argued that epistemic relationships can help us accomplish such variegated tasks as: setting a principled limit on appropriate targets of epistemic blame; explaining why some people but not others have the standing to epistemically blame; and explaining why our epistemic blaming practice has distinctive value. This is a wide-ranging set of theoretical virtues. Of course, friends of alternative frameworks may argue that they, too, have resources for explaining all this. And I look forward to hearing more about that. Indeed, my bigger picture aim in engaging with the ethics of epistemic blame is not so much demonstrating the relationship-based account's ability to answer lots of questions. Rather, it is to point out that those questions are *there*. This is just one area of inquiry that a resolution of the puzzle of epistemic blame makes visible—one that I hope to engage more with in future debate.

One thing that readers may wonder at this point is how my conclusions fit with my point of departure. In Chapter 1, I offered three arguments motivating the importance of the concept of epistemic blame. How does the account of the nature

---

Epistemic Blame: The Nature and Norms of Epistemic Relationships. Cameron Boult, Oxford University Press.
© Cameron Boult 2024. DOI: 10.1093/oso/9780192890580.003.0009

of epistemic blame I ended up with—and the questions I am now claiming the account makes possible—fit with the claims I made in those three arguments? Recall the three interconnected arguments I focused on: (i) normative parallels, (ii) blame in epistemology, and (iii) the authority of epistemic normativity.

Starting with normative parallels, the simple but important observation to make is that the conclusions of this book lend further depth to the idea that there are deep parallels between ethics and epistemology. In Chapter 1, I argued that if the parallels between ethics and epistemology run deep, we should expect there to be an epistemic kind of blame. We should expect parallel concepts of (epistemic) "ought," (epistemic) permission, and (epistemic) reasons to bear a family connection to epistemic blame and blameworthiness. I have now argued that there is an epistemic kind of blame. So, running this reasoning in reverse, it seems we gain support for the idea that the parallels between ethics and epistemology run deep. Of course, we have also discussed at length how, rather than standing in austere isolation, these domains interact in complex ways. Our practice of epistemic blame is just one important site of interaction between the normative domains. Epistemic relationships provide ways of structuring this central site of interaction: expectations constituting our professional, personal, and other sorts of relationships can impact the GER, which explains how epistemic blame interacts with other normative domains.

On blame in epistemology, one question is how the account of epistemic blame I have arrived at fits with blame-talk in the justification debates. As it happens, I think it fits nicely. When Tim Williamson (forthcoming) says that the BIV is unjustified but "blameless," a natural gloss on what this actually amounts to is that the BIV's conduct does nothing to warrant others modifying their epistemic relations with him as a reflection of epistemic relationship impairment. Sure, the case is strange because we are talking about a BIV. But as with other less fantastical cases of excused epistemic agents, the point is simply that their conduct does not constitute an impairment of the epistemic relationship. We may want to regard them differently out of prudence. But not out of a judgment of epistemic blameworthiness (see Chapter 4, section 4.3). This is a more natural way of understanding what is going on in the justification debates than how we seem forced to construe blame-talk on an emotion-based approach, for example. To return to an old theme, it seems odd to suggest that what the massively deceived subject is exculpated from is some kind of heated emotional response. The real difference lies in how we are inclined to adjust our epistemic relations with these subjects.

Two other areas of epistemology involving lots of blame-talk are the epistemic norms debates and the doxastic voluntarism literature. I think it's clear that the account of epistemic blame I have ended up with interacts with both of those areas in significant ways. For example, I have explicitly argued that the relationship-based approach to epistemic blame has resources for making sense of how people could be blameworthy for their doxastic states, despite seeming to lack direct voluntary control over those states (Chapter 5, section 5.1.1). Regarding the epistemic norms debates, I have argued that the relationship-based account makes sense of how people can be epistemically blameworthy for their assertions. One way this interacts with the debate about the epistemic norm of assertion is by creating room for maneuver in dealing with worries, like Kauppinen's (2018), about whether assessments of candidate norms of assertion confuse kinds of blameworthiness.

Returning finally to the authority of epistemic normativity, a central claim linking debates about the authority of epistemic normativity and epistemic blame is of course the linking principle which says these things are necessarily connected. I have done nothing in this book to argue in support of that idea. And I don't intend to do so here.[1] But one further observation we are now in a position to appreciate is that a natural way of understanding this linking principle is in terms of the idea that a central difference between agents who violate norms, and agents who violate *authoritative* norms, is what violating the latter tends to say about our relations with one another.

We violate all kinds of norms on a daily basis—norms of etiquette, games, and grammar. None of this need make any real difference to our relationships. Impairing one's relations with others typically involves flouting norms that are in some sense weightier than norms of etiquette, games, or grammar. Perhaps the sort of weight at issue here is authoritative normativity. I have acknowledged that there is room to argue about the principle linking normative authority and blame, and whether there is a meaningful distinction between authoritative and formal normativity. But for those who find these ideas plausible, a natural way of understanding *why* blame for a norm violation is only fitting if the norm is authoritative, is because blame is a kind of relationship modification. It takes more than just formal norm violations to justify genuine relationship modification, of the kind that constitutes blame in my framework—that is, the kind reflecting a judgment that someone has fallen short of a legitimate set of intentions and *normative expectations* you have of them.

Of course, if you know that Chris cares a great deal about chess, but willingly makes a bad move for no apparent reason, that bad chess move may tell you something about Chris—something you may want to keep an eye on from the point view of your relations with him. But it seems to me that, if anything, this is simply a reflection of the authority of *prudence*, not norms of chess. If Chris's strange chess behavior has implications for his relations with others (or himself), that is because it seems practically irrational. If Chris happened to care nothing about chess—and nothing of any prudential or moral significance hangs on the

---

[1] Again, see Schmidt (2021) and Kauppinen (2018; forthcoming) for helpful discussion.

CONCLUSION 199

matter—then the fact that he willingly makes a bad move does not, or at least should not, have any significant implications for his relations with others (nor himself). It's just chess.[2]

The thought for epistemology is this: it does seem right that certain kinds of epistemic failing—considered on their own, independently of downstream practical consequences (in the *target-based* sense)—can give us good reason to modify our epistemic relations with a person. This is what I argued in Chapter 4. If that is right, and if I am right that it amounts to a kind of blame, then we have developed considerable resources for those defending the authority of epistemic normativity.

Many of the conclusions I have reached in this book are just starting points for future work on epistemic blame and related concepts. I see this work as comprising an underdeveloped area of social epistemology. The study of epistemic blame fits neatly within social epistemology because epistemic blame is a social phenomenon. That there is a central role for social epistemology in our theoretical and practical lives has only become increasingly clear over the last twenty years or more. But so far, our understanding of social epistemology's role has largely been limited to how our social nature interacts with the *norms* that govern various facets of our epistemic lives—from testimony, to reliance on experts, to disagreement, to belief itself.

Our practice of *responding* to one another, for failing to comply with those norms, is an area for investigation in its own right. It is a practice with its own nature, and its own norms. Epistemic normativity and epistemic blame are of course deeply related. As I put it earlier, epistemic blame is a kind of *mirror* of epistemic normativity. It reflects properties of the norms that govern our intellectual lives. But this only shows the importance of framing the mirror well. This book has developed a way—a decidedly social one—of framing the mirror.

---

[2] For those inclined to disagree here, recall my suggestion in Chapters 1 and 4 that "chess blame" is epistemic blame.

Bibliography

Abramson, K. 2014. Turning up the lights on gaslighting. *Philosophical Perspectives*, 28(1): 1–30.

Adams, R.M. 1985. Involuntary sins. *Philosophical Review*, 94(1): 3–31.

Alston, W. 1988. The deontological conception of epistemic justification. *Philosophical Perspectives*, 2: 258–99.

Anderson, E. 1995. Feminist epistemology: An interpretation and a defense. *Hypatia*, 10(3): 50–84.

Arneson, R. 2003. The smart theory of moral responsibility and desert. In Serena Olsaretti (Ed.), *Desert and Justice*. Oxford: OUP.

Baehr, J. 2011. *The Inquiring Mind*. Oxford: OUP.

Bartolotti, L. and Miyazono, K. 2015. The ethics of delusional belief. *Erkenntnis*, 81: 275–96.

Basu, R. 2018. Can beliefs wrong? *Philosophical Topics*, 46(1): 1–17.

Basu, R. 2019. The wrongs of racist beliefs. *Philosophical Studies*, 176: 2497–515.

Basu, R. 2020. The spectre of normative conflict. In E. Beeghly and A. Madva (Eds), *An Introduction to Implicit Bias: Knowledge and the Social Mind*. New York: Routledge.

Basu, R. 2021. A take of two doctrines: Moral encroachment and doxastic wronging. In J. Lackey (Ed.), *Applied Epistemology*, pp. 99–118. Oxford: OUP.

Basu, R. Forthcoming. The ethics of expectations. *Oxford Studies in Normative Ethics*, Vol. 13, pp. 149–69. Oxford: OUP.

Basu, R. and Schroeder, M. 2019. Doxastic wronging. In B. Kim and M. McGrath (Eds), *Pragmatic Encroachment in Epistemology*, pp. 181–205. New York: Routledge.

Beddor, B. 2019. Noncognitivism and epistemic evaluations. *Philosophers' Imprint*, 19(10): 1–27.

Begby, E. 2018. Doxastic morality: A moderately skeptical perspective. *Philosophical Topics*, 46: 155–72.

Begon, J. 2016. Paternalism. *Analysis*, 76(3): 355–73.

Bell, M. 2013. The standing to blame: A critique. In D. Coates and N. Tognazzini (Eds), *Blame: Its Nature and Norms*. Oxford: OUP.

Bennett, J. 1974. The conscience of Huckleberry Finn. *Philosophy*, 49: 123–34.

Berenstain, N. 2016. Epistemic exploitation. *Ergo: An Open Access Journal of Philosophy*, 3: 569–90.

Bollinger, R.J. 2020a. Varieties of moral encroachment. *Philosophical Perspectives*, 34(1): 5–26.

Bollinger, R.J. 2020b. The rationality of accepting (some) racial generalizations. *Synthese*, 197(6): 2415–31.

Boult, C. 2017a. Epistemic normativity and the justification-excuse distinction. *Synthese*, 194(10): 4065–81.

Boult, C. 2017b. Knowledge and attributability. *Pacific Philosophical Quarterly*, 98(1): 329–50.

Boult, C. 2017c. Categorical norms and convention-relativism about epistemic discourse. *Dialectica*, 71: 85–99.

Boult, C. 2019. Excuses, exemptions, and derivative norms. *Ratio*, 32(2): 150–8.

BIBLIOGRAPHY

Boult, C. 2021a. There is a distinctively epistemic kind of blame. *Philosophy and Phenomenological Research*, 103(3): 518–34.

Boult, C. 2021b. Standing to epistemically blame. *Synthese*, 199(3–4): 11355–75.

Boult, C. 2021c. Epistemic blame. *Philosophy Compass*, 16(8).

Boult, C. 2021d. The epistemic responsibilities of citizens in a democracy. In M. Hannon and J. DeRidder (Eds), *The Routledge Handbook of Political Epistemology*. New York: Routledge.

Boult, C. 2023. The significance of epistemic blame. *Erkenntnis*, 88(2): 807–28.

Boult, C. Forthcoming. Epistemic complicity. *Episteme*.

Boult, C. and Kohler, S. 2020. Epistemic judgment and motivation. *Philosophical Quarterly*, 70(281): 738–58.

Blustein, J. 2014. Forgiveness and the moral psychology of sadness. In A. Gotlib (Ed.), *The Moral Psychology of Sadness*. Lanham, MD: Rowman & Littlefield.

Brennan, J. 2016. *Against Democracy*. Princeton, NJ: Princeton University Press.

Brennan, J. 2020. In defense of epistocracy: Enlightened preference voting. In M. Hannon and J. de Ridder (Eds), *The Routledge Handbook of Political Epistemology*. New York: Routledge.

Brown, J. 2011. Assertion and practical reasoning: Common or divergent epistemic standards? *Philosophy and Phenomenological Research*, 84: 123–57.

Brown, J. 2017. Blame and wrongdoing. *Episteme*, 14: 3.

Brown, J. 2020a. What is epistemic blame? *Noûs*, 54(2): 389–407.

Brown, J. 2020b. Epistemically blameworthy belief. *Philosophical Studies*, 177(12): 3595–614.

Buchak, L. 2014. Belief, credence and norms. *Philosophical Studies*, 169: 285–311.

Carter, J.A., Clark, A., Kallestrup, J., Palermos, O., and Pritchard, D. Forthcoming. *Socially Extended Knowledge*. Oxford: OUP.

Carter, J.A. and Nickel, P.J. 2014. On testimony and transmission. *Episteme*, 11(2): 145–55.

Carter, J.A. and Simion, M. 2020. The ethics and epistemology of trust. *Internet Encyclopedia of Philosophy*. https://iep.utm.edu/trust/

Cassam, Q. 2019. *Vices of the Mind: From the Intellectual to the Political*. Oxford: OUP.

Cassam, Q. 2021. Bullshit, post truth, and propaganda. In M. Hannon and E. Edenberg (Eds), *Political Epistemology*, pp. 49–63. Oxford: OUP.

Cherry, M. 2021. *The Case for Rage: Why Anger is Essential to Anti-Racist Struggle*. New York: OUP.

Chislenko, E. 2020. Scanlon's theories of blame. *Journal of Value Inquiry*, 54(3): 371–86.

Chrisman, M. 2008. Ought to believe. *Journal of Philosophy*, 105(7): 346–70.

Chrisman, M. 2012. Epistemic expressivism. *Philosophy Compass*, 7(2): 110–26

Chrisman, M. 2022. *Belief, Agency, and Knowledge: Essays on Epistemic Normativity*. Oxford: OUP.

Chuard, P. and Southwood, N. 2009. Epistemic norms without voluntary control. *Noûs* 43: 4.

Coady, C.A.J. 1992. *Testimony: A Philosophical Study*. Oxford: OUP.

Coates, A. 2016. The epistemic norm of blame. *Ethical Theory and Moral Practice*, 19: 457–73.

Coates, A. 2020. The ethics of blame: a primer. In G. Ernst and S. Schmidt (Eds), *The Ethics of Belief and Beyond. Understanding Mental Normativity*, pp. 192–214. Abingdon: Routledge.

Coates, A. and Tognazzini, N. (Eds). 2013a. *Blame: Its Nature and Norms*. Oxford: OUP.

BIBLIOGRAPHY   203

Coates, A. and Tognazzini, N. 2013b. The contours of blame. In D. Coates and N. Tognazzini (Eds), *Blame: Its Nature and Norms*. Oxford: OUP.

Coates, A. and Tognazzini, N. 2014. Blame. *The Stanford Encyclopedia of Philosophy*.

Cogley, Z. 2013. The three-fold significance of the blaming emotions. In D. Shoemaker (Ed.), *Oxford Studies in Agency and Responsibility*, Vol. 1, pp. 205–24. New York: OUP.

Cohen, G.A. 2006. Casting the first stone: Who can, and who can't, condemn the terrorists? *Royal Institute of Philosophy Supplement*, 58: 113–36.

Collins, P.H. 2000. *Black Feminist Thought: Knowledge, Consciousness, and the Politics of Empowerment*. New York: Routledge.

Cornell, N. and Sepinwall, A. 2020. Complicity and hypocrisy. *Politics, Philosophy and Economics*, 19(2): 154–81.

Côté-Bouchard, C. 2017. Is epistemic normativity value based? *Dialogue*, 56(3): 407–30.

Cowie, C. 2019. *Morality and Epistemic Judgment*. Oxford: OUP.

Craig, E. 1990. *Knowledge and the State of Nature*. Oxford: OUP.

Crasnow, S. 2013. Feminist philosophy of science: Values and objectivity. *Philosophy Compass*, 8(4): 413–23.

Cuneo, T. 2007. *The Normative Web*. Oxford: OUP.

Davis, E. 2016. Typecasts, tokens, and spokespersons: A case for credibility excess as epistemic injustice. *Hypatia*, 31: 485–501.

Dembroff, R. and Whitcomb, D. Forthcoming. Content focused epistemic injustice. In T. Gendler and J. Hawthorne (Eds), *Oxford Studies in Epistemology*. Oxford: OUP.

DeRose, K. 2002. Assertion, knowledge, and context. *Philosophical Review*, 111: 167–203.

DeRose, K. 2005. The ordinary language basis for contextualism, and the new invariantism. *Philosophical Quarterly*, 55: 172–98.

DeRose, K. 2009. *The Case for Contextualism*. Oxford: OUP.

Dogramaci, S. 2012. Reverse engineering epistemic evaluations. *Philosophy and Phenomenological Research*, 84(3): 513–30.

Dormandy, K. 2020. Introduction: An overview of trust and some key epistemological applications. In K. Dormandy (Ed.), *Trust in Epistemology*, pp. 1–40. New York: Routledge.

Dotson, K. 2011. Tracking epistemic violence, tracking practices of silencing. *Hypatia*, 26(2): 236–57.

Dougherty, T. 2012. Reducing responsibility: An evidentialist account of epistemic blame. *European Journal of Philosophy*, 20: 4.

Dougherty, T. 2014. The ethics of belief is ethics (period). In J. Matheson and R. Vitz (Eds), *The Ethics of Belief*. Oxford: OUP.

Dover, D. 2019. The walk and the talk. *Philosophical Review*, 128: 387–422.

Dworkin, G. 2010. Paternalism. In E.N. Zalta (Ed.), *The Stanford Encyclopedia of Philosophy*. https://plato.stanford.edu/entries/paternalism/

Engen, A. 2020. Punishing the oppressed and the standing to blame. *Res Philosophica*, 97(2): 271–95.

Enoch, D. and Spectre, L. Forthcoming. There is no such thing as doxastic wronging. *Philosophical Perspectives*.

Fantl, J. and McGrath, M. 2009. *Knowledge in an Uncertain World*. Oxford: OUP.

Fassio, D. 2019. Are epistemic reasons perspective-dependent? *Philosophical Studies*, 176(12): 3253–83.

Faulkner, P. 2007. On telling and trusting. *Mind*, 116(484): 875–902.

Faulkner, P. and Simpson, T. 2017. *The Philosophy of Trust*. Oxford: OUP.

BIBLIOGRAPHY

Feldman, R. 2004. The ethics of belief. In E. Conee and R. Feldman, *Evidentialism*. Oxford: OUP.

Fischer, J.M. and Ravizza, M. 1998. *Responsibility and Control*. Cambridge: CUP.

Fiske, S. and Stevens, L. 1993. *What's So Special About Sex? Gender Stereotyping and Discrimination*. Thousand Oaks, CA: Sage Publications.

FitzPatrick, W. 2008. Moral responsibility and normative ignorance: Answering a new skeptical challenge. *Ethics*, 118: 589–613.

Frankfurt, H. 1988. The importance of what we care about. In *The Importance of What We Care About: Philosophical Essays*, pp. 80–94. Cambridge: CUP.

Franklin, C.E. 2013. Valuing blame. In D. Coates and N. Tognazzini (Eds), *Blame: Its Nature and Norms*. Oxford: OUP.

Fricker, M. 2007. *Epistemic Injustice*. Oxford: OUP.

Fricker, M. 2016. What's the point of blame? *Noûs*, 50: 165–83.

Friedman, M. 2013. How to blame people responsibly. *Journal of Value Inquiry*, 47: 271–84.

Fritz, K. 2017. Pragmatic encroachment and moral encroachment. *Pacific Philosophical Quarterly*, 98: 643–61.

Fritz, K. and Miller, D. 2018. Hypocrisy and the standing to blame. *Pacific Philosophical Quarterly*, 99: 1.

Fritz, K. and Miller, D. 2019. The unique badness of hypocritical blame. *Ergo: An Open Access Journal of Philosophy*, 6.

Gardiner, G. 2020. Relevance and risk: How the relevant alternatives framework models the epistemology of risk. *Synthese*, 199(1–2): 481–511.

Gerken, M. 2011. Warrant and action. *Synthese*, 178(3): 529–47.

Gibbons, J. 2006. Access externalism. *Mind*, 115(457): 19–39.

Glover, J. 1970. *Responsibility*. London: Routledge.

Goldberg, S. 2010. *Relying on Others: An Essay in Epistemology*. Oxford: OUP.

Goldberg, S. 2017. Should have known. *Synthese*, 194(8): 2863–94.

Goldberg, S. 2018. *To the Best of Our Knowledge: Social Expectations and Epistemic Normativity*. Oxford: OUP.

Goldberg, S. 2020. *Conversational Pressure*. Oxford: OUP.

Goldberg, S. 2022. What is a speaker owed? *Philosophy and Public Affairs*, 50(3): 375–407.

Goldman, A. 2001. Experts: Which ones should you trust? *Philosophy and Phenomenological Research*, 63(1): 85–110.

Goldman, A. and McGrath, M. 2014. *Epistemology: A Contemporary Introduction*. Oxford: OUP.

Goldman, A. and Whitcomb, D. 2010. *Social Epistemology: Essential Readings*. In A. Goldman and D. Whitcomb (Eds). Oxford: OUP.

Goldman, D. 2014. Modification of the reactive attitudes. *Pacific Philosophical Quarterly*, 95 (1): 1–22.

Graham, P. 2014. Functions, warrant, history. In A. Fairweather and O. Flanigan (Eds), *Naturalizing Epistemic Virtue*. Cambridge: CUP.

Graham, P.A. 2014. A sketch of a theory of moral blameworthiness. *Philosophy and Phenomenological Research*, 88(2): 388–409.

Greco, D. 2019. Justifications and excuses in epistemology. *Noûs*, 55(3): 517–37.

Green, A. 2021. Forgiveness and the repairing of epistemic trust. *Episteme*, Online First, pp. 1–17.

Grill, K., and Hanna, J. 2018. *The Routledge Handbook of the Philosophy of Paternalism*. New York: Routledge.

BIBLIOGRAPHY 205

Guerrero, A. 2007. Don't know, don't kill: Moral ignorance, culpability, and caution. *Philosophical Studies*, 136: 59–97.

Haddock, A., Millar, A., and Pritchard, D. 2009. *Epistemic Value*. Oxford: OUP.

Hänel, H.C. 2020. Hermeneutical injustice, (self)-recognition, and academia. *Hypatia*, 35: 1–19.

Hannon, M. 2019. *What's the Point of Knowledge? A Function-First Epistemology*. Oxford: OUP.

Hawthorne, J. 2003. *Knowledge and Lotteries*. Oxford: OUP.

Hawthorne, J. and Stanley, J. 2008. Knowledge and action. *Journal of Philosophy*, 105: 10.

Hazlett, A. 2013. *A Luxury of the Understanding*. Oxford: OUP.

Heilman, M.E. 2001. Descriptions and prescription: how gender stereotypes prevent women's ascent up the organizational ladder. *Journal of Social Issues*, 57(4): 657–74.

Hieronymi, P. 2004. The force and fairness of blame. *Philosophical Perspectives*, 18: 115–48.

Hieronymi, P. 2008. Responsibility for believing. *Synthese*, 161(3): 357–73.

Howard, N. and Laskowski, N.G. Forthcoming. Robust vs. formal normativity II, or: No gods, no masters, no authoritative normativity. In *Oxford Handbook of Meta-Ethics*. Oxford: OUP.

Hughes, N. 2019. Dilemmic epistemology. *Synthese*, 196(1): 4059–90.

Hughes, N. 2021. Who's afraid of epistemic dilemmas? In K. McCain, S. Stapleford, and M. Steup (Eds), *Epistemic Dilemmas: New Arguments, New Angles*. New York: Routledge.

Hughes, N. (Ed.). Forthcoming. *Epistemic Dilemmas*. Oxford: OUP.

Ivy, V. [McKinnon, R.]. 2017. Allies behaving badly: Gaslighting as epistemic injustice. In Ian James Kidd, José Medina, and Gaile Pohlhaus, Jr. (Eds), *The Routledge Handbook of Epistemic Injustice*. Routledge: New York.

Ivy, V. 2019. Gaslighting as epistemic violence. In B.R. Sherman and S. Goguen (Eds), *Overcoming Epistemic Injustice: Social and Psychological Perspectives*. Lanham, MD: Rowman & Littlefield.

Jackson, D. L. 2019. Date rape: The intractability of hermeneutical injustice. In W. Teays (Ed.), *Analyzing Violence Against Women*, pp. 39–50. New York: Springer.

Jackson, L. 2022. What's epistemic about epistemic paternalism? In J. Matheson and K. Lougheed (Eds), *Epistemic Autonomy*. New York: Routledge.

Johnson-King, Z. and Babic, B. 2020. Moral obligation and epistemic risk. In M. Timmons (Ed.), *Oxford Studies in Normative Ethics* (Vol. 10). Oxford: OUP.

Kauppinen, A. 2018. Epistemic norms and epistemic accountability. *Philosophers' Imprint*. 18(8): 1–16.

Kauppinen, A. Forthcoming. The epistemic vs. the practical. In *Oxford Studies in Metaethics*. Oxford: OUP.

Kelly, T. 2003. Epistemic rationality as instrumental rationality: A critique. *Philosophy and Phenomenological Research*, 66(3): 456–64.

Kelp, C. 2018. *Good Thinking: A Knowledge First Virtue Epistemology*. London: Routledge.

Kelp, C. 2020. The knowledge norm of blaming. *Analysis*, 80(2): 256–61.

Kelp, C. and Simion, M. 2017. Criticism and blame in action and assertion. *Journal of Philosophy*, 114(2): 76–93.

Kiesewetter, B. 2022. Are epistemic reasons normative? *Noûs*, 56(3): 670–95.

King, A. 2019. *What We Ought and What We Can*. New York: Routledge.

King, M. 2019. Skepticism about the standing to blame. In D. Shoemaker (Ed.), *Oxford Studies in Agency and Responsibility 6*. Oxford: OUP.

King, M. 2020. Attending to blame. *Philosophical Studies*, 177(5): 1423–39.

Kirk-Giannini, C. 2022. Dilemmatic gaslighting. *Philosophical Studies*, 180(3): 745–72.

206 BIBLIOGRAPHY

Kristjansson, K. 2003. On the very idea of negative emotions. *Journal for the Theory of Social Behaviour*, 33(4): 351–64.

Kvanvig, J. 2003. *The Value of Knowledge and the Pursuit of Understanding*. Cambridge: CUP.

Lackey, J. 2008. *Learning from Words: Testimony as a Source of Knowledge*. Oxford: OUP.

Lackey, J. 2011. Assertion and isolated secondhand knowledge. In J. Brown and H. Cappelen (Eds), *Assertion: New Philosophical Essays*, pp. 251–76. Oxford: OUP.

Lackey, J. 2021. False confessions and testimonial injustice. *The Journal of Criminal Law and Criminology*, 110(1): 43–68.

Lippert-Rasmussen, K. 2020. Why the moral equality account of the hypocrite's lack of standing to blame fails. *Analysis* 80(4): 666–74.

Littlejohn, C. 2012. *Justification and the Truth Connection*. Cambridge: CUP.

Littlejohn, C. Forthcoming. A plea for epistemic excuses. In J. Dutant, *The New Evil Demon: New Essays on Knowledge, Justification and Rationality*. Oxford: OUP.

Lupia, A. 2016. *Uninformed: Why People Know so Little about Politics and What We Can do about It*. Oxford: OUP.

Luzzi, F. 2016. Testimonial injustice without credibility deficit. *Thought: A Journal of Philosophy*, 5: 203–11.

Mackenzie, C. 2021. Culpability, blame, and the moral dynamics of social power. *Aristotelian Society Supplementary Volume*, 95(1): 163–82.

Madison, B.J.C. 2018. On justifications and excuses. *Synthese*, 195(10): 4551–62.

Maguire, B. and Woods, J. 2020. The game of belief. *The Philosophical Review*, 129: 211–49.

Maheshwari, K. 2021. On the harm of imposing risk of harm. *Ethical Theory and Moral Practice*, 24(4): 965–80.

Maitra, I. 2010. The nature of epistemic injustice. *Philosophical Books*, 51: 195–211.

Mantel, S. 2019. Do epistemic reasons bear on the ought simpliciter? *Philosophical Issues*, 29(1): 214–27.

Marusic, B and White, S. 2018. How can beliefs wrong? A Strawsonian epistemology. *Philosophical Topics*, 46(1): 97–114.

McCain, K., Stapleford, S., and Steup, M. (Eds). 2021. *Epistemic Dilemmas: New Arguments, New Angles*. New York: Routledge.

McCraw, B. 2015. The nature of epistemic trust. *Social Epistemology*, 29: 413–30.

McGeer, V. 2013. Civilizing blame. In D. Coates and N. Tognazzini (Eds), *Blame: Its Nature and Norms*. Oxford: OUP.

McGlynn, A. 2020. Objects or others? Epistemic agency and the primary harm of testimonial injustice. *Ethical Theory and Moral Practice*, 23(5): 831–45.

McGlynn, A. 2021. Epistemic objectification as the primary harm of testimonial injustice. *Episteme*, 18(2): 160–76.

McHugh, C. 2012. Epistemic deontology and voluntariness. *Erkenntnis*, 77.

McHugh, C. 2017. Attitudinal control. *Synthese*, 194(8): 2745–62.

McKenna, R. 2015. Epistemic contextualism defended. *Synthese*, 192(2): 363–83.

McKenna, R. and Hannon, M. 2020. Assertion, action, and context. *Synthese*, 199(1–2): 731–43.

McKiernan, A. 2016. Standing conditions and blame. *Southwest Philosophy Review*, 32(1): 145–51.

Medina, J. 2012a. *The Epistemology of Resistance: Gender, Racial Oppression, Epistemic Injustice, and the Social Imagination*. OUP: Oxford.

Medina, J. 2012b. Hermeneutical injustice and polyphonic contextualism: Social silences and shared hermeneutical responsibilities. *Social Epistemology*, 26: 201–20.

BIBLIOGRAPHY   207

Meeker, K. 2004. Justification and the social nature of knowledge. *Philosophy and Phenomenological Research*, 69: 156–72.

Menges, L. 2017. The emotion account of blame. *Philosophical Studies*, 174.

Menges, L. 2020. Blame it on disappointment. *Public Affairs Quarterly*, 34: 169–84.

Milam, P. 2016. Reactive attitudes and personal relationships. *Canadian Journal of Philosophy*, 46(1): 102–22.

Mill, J.S. 1869. On liberty. London: Longman, Roberts & Green.

Miller, B. and Record, I. 2013. Justified belief in a digital age: On the epistemic implications of secret internet technologies. *Episteme*, 10: 117–34.

Millikan, R. 1984. *Language, Thought, and Other Biological Categories*. Cambridge, MA: MIT Press.

Mills, C. 1997. *The Racial Contract*. Ithaca, NY: Cornell University Press.

Mills, C. 2007. White ignorance. In Shannon Sullivan and Nancy Tuana (Eds), *Race and Epistemologies of Ignorance*. Albany, NY: SUNY Press.

Mills, C. 2013. White ignorance and hermeneutical injustice: A comment on Medina and Fricker. *Social Epistemology Review and Reply Collective*, 3: 38–43.

Mitova, V. 2011. *Believable Evidence*. Cambridge: CUP.

Montmarquet, J. 1992. Epistemic virtue and doxastic responsibility. *American Philosophical Quarterly*, 29: 331–41.

Montmarquet, J. 1999. Zimmerman on culpable ignorance. *Ethics*, 109: 842–5.

Moody-Adams, M. 1994. Culture, responsibility, and affected ignorance. *Ethics*, 104: 91–309.

Moss, S. 2018. Moral encroachment. *Proceedings of the Aristotelian Society*, 118(2): 177–205.

Narayan, Uma. 1997. *Dislocating Cultures: Identities, Traditions, and Third World Feminism*. New York: Routledge.

Nottelmann, N. 2007. *Blameworthy Belief: A Study in Epistemic Deontologism*. Dordrecht: Springer.

Owens, D. 2000. *Reason Without Freedom: The Problem of Epistemic Normativity*. New York: Routledge.

Pace, M. 2011. The epistemic value of moral considerations: justification, moral encroachment, and James' "will to believe." *Noûs*, 45(2): 239–68.

Papineau, D. 2012. There are no norms of belief. In T. Chan (Ed.), *The Aim of Belief*. Oxford: OUP.

Peels, R. 2016. *Responsible Belief: A Theory in Ethics and Epistemology*. Oxford: OUP.

Peels, R., Kindermann, N., and Ranalli, C. 2023. Normativity in studying conspiracy theory belief: Seven guidelines. *Philosophical Pscyhology*, 36(6): 1125–59.

Pereboom, D. 2001. *Living Without Free Will*. New York: CUP.

Pereboom, D. 2014. *Free Will, Agency, and Meaning in Life*. New York: OUP.

Pickard, H. 2013. Irrational blame. *Analysis*, 73(4): 613–26.

Piovarchy, A. 2020. Hypocrisy, standing to blame, and second-personal authority. *Pacific Philosophical Quarterly* 101(4): 603–27.

Piovarchy, A. 2021a. What do we want from a theory of epistemic blame? *Australasian Journal of Philosophy*, 99(4): 791–805.

Piovarchy, A. 2021b. Responsibility for testimonial injustice. *Philosophical Studies*, 178(2): 597–615.

Piovarchy, A. 2023. Situationism, subjunctive hypocrisy, and standing to blame. *Inquiry*, 66(4): 514–38.

Placani, A. 2017. When the risk of harm harms. *Law and Philosophy*, 36(1): 77–100.

BIBLIOGRAPHY

Podosky, P.M.C. 2021. Gaslighting, first- and second-order. *Hypatia*, 36: 207–27.

Pohlhaus, G. 2012. Relational knowing and epistemic injustice: Toward a theory of willful hermeneutical ignorance. *Hypatia*, 27: 715–35.

Pohlhaus, G. 2014. Discerning the primary epistemic harm in cases of testimonial injustice. *Social Epistemology*, 28: 99–114.

Pollock, J. 1986. *Contemporary theories of knowledge*. Lanham, MD: Rowman & Littlefield.

Pritchard, D. 2015. *Epistemic Angst: Radical Skepticism and the Groundlessness of Our Believing*. Princeton, NJ: Princeton University Press.

Queloz, M. 2021. The self-effacing functionality of blame. *Philosophical Studies*, 178: 1361–79.

Radzik, L. 2011. On minding your own business: Differentiating accountability relations within the moral community. *Social Theory and Practice*, 37(4): 574–98.

Radzik, L. 2012. On the virtue of minding our own business. *Journal of Value Inquiry*, 46(2): 173–82.

Record, I. 2013. Technology and epistemic possibility. *Journal for General Philosophy of Science*, 28: 1–18.

Reis-Denis, S. 2019. Anger: Scary good. *Australasian Journal of Philosophy*, 97(3): 451–64.

Reisner, A. 2018. Two theses about the distinctness of practical and theoretical normativity. In C. McHugh, J. Way, and D. Whiting (Eds), *Normativity: Epistemic and Practical*, pp. 221–40. Oxford: OUP.

Rettler, L. 2018. In defense of doxastic blame. *Synthese*, 195(5): 2205–26.

Roberts, R. and Wood, W.J. 2007. *Intellectual Virtues: An Essay in Regulative Epistemology*. Oxford: OUP.

Robichaud, P. and Weiland, J. 2017. *Responsibility: The Epistemic Condition*. Oxford: OUP.

Rosen, G. 2003. Culpability and ignorance. *Proceedings of the Aristotelian Society*, 103: 61–84.

Ross, J. and Schroeder, M. 2012. Belief, credence, and pragmatic encroachment. *Philosophy and Phenomenological Research*, 88(2): 259–88.

Rossi, B. 2018. The commitment account of hypocrisy. *Ethical Theory and Moral Practice*, 21(3): 553–67.

Rossi, B. 2020. Hypocrisy is vicious, value-expressing inconsistency. *Journal of Ethics*, 25(1): 57–80.

Rowe, T. 2022. Can the risk of harm itself be a harm? *Analysis*, 81(4): 694–701.

Russel, B. 2001. Epistemic and moral duty. In M. Steup (Ed.), *Knowledge, Truth, and Duty. Essays on Epistemic Justification, Responsibility, and Virtue*. Oxford: OUP.

Ryan, S. 2003. Doxastic compatibilism and the ethics of belief. *Philosophical Studies*, 114 (1–2): 47–79.

Saint-Croix, C. 2022. Rumination and wronging: The role of attention in epistemic morality. *Episteme*, 19(4): 491–514.

Scanlon, T.M. 1998. *What We Owe to Each Other*. Cambridge, MA: Harvard University Press.

Scanlon, T.M. 2008. *Moral dimensions: Permissibility, Meaning, Blame*. Cambridge, MA: Belknap Press.

Scanlon, T.M. 2013. Interpreting blame. In D. Coates and N. Tognazzini (Eds), *Blame: Its Nature and Norms*. Oxford: OUP.

Schleifer-McCormick, M. 2021. Believing badly: Doxastic duties are not epistemic duties. In K. McCain, S. Stapleford, and M. Steup (Eds), *Epistemic Dilemmas: New Arguments, New Angles*. New York: Routledge.

BIBLIOGRAPHY 209

Schmidt, S. 2021. Epistemic blame and the normativity of evidence. *Erkenntnis*, Online First.

Schmidt, S. ms. Doxastic dilemmas and epistemic blame: on the normativity of the epistemic "ought."

Schroeder, M. 2011. Ought, agents, actions. *The Philosophical Review*, 120: 1–41.

Schroeder, M. 2018. When beliefs wrong. *Philosophical Topics*, 46(1): 115–27.

Seim, M. 2019. The standing to blame and meddling. *Teorema*, 38(2): 7–26.

Senor, T. 2007. Preserving preservationism: A reply to Lackey. *Philosophy and Phenomenological Research*, 74: 199–208.

Shah, N. 2002. Clearing space for doxastic voluntarism. *The Monist*, 85(3): 436–45.

Sher, G. 2006. *In Praise of Blame*. Oxford: OUP.

Sher, G. 2013. Wrongdoing and relationships: The problem of the stranger. In D. Coates and N. Tognazzini (Eds), *Blame: Its Nature and Norms*. Oxford: OUP.

Shoemaker, D. and Vargas, M. 2021. Moral torch fishing: A signaling theory of blame. *Noûs*, 55(3): 581–602.

Sliwa, P. 2019. Reverse engineering blame. *Philosophical Perspectives*, 33: 200–19.

Smart, J.J.C. 1970. Free will, praise, and blame. In G. Dworkin (Ed.), *Determinism, Free Will and Moral Responsibility*, pp. 196–213. Englewood Cliffs, NJ: Prentice Hall.

Smartt, T. 2023. Scepticism about epistemic blame. *Philosophical Studies*, 180: 1813–828.

Smith, A. 2005. Responsibility for attitudes: Activity and passivity in mental life. *Ethics*, 115: 236–71.

Smith, A. 2007. On being responsible and holding responsible. *Journal of Ethics*, 11: 4.

Smith, A. 2012. Attributability, Answerability, and Accountability: In Defense of a Unified Account. *Ethics*, 122: 575–89.

Smith, A. 2013. Moral blame and moral protest. In D. Coates and N. Tognazzini (Eds), *Blame: Its Nature and Norms*. Oxford: OUP.

Spear, A.D. 2020. Gaslighting, confabulation, and epistemic innocence. *Topoi*, 39: 229–41.

Spear, A.D. 2023. Epistemic dimensions of gaslighting: Peer disagreement, self-trust, and epistemic injustice. *Inquiry*, 66(1): 68–91.

Srinivasan, A. 2018. The aptness of anger. *Journal of Political Philosophy*, 26(2): 123–44.

Stanley, J. 2005. *Knowledge and Practical Interests*. Oxford: OUP.

Stark, C. A. 2019. Gaslighting, misogyny, and psychological oppression. *The Monist*, 102: 221–35.

Steup, M. 2008. Doxastic freedom. *Synthese*, 161(3): 375–92.

Stout, N. 2020. On the significance of praise. *American Philosophical Quarterly*, 57(3): 215–26.

Strawson, P. 1962. Freedom and resentment. In G. Watson (Ed.), *Proceedings of the British Academy, Vol. 48*. Oxford: OUP.

Sutton, J. 2007. *Without Justification*. Cambridge, MA: MIT Press.

Talbert, M. 2008. Blame and responsiveness to moral reasons. Are psychopaths blameworthy? *Pacific Philosophical Quarterly*, 89(4): 516–35.

Telech, D. 2022. Praise. *Philosophy Compass*, 17(10): 1–19.

Telech, D. and Katz, L.D. 2022. Condemnatory disappointment. *Ethics*, 132(4): 851–80.

Tierney, H. 2021. Hypercrisy and standing to self-blame. *Analysis*, 81(2): 262–9.

Todd, P. 2019. A unified account of the moral standing to blame. *Noûs*, 53(2): 347–74.

Tognazzini, N. 2013. Blameworthiness and the affective account of blame. *Philosophia*, 41(4): 1299–312.

Toole, B. 2021a. Demarginalizing standpoint epistemology. *Episteme*, 19: 47–65.

Toole, B. 2021b. Recent work in standpoint epistemology. *Analysis*, 81: 338–50.

BIBLIOGRAPHY

Toole, B. 2022. Objectivity in feminist epistemology. *Philosophy Compass*, 17(11): 1–13.

Tsai, G. 2014. Rational persuasion as paternalism. *Philosophy and Public Affairs*, 42: 78–112.

Tuana, N. 2006. The speculum of ignorance: The women's health movement and epistemologies of ignorance. *Hypatia*, 21(2): 1–13.

Van Woudenberg, R. 2009. Responsible belief and our social institutions. *Philosophy*, 84: 47–73.

Vargas, M. 2013. *Building Better Beings: A Theory of Moral Responsibility*. Oxford: OUP.

Wallace, R.J. 1994. *Responsibility and the Moral Sentiments*. Cambridge, MA: Harvard University Press.

Wallace, R.J. 2011. Dispassionate opprobrium. In R.J. Wallace, R. Kumar, and S. Freeman (Eds), *Reasons and Recognition: The Philosophy of T.M. Scanlon*. Oxford: OUP.

Wanderer, J. 2012. Addressing testimonial injustice: Being ignored and being rejected. *Philosophical Quarterly*, 62: 148–69.

Wanderer, J. 2017. Varieties of testimonial injustice. In I. Kidd, J. Medina, and G. Pohlhaus (Eds), *The Routledge Handbook of Epistemic Injustice*. London: Routledge.

Watson, G. 1996. Two faces of responsibility. In *Agency and Answerability: Selected Essays*, pp. 260–88. New York: OUP.

Watson, L. 2021. *The Right to Know: Epistemic Rights and Why We Need Them*. London: Routledge.

Wedgwood, R. 2007. *The Nature of Normativity*. Oxford: OUP.

Wertheimer, R. 1998. Constraining condemning. *Ethics*, 108(3): 489–501.

Williams, B. 1973. *Problems of the Self*, pp. 207–29. Cambridge: CUP.

Williamson, T. 1996. Knowing and asserting. *Philosophical Review* 105(4): 489–523.

Williamson, T. 2000. *Knowledge and Its Limits*. Oxford: OUP.

Williamson, T. Forthcoming. Justifications, excuses, and sceptical scenarios. In J. Dutant (Ed.), *The New Evil Demon: New Essays on Knowledge, Justification and Rationality*. Oxford: OUP.

Wolf, S. 2011. Blame, Italian style. In R.J. Wallace, R. Kumar, and S. Freeman (Eds), *Reasons and Recognition: The Philosophy of T.M. Scanlon*. Oxford: OUP.

Woodard, E. Forthcoming. Epistemic atonement. In R. Schafer-Landau (Ed.), *Oxford Studies in Metaethics, Vol. 18*. Oxford: OUP.

Wright, L. 1973. Functions. *The Philosophical Review*, 82: 139–68.

Wright, S. 2018. Epistemic harm and virtues of self-evaluation. *Synthese*, 198(7): 1691–709.

Zagzebski, L. 1996. *Virtues of the Mind*. Cambridge: CUP.

Zimmerman, M. 1988. *An Essay on Moral Responsibility*. Totowa, NJ: Rowman & Littlefield.

Zimmerman, M. 2008. *Living With Uncertainty: The Moral Significance of Ignorance*. Cambridge: CUP.

Index

For the benefit of digital users, indexed terms that span two pages (e.g., 52–53) may, on occasion, appear on only one of those pages.

Affective trust 77–8 (*see also* trust; epistemic trust; reliance)
Apology 51, 53, 62
Assertion 76, 97, 116–20
  Epistemic norm of assertion 16, 117, 119–20, 197–8
Attributability 113, 122n.18 (*see also* moral responsibility)

Basu, Rima 31–2, 84
Begon, Jessica 187
Berenstain, Nora 136–8
Bias 8, 41, 89–90, 108–10, 124, 145, 169n.26, 191
Blame (*see also* theories of blame; epistemic blame; ethics of blame; standing to blame)
  Affectless blame 38–9, 52, 103
  Engagement characteristic of blame 23–4, 143
  Fineness of grain 100–1
  Function of blame 11, 11n.2, 36
  Private blame 37, 52
  Significance of blame 23–4, 27–9, 37, 73, 106–7
Blameworthy belief 12n.3, 17–19, 108–16
  (*see also* epistemic responsibility)
Brown, Jessica 12n.5, 16, 29, 54–63, 98, 143–4, 146n.12, 151–2, 181
Bullshit 118–19

Cassam, Quassim 12, 118–19
Cherry, Myisha 182–3
Chess 19, 21–2, 21n.22, 103–4, 198–9
Chislenko, Eugene 7, 68
'Civilizing blame' 194n.23
Coates, Adam 10, 141, 142n.6, 143n.8
Conspiracy theories 190–2
Contaminated evidence 130–1 (*see also* misleading evidence)
Craig, Edward 94–5
Culpable ignorance 24, 115n.11, 148

Davis, Emmalon 133–7, 134n.29
Defeat 17, 148–50

Democracy 8–9, 173 (*see also* representative democracy; epistocracy; lottocracy)
  Epistemic conceptions of democracy 175n.3
  Pure proceduralist conceptions of democracy 175n.3
Democratic participation 8–9, 173–8, 182–3
Directly personal harm 33–4, 42, 145–7 (*see also* harm; epistemic harm)
Disappointment 44–6, 58n.20, 180n.10 (*see also* reactive attitudes; blame)
  Propositional disappointment 44
  Reactive disappointment 45, 180n.10
Dogmatism 17, 57–8, 80, 82, 94, 108–10, 115, 124
Dogramaci, Sinan 28–9
Doxastic control 17–19, 109–13, 197–8 (*see also* doxastic voluntarism; voluntary control)
Doxastic voluntarism 17–18, 24, 109–12, 197–8 (*see also* doxastic control; voluntary control)
Doxastic wronging 12n.3 (*see also* moral encroachment)

Entitlement to expect 143, 147–55 (*see also* expectations)
  Practice based 149–54
Epistemic blame (*see also* blame)
  Concept of epistemic blame 12–13
  Coolness of epistemic blame 24–5, 66, 104–5
  Fittingness of epistemic blame 6–7, 90, 177
  Puzzle of epistemic blame 2–3, 6, 23–6, 162
  Significance of epistemic blame 6–7, 27–9, 48–9, 82–93, 177
  Variable strength of epistemic blame 56, 99–100, 161
Epistemic dilemmas 15
Epistemic harms 8, 120–1, 124–5, 127–8, 132–9, 146n.11, 193 (*see also* harms; directly personal harms)
Epistemic injustice 5–6, 25n.27, 120–39, 146n.11, 193
  Epistemic exploitation 8, 136–8
  Gaslighting 8, 138–9
  Testimonial injustice 8, 33, 89n.2, 120–32

212 INDEX

Epistemic injustice (*cont.*)
  Testimonial injustice through credibility
    excess 119n.14, 133–8
Epistemic justification 14, 16–17, 197
Epistemic norm debates 15–16, 20–1, 117, 197–9
Epistemic objectification 133–4, 139n.31 (*see also*
  epistemic harms; epistemic othering)
Epistemic othering 133–4, 139n.31 (*see also*
  epistemic harms; epistemic objectification)
Epistemic paternalism 187–8
Epistemic praise 1n.1
Epistemic reasons 13–14 (*see also* practical
  reasons for belief)
Epistemic relationship 7, 64, 105–7, 123–9, 154,
  183–5, 191–2, 197
Epistemic responsibility 39–40, 144–5, 174–8
  (*see also* political responsibility)
  Epistemic responsibilities of citizens in a
    democracy 175–83
Epistemic rights 15
Epistemic trust 49, 77–8, 95–6, 181, 186–7
  (*see also* affective trust; reliance)
  Reductions of epistemic trust 49, 91, 182–3
Epistemic virtues 15
Epistocracy 173–4 (*see also* democracy;
  lottocracy)
Ethics of moral blame 18–19, 74, 194n.23 (*see also*
  blame; standing to blame; theories of blame)
Evidentialism 16–17
Excuses 14, 18–19, 24, 68n.6, 76n.13, 89–90, 122
Expectations 27–8, 33–4, 58, 75–7, 82–6, 92–3,
  123–9, 143, 198
  Normative vs predictive expectations 27–8,
    84, 125–8, 151–4
  Peremptory expectations 85
  Proleptic expectations 84–5
Experts 164–6
Externalism 17

Factive norm 17
Feminist epistemology 130, 193n.21
Formal normativity 19, 198 (*see also* authority of
  normativity)
Fricker, Miranda 38, 120–1, 133
Friendship 33, 65–6, 68n.6, 87, 111–12, 162,
  166–8 (*see also* relationships)

General epistemic relationship 76–9, 114–16,
  118, 123–9, 147–55 (*see also* epistemic
  relationship)
Gibbons, John 167
Goldberg, Sandy 8, 129–32, 148–54, 158, 163–4,
  166–7
Goldman, Alvin 164

Harm 33–4 (*see also* epistemic harm; directly
  personal harm)
Hermeneutical injustice 119n.14
Hieronymi, Pamela 25, 27, 50, 92

Identity prejudicial credibility excess 133–5
  (*see also* epistemic injustice)
Inequality 192–5
Inquiry 109–10, 113–16
Intellectual act 76, 115–16
Internalism 17
Irrational blame 68–9, 88–9 (*see also* blame;
  theories of blame; epistemic blame)

Jackson, Elizabeth 187–8
Justified belief (*see* epistemic justification)

Kauppinen, Antti 19–20, 22, 49, 77n.15, 117,
  197–8
Kelp, Christoph 21n.22
Kirk-Giannini, Cameron Domenico 138–9
Know-how 159–60

Lackey, Jennifer 119
Lottocracy 173–4 (*see also* democracy;
  epistocracy)

Mackenzie, Catriona 194n.23
Maitra, Ishani 122n.19
McHugh, Connor 109n.2, 144
Meaning 64–5, 73, 90, 112–13 (*see also*
  permissibility)
Menges, Leonhard 45n.7, 46
Misleading evidence 130–1 (*see also*
  contaminated evidence)
Moral encroachment 4–5, 31–2, 161–2 (*see also*
  doxastic wronging)
Moral responsibility 115n.11, 122, 148 (*see also*
  attributability)

Nayaran, Uma 133–4
Negative emotions 6–7, 24–5, 25n.26, 36n.1,
  37–49, 66, 102–3, 145–6, 179–81 (*see also*
  reactive attitudes)
  Emotion episodes 46, 180
  Emotion stances 46–7, 180
Negative valance 72, 184
Normative authority 14n.10, 19–23, 147–8, 198–9
  (*see also* formal normativity)
  Definition of normativity authority 19
  Grounds of normative authority 147–8
  Skepticism about normative authority 19n.17
Normative domains
  Clash of normative domains 129–32

Independence of normative domains 29–34, 43n.5, 93–8
Interaction of normative domains 4, 97–100, 158, 160–3, 167, 197
Parallels between normative domains 4, 13–16, 197
Nottelmann, Nikolaj 39, 47n.9

Ought implies can 24

Paternalism 173, 186–9 (*see also* epistemic paternalism)
Peels, Rik 39–40, 110n.3, 144–5
Permissibility 64–5 (*see also* meaning)
Pickard, Hannah 68–9, 89
Piovarchy, Adam 122
Pohlhaus, Gaile 133–4, 139n.31
Political epistemology 174–84 (*see also* democracy; democratic participation; epistocracy; lottocracy; political ignorance; political responsibility)
Political ignorance 175n.4
Political responsibility 175–84
Positive stereotyping 135
Positive valance 184
Practical considerations (dependence on) 29–34, 41–2, 93–8, 145, 150n.18
Practical reasons for belief 4–5
Pragmatic encroachment 4–5, 30–2, 43n.5, 161–2 (*see also* moral encroachment)

Racial injustice 182–3, 192–3
Rage 182–3
Rational persuasion 188–9 (*see also* paternalism; epistemic paternalism)
Reactive attitudes 24, 27–8, 37–8, 41, 45, 71, 83–4, 102–3, 179–80 (*see also* negative emotions)
Reasons responsiveness 110n.4
Relationship (*see also* epistemic relationship)
 Definition of a relationship 65–6
 Impairment of relationships 49, 66, 86–7, 91, 115, 123–9, 132–9
 Modification to relationships 66–7, 70–1, 86–8, 105–7, 184–5
 Normative ideal of a relationship 65–6, 68, 87
Reliable informant 94–5
Reliabilism 16–17
Reliance 77–8 (*see also* affective trust; epistemic trust)
Representative democracy 173–4, 176–7, 182–3 (*see also* democracy; democratic participation)
Reproach 51, 53, 61

Scanlon, T.M. 7, 26, 64–5, 102–6
Schmidt, Sebastian 20–1
Self-blame 103–4, 155n.21
Sher, George 25, 37, 46, 47n.8, 51–4, 57, 59, 61–2, 104
Smith, Angela 7, 25, 50, 56, 72, 111, 141–2, 185
Stakes 30–1, 150n.19, 161–2
Standing to blame 8, 18–19, 23, 92, 140–3, 168–71
 Business condition 8, 23, 141–3, 146, 155, 163, 165–6
 Moral-fragility condition 141
 Non-complicity condition 23, 141, 168–71
 Non-hypocrisy condition 23, 141, 168–71
 Skepticism about standing 141, 169
 Warrant-condition 141
Standpoint epistemology 193n.21
Strawson, P.F. 10–11, 37, 143
Structural inequality 192–5
Subject sensitive invariantism 30

Theories of blame (*see also* blame; epistemic blame)
 Cognitive approaches to blame 10–11, 23, 37
 Desire-based approach to blame 10–11, 51–4, 98, 146n.12
 Emotion-based approach to blame 24, 37–9, 96–7, 145–6
 Functional approach to blame 11, 11n.2, 36
 Relationship-based approach to blame 64–7, 102
 Revisionism about the concept of blame 104–5, 120, 139
Todd, Patrick 142–3
Tognazzini, Neil 10, 141, 142n.6
Tokening 133–4 (*see also* typecasting)
Trivial truths 24–5, 55
Trust 77–8, 78n.17 (*see also* affective trust; reliance; epistemic trust)
Tsai, George 187–9
Typecasting 133–4 (*see also* tokening)

Voluntary control 110–13 (*see also* doxastic control; doxastic voluntarism)

Wallace, R.J. 23, 27–8, 38, 48–50, 83, 85, 102, 143, 145
What speakers are owed 129–32
Wishful thinking 17, 25–6, 31, 108–10, 124
Wolf, Susan 86–7, 102

Zagzebski, Linda 15n.13